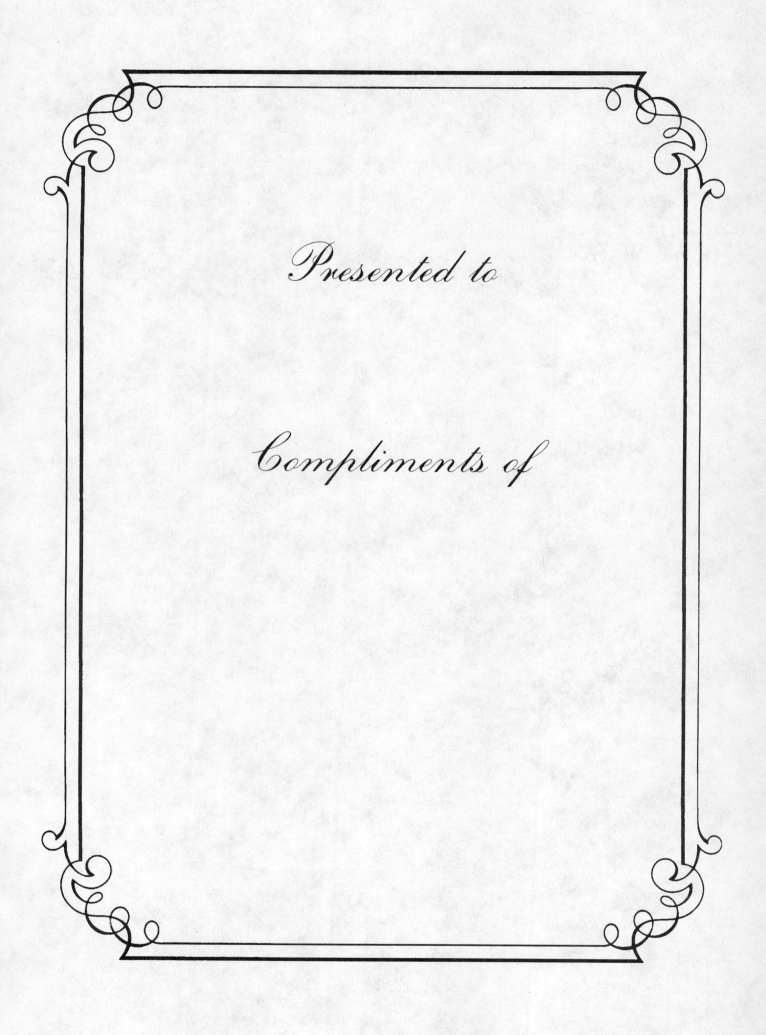

Presented to

Compliments of

MISSOURI

ON THE EVE OF THE TWENTY-FIRST CENTURY

MISSOURI

ON THE EVE OF THE TWENTY-FIRST CENTURY

BY ANN WYLIE & DAWN J. GRUBB
AND ROBERT L. DYER

CHERBO PUBLISHING GROUP, INC.
ENCINO, CALIF.

The Missouri River. © Kevin Sink/Midwestock

CHERBO
PUBLISHING
GROUP, INC.

PRESIDENT **Jack C. Cherbo**

EXECUTIVE VICE PRESIDENT **Elaine Hoffman**

EDITORIAL DIRECTOR **Christina M. Beausang**

MANAGING FEATURE EDITOR **Margaret L. Martin**

SENIOR EDITOR **Gina K. Thornburg**

PROFILES EDITOR **J. Kelley Younger**

ESSAY EDITOR **Tina G. Rubin**

SENIOR DESIGNER **Mika Toyoura**

CONTRIBUTING DESIGNER **Mary Cameron**

PHOTO EDITOR **Catherine A. Vandenberg**

SALES ADMINISTRATOR **Joan K. Baker**

PRODUCTION SERVICES MANAGER **Ellen T. Kettenbeil**

ADMINISTRATIVE COORDINATOR **Jahnna Biddle**

REGIONAL DEVELOPMENT MANAGER **Merle Gratton**

PUBLISHER'S REPRESENTATIVES **Tim Burke, Roger Leesberg, David Merritt, Tom Spitz**

Cherbo Publishing Group, Inc., Encino, Calif. 91316

© 1999 by Cherbo Publishing Group, Inc.

All rights reserved. Published 1999

Printed in the United States of America

Visit CPG's Web site at www.cherbo-publishing.com

Library of Congress Cataloging-in-Publication Data

Wylie, Ann, and Grubb, Dawn J., and Dyer, Robert L.

A pictorial guide highlighting 20th-century Missouri lifestyle and economic history. 1. Missouri. 2. Economic history—Missouri. 3. Lifestyle—Missouri.

98-071767

ISBN 1-882933-24-9

ACKNOWLEDGMENTS

ANN WYLIE AND DAWN GRUBB

WOULD LIKE TO GIVE SPECIAL THANKS TO THE

MISSOURI DEPARTMENT OF COMMERCE AND

ECONOMIC DEVELOPMENT,

ST. LOUIS REGIONAL COMMERCE AND GROWTH

ASSOCIATION, GREATER KANSAS CITY CHAMBER OF

COMMERCE, SPRINGFIELD CONVENTION AND VISITORS

BUREAU, SPRINGFIELD AREA CHAMBER OF COMMERCE,

STE. GENEVIEVE CHAMBER OF COMMERCE,

BOOTHEEL REGIONAL PLANNING AND

ECONOMIC DEVELOPMENT COMMISSION, SOUTHEAST

MISSOURI REGIONAL PLANNING AND ECONOMIC

DEVELOPMENT COMMISSION, AND THE JEFFERSON CITY

CHAMBER OF COMMERCE FOR SHARING THEIR

ECONOMIC FORECASTS, FACT SHEETS, ANNUAL REPORTS,

EXECUTIVE SUMMARIES, PRESS RELEASES, BROCHURES,

AND ON-LINE INFORMATION.

...uri wetlands at sunset. © Kevin Sink/Midwestock

Office of the Governor
State of Missouri
Jefferson City

Greetings!

Since the days of the first pioneers, Missourians have exemplified a progressive, determined spirit that has earned us the reputation as the Show Me State. Within our borders you will find the last city of the East, St. Louis, as well as the first city of the West, Kansas City. Missouri was the destination of those looking to start a new life on the western frontier and was the point of departure for those wanting to cross the Continental Divide and explore new opportunities in new territories.

Missouri has always been a state that believes in honesty, integrity, hard work, and family values. It is a blend of these attributes from our parents and forefathers that helped build the Missouri we see today.

We can be proud of what we have built and what we have accomplished. Missouri now boasts what is perhaps one of the most progressive and well-diversified economies in the nation. Currently, Missouri is enjoying the best economy in the past quarter century, and it would not have been possible without the work of those who went before us.

As we embark on a new century, it is only appropriate for us to look at where we have been, where we are now, and where we are going. From our economic roots in agriculture to the burgeoning industries of the present day, such as aerospace and plant science research, I feel confident in saying that our future will be just as bright as our colorful past. It is our hope that everyone will join us in celebrating our past and be a part of Missouri's exciting future as we proceed into a new millennium.

Very truly yours,

Mel Carnahan

Mel Carnahan

Kansas City skyline. © Bruce Mathews/Midwestock

CONTENTS

PROFILES OF CORPORATIONS AND ORGANIZATIONS

THE FOLLOWING COMPANIES AND ORGANIZATIONS HAVE MADE
A VALUABLE COMMITMENT TO THE QUALITY OF THIS PUBLICATION.
CHERBO PUBLISHING GROUP GRATEFULLY ACKNOWLEDGES THEIR PARTICIPATION
IN *MISSOURI ON THE EVE OF THE TWENTY-FIRST CENTURY*.

ESSAYISTS

CHERBO PUBLISHING GROUP WOULD LIKE TO THANK THE FOLLOWING INDIVIDUALS FOR THEIR PARTICIPATION IN *MISSOURI ON THE EVE OF THE TWENTY-FIRST CENTURY*

INTRODUCTION

Long before the United States earned its name, European adventurers were discovering the abundance of a land where two great rivers met. Spanish and French explorers, and after them, restless American colonists, made their way overland or upriver to a place rich in wildlife, vegetation, and mineral ore. Their early settlements at the frontier of the colonized East soon established Missouri's importance as the gateway to the West. Missouri's first towns became vital crossroads of travel and commerce, and soon economies in all directions depended on the lively trade that radiated out from them. As the state and the nation grew, Missouri's location near the geographic center of the United States forever sealed its role as a transportation hub. Today, important hubs of rail, river, road, and air traffic all center in the state once known as the principal launching point for wagons heading west on America's fabled trails.

State businesses of every size still bank on Missouri's central location. From St. Joseph to Springfield, Kansas City to St. Louis, Kirksville to New Madrid, and all points in between, the key to the state's optimistic economic outlook is variety. Agriculture and mining continue to hold important places in the state's economy, while service industries, wholesale and retail trade, and manufacturing provide a solid base for future growth. In addition, the tourism industry expands every year. As one of the two states in the nation bordered by eight others, Missouri entices people from near and far to come enjoy its natural beauty and limitless recreational opportunities. In 1993 alone, travelers spent about $9.1 billion in the Show Me State, generating more than $888 million in state tax revenues, as well as $471 million for local governments. Tourism, in fact, is one of the state's top revenue-producing sectors and is expected to remain thus for many years to come.

Livable cities and towns, excellent educational systems, and awe-inspiring countryside make Missouri a place where both entrepreneurial and personal dreams can bear fruit. As the fourth most populous state west of the Mississippi (ranking behind California, Texas, and Washington), Missouri continues to attract newcomers. With so much to enjoy, it's no wonder that, as the twenty-first century approaches, most native families and businesses stay in Missouri and many others choose to relocate to the Show Me State.

Completed in 1965, the Gateway Arch is an engineering marvel. Designed by Eero Saarinen, the Arch soars 630 feet above the city of St. Louis and is the centerpiece of the Jefferson National Expansion Memorial Park along the Mississippi River. © Lewis Portnoy/ Spectra-Action, Inc.

HISTORICAL HIGHLIGHTS

© Hilber Nelson

AREA: 69,709 square miles
POPULATION: 5,402,058
STATE CAPITAL: Jefferson City
STATE MOTTO: *Salus Populi Suprema Lex Esto*
(The welfare of the people shall be the supreme law)
STATEHOOD: Admitted as the twenty-fourth state on August 10, 1821
STATE BIRD: Bluebird
STATE FLOWER: Hawthorn
STATE NICKNAMES: Show Me State, Cave State, Mother of the West

PEOPLE

MAYA ANGELOU, born in St. Louis in 1928; award-winning poet, playwright, and novelist. Among her works are *I Know Why the Caged Bird Sings* (1970), *And Still I Rise* (1978), and *All God's Children Need Traveling Shoes* (1986).

JOSEPHINE BAKER (1906–1975), St. Louis–born dancer, singer, actress. After stints dancing in New York City, Baker went to Paris, where she settled in 1925. She starred at the Folies-Bergère and the Casino de Paris. After her 1956 retirement, she supported the orphanage she had established.

WALTER CRONKITE, born in St. Joseph in 1916; broadcast journalist. In World War II, Cronkite covered the major battles in Europe. From 1962 to 1981, he served as anchor of the "CBS Evening News with Walter Cronkite."

WALT DISNEY (1901–1966), born in Chicago, grew up in Marceline; animated-film producer and pioneer. He created Donald Duck and Mickey Mouse. Among his many works are *Snow White and the Seven Dwarfs* (1937) and *Fantasia* (1940).

CHARLES EAMES (1907–1978), St. Louis–born architect and designer. The chair he created in collaboration with his wife, Ray (Kaiser), in 1946 became the prototype for much of the mass-produced seating of the 1950s and 1960s.

T. S. ELIOT (1888–1965), born Thomas Stearns Eliot in St. Louis; Nobel Prize–winning poet, playwright, literary critic. Among his many works are the poem "The Love Song of J. Alfred Prufrock" and the collection *Prufrock and Other Observations* (1917).

LANGSTON HUGHES (1902–1967), Joplin-born award-winning writer and poet. Hughes published his first book of poems in 1926, *The Weary Blues.* His work marked a turning point in how Black writers interpreted their experiences in U.S. society. His 1951 collection, *Montage of a Dream Deferred*, contains the poem "Harlem."

SCOTT JOPLIN (1868–1917), composer, musician; moved to St. Louis as a teen. In Sedalia, Joplin studied music at George R. Smith College for Negroes and went on to become the "father" of ragtime music. His compositions include "Maple Leaf Rag" (1897) and "The Entertainer: A Ragtime Two Step" (1902).

MARIANNE MOORE (1887-1972), St. Louis–born poet and editor. Her first poetry volume published in the United States was *Observations* (1924). From 1925 until 1929 she edited the literary journal *The Dial*. In 1952, her *Collected Poems* won the Pulitzer Prize.

REINHOLD NIEBUHR (1892–1971), born in Wright City; religious and social thinker whose works deeply influenced Martin Luther King, Jr. His works include *Moral Man and Immoral Society* (1932), *Christianity and Power Politics* (1940), and *The Nature and Destiny of Man* (two volumes, 1941 and 1943).

BRAD PITT, born in Oklahoma in 1964, raised in Springfield; actor. His films include *Thelma & Louise* (1991), *A River Runs Through It* (1992), and *Twelve Monkeys* (1995).

SARA TEASDALE (1884–1933), St. Louis–born Pulitzer Prize–winning poet. Her classically simple work includes *Love Songs* (1917), *Rivers to the Sea* (1915), and *Strange Victory* (1933).

HELEN TRAUBEL (1899–1972), born in St. Louis; operatic and concert singer. She was a leading Wagnerian soprano at the Metropolitan Opera.

TINA TURNER, born in Tennessee in 1939, relocated to St. Louis in 1956; Grammy Award–winning musical artist. While part of The Ike & Tina Turner Revue, her hits included "River Deep, Mountain High" and "Proud Mary." Later, as an accomplished artist on her own, Turner achieved enormous success with her album *Private Dancer* (1984).

DICK VAN DYKE, born in West Plains, Missouri, in 1925; film and television actor. Among his work are the films *Bye*

Bye Birdie (1963), *Mary Poppins* (1964), and *Chitty Chitty Bang Bang* (1968), as well as the television series *The Dick Van Dyke Show* (1961–1966) and *Diagnosis: Murder* (1993–).

LAURA INGALLS WILDER (1867–1957), settled in Mansfield with her  husband and small daughter in 1894; editor, novelist. At the age of sixty-five, she began writing her much-loved *Little House on the Prairie* series of children's novels. Prior to that, she edited the *Missouri Ruralist* for twelve years.

MEMORABLE MOMENTS OF THE TWENTIETH CENTURY

1904 The first Olympic Games held in the United States take place in St. Louis.

1917–1918 General John Joseph Pershing (of Laclede, Missouri) commands the American Expeditionary Force in World War I in Europe.

1919–1925 While manager of the St. Louis Cardinals, Wesley Branch Rickey creates the minor-league "farm system" to develop young players. After 1925, he serves as vice president and general manager. His many innovations lead the team to win six pennants and four world titles.

1926 The Cardinals win the World Series for the first time, defeating the New York Yankees.

1927 On May 20, Minnesotan Charles Lindbergh flies the *Spirit of St. Louis* from New York to France. His feat, financed by St. Louis businessmen, is the first nonstop, solo flight across the Atlantic Ocean.

1931 The Bagnell Dam is completed, creating Lake of the Ozarks.

1943 The George Washington Carver National Monument in Diamond is authorized to commemorate one of the century's most prolific botanists and scientists.

1945 Vice President Harry S. Truman, a Missourian, becomes the thirty-third president of the United States upon President Franklin D. Roosevelt's death. In August, he authorizes the atomic  bombing of Hiroshima and Nagasaki, Japan. In 1947, Truman spurs the creation of the Marshall Plan. In 1948, he helps found NATO (1949).

1965 The 630-foot-tall Gateway Arch is completed in St. Louis. Not one worker dies during its construction.

1971 Southwestern Bell in St. Louis enables its customers to dial long distance without an operator's assistance for the first time.

1985 The Kansas City Royals beat the St. Louis Cardinals in the World Series, nicknamed that year the "I-70 Series."

1986 Chuck Berry, the legendary St. Louis–born musician, is inducted into the Rock 'n' Roll Hall of Fame.

1987 On May 8, the Santa Fe National Historic Trail is established.

1990 Debbye Turner, from Mexico, Missouri, becomes the first Miss America from the Show Me State.

1993 Freeman Bosley, Jr., is elected as St. Louis's first African American mayor.

1993 After heavy summer rains, floods across the state cause more than $5 billion in damages.

1998 On September 8, the Cardinals' Mark McGwire breaks Roger Maris's sea-sonal home-run record when he hits his sixty-second homer of the season. He topped out his record-breaking streak with a total of seventy.

1999 Pope John Paul II celebrates Mass in front of more than 100,000 at Trans World Dome in St. Louis, the only U.S. stop on his tour of North America.

DID YOU KNOW...?

! Big Spring, near Van Buren in southeast Missouri, is the largest single-outlet spring in the United States. Its average daily flow is 276 million gallons.

! The Kansas City area has the most underground storage capacity in the country, thanks to several abandoned limestone mines. Four of the area's five largest industrial parks are underground, filling 16.5 million square feet of space.

! Kemper Military School and College in Boonville, the oldest of Missouri's three military schools, was attended by American humorist Will Rogers and actors Hugh O'Brien (star of the television series *Wyatt Earp*) and George "Goober" Lindsey (co-star of the television series *Mayberry R.F.D.*).

! The highest earthquake risk in the United States outside of the West Coast is along the New Madrid Fault in southeastern Missouri. The strongest recorded U.S. earthquakes occurred in New Madrid over a five-month period during the winter of 1811–1812. Of the more than two thousand temblors, five measured 8.0 or greater in magnitude.

! Missouri ranks fourth in the nation in the number of rural roads and street mileage: 106,333 miles.

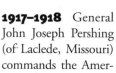

FIRSTS AND INNOVATIONS

1874 Construction of the world's first steel-truss bridge is completed across the Mississippi River in St. Louis.

1884 The Switzer Clark company introduces Switzer's licorice. The St. Louis company is also the creator of Good 'n' Plenty.

1891 A patent for the first automated telephone exchange is granted to Kansas City resident Almon Brown Strowger. His invention allowed callers to make direct connections without the need for an operator.

1898 The St. Louis Iron and Marine Works builds the first diesel engine.

1899 Scott Joplin's famous ragtime song "Maple Leaf Rag" is published by John Stark in Sedalia. The song is named for a popular dance club in that town.

1902 Monsanto produces the first saccharin.

1904 The St. Louis World's Fair introduces iced tea, hot dogs, peanut butter, ice cream cones, and the coin-slot turnstile to the public.

1908 The first degree-granting journalism school in the world is established at the University of Missouri in Columbia.

1912 The first parachute descent from an airplane is made over Jefferson Barracks, Missouri. Captain Albert Berry makes the jump.

1914 The *St. Louis Post-Dispatch* becomes one of the country's first newspapers to use the rotogravure process.

1917 Using a portion of the $2.5 million endowment of Missouri publisher Joseph Pulitzer, the Columbia University School of Journalism in New York establishes the Pulitzer Prizes.

1922 Hallmark Cards, Inc., produces the first decorative gift wrap.

1922 Kansas City developer J. C. Nichols builds Country Club Plaza, the nation's first shopping center designed for automobile traffic.

1920s James Howe creates the stomach-upset remedy Tums for his uncle's business. Today, SmithKline Beecham produces 18 million tablets of Tums every day at its St. Louis facility.

1923 Radio station KSD in St. Louis is the first to transmit the voice of a U.S. president—Warren G. Harding.

1929 C. L. Grigg, a soft-drink salesman and general store owner in St. Louis, invents Bib-Label Lithiated Lemon-Lime Soda. The soft drink later becomes 7-Up.

1930 At the drive-in restaurant Parkmoor in St. Louis, proprietor W. L. McGinley introduces the curbside serving tray. Stainless steel and square, it affixes to car windows. It quickly becomes an indelible icon of Americana.

1933 The first medical fiberglass sutures are used, in a mastoid operation.

1934 On the banks of the Mississippi in St. Louis in the place where One Memorial Drive is today, the powerful liqueur Southern Comfort is concocted and bottled for the first time.

1939 The General Pershing Zephyr, the first train with fluorescent lights, makes its first run—between St. Louis and Kansas City—on April 30.

1940s In a project for the J. A. Folger Company, scientists at the Midwest Research Institute in Kansas City invent the process for making freeze-dried coffee.

1948 With his mother's Sicilian recipe, Kansas City restaurateur Phillip Sollomi, owner of The Wish-Bone restaurant, creates the first Wish-Bone Salad Dressing. The Thomas J. Lipton Company buys the dressing business in 1957.

1946 The first nighttime baseball World Series takes place in St. Louis, between the Red Sox and the Cardinals on October 6.

1946 The mobile telephone is first put into commercial service by the Southwestern Bell Telephone Company.

1946 McDonnell Aircraft of St. Louis builds the FH-1 Phantom, the first jet to operate from a U.S. aircraft carrier.

1947 Drs. Carl Ferdinand Cori and Gerty Theresa Cori of the Washington University School of Medicine receive a joint Nobel Prize for their discovery of how sugar is converted into glycogen in humans.

1948 Stan Musial of the St. Louis Cardinals becomes the first baseball player to win the Most Valuable Player Award three times (he also won in 1943 and 1946).

This page, top to bottom, first column: ©Courtesy, GTE Corporation; ©Corbis-Bettmann; ©Archive Photos; second column: ©Museum of the City of New York/Archive Photos; ©Library of Congress; third column: sticker courtesy of Vicky Matranga, image ©Karen Kohn & Associates, Ltd.; ©Midwest Research Institute; ©Archive Photos

FROM THE SHOW ME STATE

1949 The first all-electric railroad dining car, the Café St. Louis, begins service on March 9 between St. Louis and Chicago.

1950s Because of a Midwest Research Institute innovation, hard candy coating, M&Ms chocolate candy "melts in your mouth, not in your hands."

1956 Missouri begins work on the first interstate highway project in the nation.

1961 The McDonnell Company builds the Mercury spacecraft MR-3 that carries the first American, Alan Shepard, into space.

1961 The first Color King press is installed at the Joplin, Missouri, facility of King Press Corporation. The Joplin facility goes on to become a pioneer in small web offset printing.

1962 The McDonnell Company introduces the Mercury spacecraft MA-6. It carries the first American to orbit the earth, John Glenn, around the globe.

1963 In Kansas City, AMC Entertainment, Inc., builds the world's first multi-screen movie theater in a mall. AMC introduces the world's first four-plex in 1966 and the first six-plex in 1969.

1964 Federal legislation creates the Ozark National Scenic Riverways, which now include passages of the Current, Jacks Fork, and Eleven Point Rivers in southern Missouri.

1965 The McDonnell Company builds the Gemini 4 spacecraft, which carries astronaut Ed White, the first American to walk in space.

1966 Southwestern Bell develops the first single-slot pay phone that distinguishes nickels, dimes, and quarters electronically.

1966 Monsanto develops the first synthetic turf, called AstroTurf, which eventually is used in stadiums and sports arenas the world over.

1967 Wayne Biggs opens the first horse motel in Marshfield. Lodging, feed, and care go for $7; lodging only, for $5.

1971 Ralston Purina Company creates the first soft-moist cat food, Tender Vittles—and launches an entire pet food category.

1971 The Rival Manufacturing Company of Kansas City invents the first Crock Pot.

1972 The Union Electric Company (now known as AmerenUE) generates the first electric power using municipal refuse as a boiler fuel.

1975 Researchers at the Washington University School of Medicine in St. Louis establish the effectiveness of taking aspirin to prevent heart attacks.

1978 The University of Missouri at Columbia establishes the nation's only federally funded arthritis rehabilitation research and training center.

1981 Bass Pro Shops in Springfield launches the first interactive sporting-goods store, bringing the outdoors inside with waterfalls, live fish, and birds.

1983 St. Louis becomes the first city in the United States to allow advertisements on parking meters.

1984 Kansas City-based Marion Laboratories introduces Nicorette Gum, the first prescription smoking-cessation aid approved by the Food and Drug Administration.

1987 Sprint completes the country's first 100 percent digital, fiber-optic network.

1989 Sprint conducts the first trans-Atlantic fiber-optic phone call.

1990 A cure for hepatitis B is announced. A Washington University School of Medicine physician headed up the multi-center research that led to the cure.

1990s Midwest Research Institute engineers develop the small thermoelectric cooling units now used by all crew members on NASA space shuttle flights.

1991 AMC Theatres introduces TeleTicket system, the first movie ticket sales system that allows patrons to purchase tickets in advance by telephone.

1996 The TeleCommunity Center Program sponsored by Southwestern Bell creates a series of high-tech communications centers throughout the state.

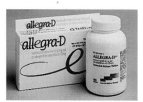

1998 Hoechst Marion Roussel introduces Allegra-D™, a nonsedating antihistamine for the relief of seasonal allergic rhinitis.

A GOOD LIVING, A GOOD LIFE

PART ONE

BY ANN WYLIE & DAWN J. GRUBB

America's heartland has a secret—and its name is Missouri. With its rivers, forests, prairies, mountains, caves, and bluffs, Missouri has been the source of inspiration for many a writer, artist, and musician, giving rise to some of the nation's greatest cultural icons. Writer and humorist Mark Twain, painter Thomas Hart Benton, animator Walt Disney, entertainer Josephine Baker, and writer Maya Angelou are just a few of the notable people who have come from the Show Me State.

Missouri offers residents everything they need and want to create the kind of lifestyle that suits them. Top-notch education, transportation, and health care are just three of the tangible assets that help build a strong foundation for growing families and companies. Intangible qualities, such as civic pride, friendliness, and enthusiasm, keep residents engaged in the myriad cultural and recreational opportunities that abound in rural and urban areas alike.

Whether Missourians call their home MissourEE or MissourAH, they are sure to agree that the state is a fine place in which to live, work, and play. President Harry Truman deemed his hometown of Independence, Missouri, "the best place in America." Today, most Missourians would swiftly extend such praise to include the entire state.

A quaint brick hotel overlooks the Missouri River in Boonville. In the early 1800s, the town's central location on a major riverway made Boonville the port of entry and market for the southwestern area of the state. Boonville also figured prominently as a stop on the Santa Fe Trail and as the site of the first Civil War battle fought on Missouri soil. © Kevin Sink/Midwestock

CULTURAL MOSAIC

CHAPTER ONE

MISSOURI HAS A CULTURAL SCENE FOR EVERY TASTE AND INCLINATION. EXCITING URBAN CENTERS, ECLECTIC COLLEGE TOWNS, AND BUCOLIC HAMLETS THAT OFFER HOMESPUN ARTS AND CRAFTS KEEP RESIDENTS AND TOURISTS COMING BACK FOR MORE. IN KANSAS CITY, FOR INSTANCE, SHOPPERS STROLL ALONG THE PLEASANT STREETS OF THE COUNTRY CLUB PLAZA, WHERE SPANISH-

style architecture, upscale shops, and fine restaurants earn it the nickname "Rodeo Drive of the Midwest." With its bronze bas-relief buffaloes, Italian marble Madonnas, red-tile roofs, and intricate wrought-iron entryways, some $1 million worth of artwork in all, the plaza has an ambience which echoes that of Kansas City's sister city of Seville, Spain. These monuments to beauty join many other aspects that make this former cow town on the Missouri River a dynamic metropolis with a European flair. Kansas City can boast more than two hundred fountains, second only to Rome, and more boulevard miles (140) than Paris. Art offerings include the Kemper Museum of Contemporary Art and Design, featuring changing exhibits, and the Nelson-Atkins Museum of Art, noted for its outstanding Asian art collection and its Henry Moore Sculpture Garden.

The arts don't stop in Kansas City, though. In Columbia, for instance, the State Historical Society dis-

plays its collection of paintings by Missouri artists, who count among them two of America's greatest painters, Thomas Hart Benton and George Caleb Bingham.

Other notable Missouri museums include the Museum of Art and Archaeology at the University of Missouri–Columbia; the Missouri State Museum in Jefferson City; the Harry S. Truman Library and Museum in Independence; and the Albrecht-Kemper Museum of Art in St. Joseph.

On the other side of the state, where the Gateway Arch commemorates the important role the state played in early westward expansion, St. Louis rivals Kansas City with its own array of cultural treasures. For starters, the St. Louis Art Museum, housed in a beautiful stone building that was the only permanent structure built for the 1904 world's fair, is considered one of the top ten art museums in the country. Its permanent collections include ancient and contemporary works and feature Renaissance art, impressionism, American art,

FACING PAGE: *The recently reopened Gem Theatre in Kansas City is part of the refurbished 18th & Vine District, home to the new Jazz Museum and the Negro Leagues Baseball Museum.* © Kevin Sink/Midwestock. THIS PAGE: *This graceful fountain soothes visitors to the garden of the Albrecht-Kemper Museum in St. Joseph, which has an extensive collection of eighteenth-, nineteenth-, and twentieth-century American art, including works by Missouri native Thomas Hart Benton.* © Aneal S. Vohra/Unicorn Stock Photos

Plaza

GERHARDT FURS

At the Missouri Repertory Theatre in Kansas City, actress Mary Proctor (aka Elvira) discovers it's not easy being a ghost in Noel Coward's Blithe Spirit. © Missouri Repertory Theatre

pre-Columbian artifacts, and German expressionism. Visual arts are also on display at many other fine museums throughout the state.

When it comes to music, Missouri offers such a selection of live music and festivals that a music lover could spend an entire year traveling around the state sampling auditory delights and never take it all in. In the east-central part of the state, for example, Sedalia stages the lively Scott Joplin Ragtime Festival in June to commemorate the best-known composer of ragtime music, which captivated a whole generation in the early 1900s. The music of the 1930s comes alive in Kansas City's newly renovated 18th & Vine Historic District, where Count Basie and Joe Turner played in dozens of jazz clubs

FACING PAGE: *Christmas lights trace the Spanish-style outline of Country Club Plaza buildings. © Jim Hays/Midwestock.* RIGHT: *This 1930s poster harks back to a musically vibrant time that solidified Kansas City's importance as a center for some of the century's greatest jazz artists. © David Morris/Midwestock*

and a young local sax player named Charlie Parker began his ascent to fame. Near the Missouri-Arkansas border, Branson shines as country music's newest mecca, boasting some sixty thousand seats in thirty-five theaters, where people enjoy singing along with stars like Glen Campbell, Andy Williams, and Wayne Newton.

Followers of the dramatic arts have much to sample in Missouri. The Missouri Repertory Theatre, St. Louis's Muny in Forest Park and Fox Theatre on Grand Boulevard, Arrowrock's Lyceum, the Little Alley Theatre in Nevada, and Kansas City's Folly Theater, Starlight Theatre, and Midland Center for the Performing Arts are just a few of the playhouses that stage recent Broadway hits, world premieres, and old favorites.

The cities also offer wilder venues, like Kansas City's spacious Zoological Gardens, where visitors can watch gorillas and giraffes roam grasslands on an overnight safari. The St. Louis Zoo, in Forest Park, features the Children's Zoo, Big Cat Country, and the Primate House, among other attractions. Just three miles away, the Missouri Botanical Garden displays a dazzling array of flora, from 515 kinds of irises to a 130-year-old ginkgo.

Sports fans, too, find plenty to cheer about in Missouri, especially in 1998, when St. Louis Cardinals slugger Mark McGwire broke Roger Maris's thirty-seven-year-old home-run record with his sixty-second homer of the season (on his way to a season total of seventy).

From 1926 to 1982, the Cardinals won the World Series nine times, and over the years the St. Louis Blues hockey team has played in two Stanley Cup Finals. In Kansas City, football enthusiasts still relish the Chiefs' 1970 win over the Minnesota Vikings in Super Bowl IV. And the victory of the Kansas City Royals over the Cardinals in the 1985 World Series really set Missouri on its ear.

History buffs need not go far to whet their appetites in Missouri. From the Jesse James House in St. Joseph to the cobblestone streets of Laclede's Landing in St. Louis, the state offers many examples of its fascinating past. The stone house near Defiance where pioneer and scout Daniel Boone lived from 1799 until his death in 1820 and the site outside St. Louis where Meriwether Lewis and William Clark launched their 1804 expedition in search of the fabled

Summer heat dissolves in the Surf City Wave Pool at Oceans of Fun in Kansas City. The sixty-acre attraction is the Midwest's largest tropically themed water park. © Cedar Fair, L.P./Worlds of Fun

Northwest Passage recall the excitement of early explorers as they ventured forth in a vast, uncharted land.

Etched into the Missouri earth are the grooves carved by thousands of wagon wheels, testimony to the country's

This cheetah pauses while pacing at the Kansas City Zoo, which features African, Australian, tropical, and domesticated fauna, among many other animals. © Rebecca Friend/Kansas City Zoo

TOP: *Frank James, shown here circa 1913, operated his infamous brother (inset) Jesse's home as a tourist attraction from 1911 to 1915. © State Historical Society of Missouri/ Courtesy of Jesse James Farm & Museum.* INSET: *© The Bettman Archive/Corbis.* RIGHT: *Arrow Rock's Lyceum Theatre is the state's oldest professional summer repertory theater. © Bruce Mathews/Midwestock*

early expansion. The National Frontier Trails Center in Independence pays tribute to the brave individuals, riding in prairie schooners and on horseback, who began their westward treks on the Santa Fe, Oregon, and California Trails. This and other destinations draw millions of visitors a year, making tourism one of the three largest industries in the state. In 1996, tourists spent over $11 billion in Missouri—and got a glimpse of the good life in America's heartland.

OF RIVERS, HILLS, AND CAVES

CHAPTER TWO

IN THE LATE 1600S, FRENCH EXPLORERS BEGAN TO ASSOCIATE THE MIGHTY RIVER THAT FLOWED INTO THE MISSISSIPPI WITH A TRIBE OF INDIANS WHO LIVED ALONG IT. THEY CALLED THEMSELVES THE *OuMISSOURI,* WHICH MEANS "PEOPLE OF THE LARGE CANOES." WHEN THE NAME *MISSOURI* STUCK, IT WAS A FITTING TRIBUTE TO THE REGION'S MANY SPRINGS, STREAMS, AND RIVERS.

In truth, Missouri isn't what it seems on a map. This "landlocked" mass is actually quite wet. The Lake of the Ozarks alone boasts 1,300 miles of shoreline, more than Lake Michigan or California's coast, and 61,000 acres of water surface. The two largest rivers in the nation, the Mississippi and the Missouri, converge in the state, and the state's rivers and lakes offer some of the country's best fishing, boating, and canoeing.

More than 140 years after Mark Twain piloted a steamboat up and down the Mississippi, the state's rivers are still important networks of transportation, both locally and nationally. St. Louis, in fact, is the busiest inland port in the country, conveying about 218 million tons of cargo every year.

In addition to crystal lakes and raging rivers, Missouri also counts eerie caves, golden prairies, rolling hills, and jagged bluffs among its natural wonders, all fringed and laced with abundant acres of greenery. One-quarter of the state is covered with red cedar, walnut, and other species of trees. Indeed, the state boasts twelve million acres within the National Forest System, home to northern harriers, barn owls, snowy egrets, red-cockaded woodpeckers, gray bats, eastern cougars, and eastern spotted skunks.

Spelunkers can play Indiana Jones among the haunting halls and exquisite rock formations of Missouri's 5,500 caves. With the largest number of caves in the country open to the public, and a total number of caves second only to Tennessee, Missouri has earned the nickname "the Cave State." Legend has it that Jesse and Frank James, the Younger Brothers, and Blackbeard the Pirate hid out and stashed their treasures in Missouri caverns. Although no such loot has been found, several Missouri caves and ancient campsites have turned out to be archaeological troves of Native American artifacts, revealing myriad items, such as tools, weapons, and stone carvings, and eagle-embossed copper pieces that suggest an early form of commerce.

FACING PAGE: *Beautiful year-round, the Missouri Ozarks region is known for its rivers, lakes, hills, caves, and forests. Encompassing about 33,000 square miles, the Ozarks offer serenity, beauty, and a chance to get away from it all. © Kevin Sink/Midwestock.* THIS PAGE: *Limestone stalagmites and stalactites and a subterranean pool glow with otherworldly hues in one of Missouri's thousands of caves, whose colorful rock formations and mysterious passageways draw thousands of tourists a year. © Bill Buchmann/Midwestock*

FACING PAGE: *The 160-acre Cupola Pond Natural Area is an out-of-the-way geologic marvel in the Mark Twain National Forest. The pond is a sinkhole formed by a collapsed limestone cave. Its native water tupelo tree grows in only two places in the Ozarks.* © *Kevin Sink/Midwestock.* TOP: *A man suns himself at Elephant Rocks State Park, near Graniteville.* © *Susan Pfannmuller/Midwestock.* BOTTOM: *The second-largest spring in Missouri, beautiful Greer Springs feeds into the Eleven Point River.* © *Kevin Sink/Midwestock*

OF RIVERS, HILLS, AND CAVES

FROM MANY NATIONS THEY CAME

CHAPTER THREE

I**N THE NORTHWESTERN MISSOURI TOWN OF JAMESPORT, WOMEN IN WHITE PRAYER CAPS AND LONG DRESSES PEDDLE OVEN-HOT PIES IN TIDY SHOPS, WHILE MEN IN BLACK-BRIMMED HATS WORK NEAT FARMS WITH HORSE-DRAWN PLOWS AND HAND-POWERED TOOLS. HOME TO THE LARGEST AMISH COMMUNITY IN MISSOURI, JAMESPORT IS JUST ONE OF THE COLORFUL CORNERS THAT**

has earned the state a reputation as less of a melting pot than a rich stew of people, cultures, and customs.

Influences of all the people who have made Missouri home are still felt across the state. The French made the earliest European mark in Missouri when they created the first permanent settlement west of the Mississippi River, in Ste. Genevieve, in 1735. Today, the town still retains a profound cultural heritage, with beautiful eighteenth-century houses, festivals, folk dancing, and traditional cuisine. German settlers also added their dimension to the state. The town of Hermann, for instance, is a picture-book village that looks much as it did when founded in 1837. It still boasts a large German community and some fine Rhinelike wine. African Americans, who make up 11 percent of Missouri's population, have contributed some of the greatest creative minds in U.S. history, among them George Washington Carver, Maya Angelou, and Chuck Berry. People of Italian descent have also brought fame to the state: Yogi Berra and Joe

Garagiola grew up on The Hill in St. Louis, where more than 75 percent of the residents trace their roots to Italy. Large Asian populations have gathered in Boone and Pulaski Counties; Hispanic communities flourish in Jackson and Pemiscot Counties; Belgians have concentrated in the town of Taos; and Irish, in Vienna.

No matter the season, an ethnic festival is in full swing somewhere, inviting visitors to discover the cultures of not-to-be-forgotten homelands. Hermann's annual Wurst Fest in March, for instance, draws some of the country's top sausage makers, who cook German bologna, summer sausage, and knackwurst to perfection in a chili-, hickory-, and sassafras-scented smokehouse. Thousands gather in St. Charles in mid-August for Fête des Petites Côtes, where French crafts, food, entertainment, and merriment abound in a nineteenth-century atmosphere. And in early fall, St. Louis's Japanese Festival features spectacular performances of taiko drums, bon odori dances, koto music, and Kabuki demonstrations.

FACING PAGE: *These handcrafted rugs are a few of the homespun attractions in and near Jamesport, a 166-family Amish settlement that preserves its traditions through foods, antiques, and crafts. Amish wares are available in many quaint area shops and at several annual festivals.* © Kevin Sink/Midwestock. THIS PAGE: *Chair caning is one of the traditional trades on display during German history weekend at Country Days at Luxenhaus Farm in Marthasville, a historic town in Missouri's wine country.* © Jim Hays/Midwestock

TOP: *The Hermannhof Winery and Vineyards, which offers tours of its 1852 winery and cellars, produces some of the fine Missouri wine that is earning renown. © Dave G. Houser.* BOTTOM: *Costumed in traditional dress, these women celebrate a Japanese festival in the Missouri Botanical Garden, a seventy-nine-acre oasis in St. Louis. © Lewis Portnoy/Spectra-Action, Inc.* FACING PAGE: *Trim houses line the streets of The Hill, a largely Italian neighborhood known since the early 1900s for its superb restaurants. © Lewis Portnoy/Spectra-Action, Inc.*

A GOOD LIVING, A GOOD LIFE

AND THE LIVING IS EASY

CHAPTER FOUR

WHEN NEW YORK LIFE RELOCATED SOME OF ITS OPERATIONS TO KANSAS CITY, ITS EMPLOYEES COULD FINALLY AFFORD THEIR OWN HOMES. "SOME EMPLOYEES HAVE FOUR-BEDROOM HOMES AND BACKYARDS FOR THE FIRST TIME IN THEIR LIVES," SAYS STAN METHENY, THE COMPANY'S MANAGEMENT CONSULTANT. "THEY WERE USED TO LIVING IN APARTMENTS." A 1990S REAL ESTATE STUDY NAMED KANSAS CITY AND ST. LOUIS AS THE SECOND AND FIFTH MOST AFFORDABLE HOUSING MARKETS IN THE COUNTRY, AND MISSOURI'S HOME OWNERSHIP RATE IS 5.2 PERCENT ABOVE THE NATION'S AVERAGE.

Living in Missouri is arguably easier than in other parts of the country. Job growth from 1992 to 1997 was higher than the national average, while personal income grew 6.6 percent from 1994 to 1995. A more secure working life is matched by plentiful creature comforts outside the office, including natural beauty, a steady infrastructure, and interesting cultural amenities. *Fortune* magazine ranked St. Louis, for instance, sixth in the nation among the fifteen "best cities to balance work and family life."

One of the most important determining factors in how comfortable a place feels is its transportation system. And in Missouri, traffic snarls aren't the norm. In fact, the Kansas City metropolitan area is so devoid of freeway

bottlenecks that long-time residents have dubbed it "The Little Easy." The average commute time from the suburbs to downtown is twenty minutes, making the city the envy of places like Chicago and Los Angeles. "Not until you've sat on a bridge in New York, wondering when you're going to get to work, do you understand Kansas City and how good it is," says Jerry Stabenow, vice president of marketing and sales at CompuSpeak Laboratories, Inc.

COMPETITIVE EDUCATIONAL PROGRAMS

Some of the best public schools in the nation make Missourians proud of their education system. *Expansion Management* magazine awarded two Missouri school districts its Gold Medal ranking and deemed nine Missouri

FACING PAGE: *A man walks down a sidewalk in charming Soulard, a St. Louis neighborhood known for its two-hundred-year-old farmers market, restored nineteenth-century homes, and venues for live music, including blues, jazz, and reggae.* THIS PAGE: *These fashionable town houses are part of St. Louis's eye-pleasing, tree-bedecked Central West End, which attracts shoppers from near and far to its mile-long row of boutiques, bookstores, and fine restaurants, pubs, and cafes. Both photos © Lewis Portnoy/Spectra-Action, Inc.*

famous for its medical school, systems engineering education, and other programs.

MISSOURI: WE'LL SHOW YOU

In 1899, U.S. Representative Willard Duncan Vandiver presented a speech that would give Missouri its nickname. "I come from a state that raises corn and cotton and cockleburs and Democrats," Vandiver thundered. "And frothy eloquence neither convinces nor satisfies me. I am from Missouri. You have got to show me."

Today, the "Show Me State" still refers to Missourians' pride, tenacity, and common sense. But insiders know that Missouri's moniker also celebrates all the attributes that this heartland state has to show off.

school districts worthy of its Blue Ribbon ranking. The students in all of these districts on average had academic performances well above those of their peers elsewhere in the nation.

Seventy-seven private colleges, public universities, and community colleges give high school graduates plenty of reasons to stay close to home. The University of Missouri is the oldest state university west of the Mississippi. Founded in 1839 in Columbia, it is among the many educational institutions in the state that offer nationally ranked programs. The University of Missouri's journalism program, for example, is among the top in the country, and its student-run newspaper has won many national awards. MU's Rolla campus is one of only two schools in the nation that offer professional training in all energy and minerals engineering disciplines. Rockhurst College in Kansas City and St. Louis University are nationally known for their physical-therapy programs. And Washington University is

Stadium Plaza surrounds Busch Stadium in downtown St. Louis. The ballpark opened in 1966 as the centerpiece of a revitalization project. © Lewis Portnoy/Spectra-Action, Inc.

Rising from a prosperous medley of well-tended suburbs and fertile farms, Kansas City offers the best in work, arts, entertainment, and recreation. Its Moorish-style Country Club Plaza and 140 miles of statue-lined boulevards and parkways, along with its museums, revitalized downtown areas, and sports arenas, make Kansas City one of the most beautiful cities in the United States. © Kevin Sink/Midwestock

AND THE LIVING IS EASY

FACING PAGE: *The St. Louis University campus has ninety-six buildings among 234 beautiful acres. Gardens, fountains, and statues, such as this realistic portrayal of an astronaut, add to a pleasing environment.* TOP: *University City is a favorite haunt for the culturally inclined. Outdoor cafes, the Center of Contemporary Arts, galleries, and a golf course are among its offerings. Both photos © Lewis Portnoy/Spectra-Action, Inc.* BOTTOM: *Students take a break at the University of Missouri–Kansas City. © Bruce Mathews/Midwestock*

THE NORTHWEST
A LAND IN MOTION

THE NORTHEAST
MARK TWAIN COUNTRY

KANSAS CITY
CONTEMPORARY TRADING POST

CENTRAL MISSOURI
POLITICAL, INTELLECTUAL HUB

ST. LOUIS
GATEWAY TO THE WEST

THE SOUTHWEST
SPORTSMAN'S PARADISE

SOUTH CENTRAL
MISSOURI'S PLAYGROUND

THE SOUTHEAST
LAND OF BEGINNINGS

Illustrations © Hilber Nelson

PART TWO
MISSOURI: REGION BY REGION

BY ANN WYLIE & DAWN J. GRUBB

From rural sights to city lights, Missouri offers a dose of heartland charm in each of its eight regions. Cultural activities abound—a reflection of the Show Me State's seventh-place national ranking in per capita state spending on the arts. Awe-inspiring topography invites residents and tourists to partake in a variety of outdoor pursuits. Across the state, a diverse economy is firmly grounded in both high-tech and traditional businesses. The educational system is excellent. These attributes and others are all the proof residents require: some 70 percent of them are native-born—and proud to hail from the Show Me State.

CHAPTER FIVE
THE NORTHWEST
A LAND IN MOTION

In 1860, executives of freight company Russell, Majors, and Waddell in St. Joseph wanted to deliver mail across the vast and perilous western landscape to Sacramento, California, in just ten days, half the time their competitors took. Using a horse-and-rider relay approach, the company established stations ten to fifteen miles apart where riders could change mounts and obtain fresh horses during their seventy-five-mile daily journey. Thus was born the Pony Express, destined to become obsolete by the advent of the telegraph one year later. The service and its daring riders are commemorated in St. Joseph's Pony Express National Memorial.

Bordered on the west by the Missouri River and on the east by the Chariton River, the rolling river-crossed plains of the northwestern region support some 270,000 residents. Lively, quaint towns such as St. Joseph, Marshall, Carrollton, Maryville, Chillicothe, Bucklin, and Cameron lend a distinctive charm. Marceline is immortalized in hometown son Walt Disney's vision of Main Street, U.S.A.

Many native sons and daughters grow up to work in the region's thriving waterborne transportation, auto parts manufacturing, publishing, food processing, retail trade, construction, and manufacturing industries. Some of the top employers in the area are Kays Engineering and Marshall Egg Products in Marshall; Meade Paper Company in St. Joseph; Worldwide Medical in Sweet Springs; and Walsworth Publishing Company in Marceline.

Agriculture is also a mainstay of the regional economy. Nodaway County, on the Iowa border, for example, is one of the state's top corn producers. Corporations, such as Princeton/Milan's Premium Standard Farms/Premium Standard Foods, till fields alongside family farms, helping to make Missouri number two in the number of farms among the fifty states. About 102,000 farms across the state produce more than $4.9 billion worth of goods annually.

The northwestern country is known among sportsmen for its deer, waterfowl, and wild-turkey hunting in the Chariton River Valley. Nature buffs flock to Swan Lake National Wildlife Refuge and the Fountain Grove Wildlife Area, where thousands of migrating waterfowl

PONY EXPRESS

Picturesque and vital, the rolling prairies of northwestern Missouri support a variety of agricultural production. © Dave G. Houser

Animator Walt Disney grew up in this tidy home in Marceline. © Martin R. Jones/Unicorn Stock Photos.

and shorebirds sojourn every spring and autumn.

Near the Nebraska border, the Squaw Creek National Wildlife Refuge stretches over 7,178 acres of Missouri Valley wetlands, which serve as a way station in the fall for countless birds, including snow geese, ducks, and bald eagles.

Area residents in search of fun and culture seek out the exhibitions, festivals, and special events in St. Joseph, Hamilton, Bethany, Gallatin, Brunswick, and other towns.

BOTTOM LEFT: *The original admissions building at Northwest Missouri State University in Maryville lends to the pleasant campus setting. © Jim Shippee/Unicorn Stock Photos.* BOTTOM RIGHT: *Frontierswoman Calamity Jane was born in Princeton, Missouri. © Corbis-Bettmann*

CHAPTER SIX
THE NORTHEAST
MARK TWAIN COUNTRY

At the turn of the century, Mark Twain eloquently depicted the spirit of river towns in *Life on the Mississippi* and *The Adventures of Huckleberry Finn.* He wrote of booming business along "the great highway" and of the many opportunities the river afforded. Today, the river is still an important part of the economy, with barges moving tons of bulk freight across and through the state every year.

A sprawling plain dissected by rivers, streams, and lakes, the northeastern region of the state is an oasis of fertile Midwest farmland. Here, farmers grow soybeans, corn, pecans, oats, and wheat, as well as sheep, hogs, and poultry. Its stunning landscape also makes this region home to important state conservation areas, including Big Creek and Sugar Creek, just outside Kirksville. The northeast also offers echoes of the past, in its friendly river towns and farming villages. Hannibal, Moberly, Kirksville, and Mexico are accented by charming riverboats, antebellum mansions, horse-drawn wagons, and trolleys.

With approximately 208,500 residents, the northeast region is Missouri's smallest, but business prospers there nonetheless. With a mere 3 percent average unemployment rate, the area offers a livelihood in various industries. Top employers include copper tubing manufacturer Cerro Copper Tube Company; wire manufacturer Optic D.D.; preprinted-office-forms producer Standard Register; dough-maker Au Bon Pain; and lunch meats processor Adair Foods, a division of Oscar Mayer. Newcomers also bring opportunities: the recent addition of two correctional facilities—Vandalia's new women's prison and Bowling Green's new men's facility—created 1,150 new jobs.

Twain country is a favorite among tourists, who may enjoy water sports on Mark Twain Lake or a stroll down the charming streets of Hannibal, where the author's boyhood home and the Becky Thatcher House are open for viewing. During the first week of July, the town erupts with the frolicking fun of National Tom Sawyer Days, held annually since 1955. The festival hosts many events, including the National Fence Painting Championships. And city leaders plan to renovate the waterfront, constructing a new harbor and park. Both will overlook the mighty Mississippi, where life keeps rolling on.

RIVERBOAT ON THE MISSISSIPPI

These Hannibal townspeople get in the spirit of National Tom Sawyer Days by dressing in period costumes. Sawyer look-alikes also compete in a fence-painting contest. © Jim Hays/Midwestock

Providing tours of the Mississippi River, the Mississippi Queen *riverboat is a twin-stacked vessel that was commissioned in 1976. Shown here docked in Hannibal, it brings tourists to several beautiful settings along the mighty river. The boat is 382 feet long, can carry 420 passengers, has a crew of 165 members, and features many amenities, including a beauty parlor. © Lewis Portnoy/Spectra-Action, Inc.*

When the first Europeans traveled up the Mississippi River, they undoubtedly were awestruck by the beauty of the landscape. Today, many historically important and culturally rich towns are found along the waterway, among them Cape Girardeau, Ste. Genevieve, and Hannibal. The Mississippi flows 2,348 miles from northwestern Minnesota to the Gulf of Mexico. © Kevin Sink/Midwestock

TOP: *Several annual festivals in the charming town of Hannibal attract thousands of tourists a year. Scenic Main Street provides the setting for a pleasant stroll or an afternoon of window-shopping. © SuperStock.* BOTTOM LEFT: *In 1839, John Clemens moved his family from Florida, Missouri, to Hannibal. Young Sam Clemens was raised in this house. To the right is Tom Sawyer's fence. © SuperStock*

Mark Twain, shown here on deck, used his experiences as a riverboat pilot along the Mississippi River in the 1850s as source material for some of his most popular written works. © Mark Twain Museum, Hannibal

CHAPTER SEVEN
KANSAS CITY
CONTEMPORARY TRADING POST

JAZZ AND BLUES CLUBS

In the early nineteenth century, Westport, the place where pioneers stocked up on supplies for the long road west, served as the jumping-off point for the Santa Fe, California, and Oregon Trails. Today, this historic district of renovated buildings near the intersection of the Missouri and Kansas Rivers is still the place to stock up, but on more contemporary items such as trendy fashion accessories and good food and drink. The boutiques, galleries, restaurants, and bars are favorite haunts of college students on both sides of the state line.

Kansas City is Missouri's second-largest economic area, the place where companies like Hallmark Cards, Inc., H&R Block, Black & Veatch, Utili-Corp United, Interstate Bakeries, Hoechst Marion Roussel USA, and Yellow Freight System produce and proffer their wares and services.

The city that straddles a state border also spawns ambitious plans. Noted as both one of the best places to own a business and a fertile location for small businesses, Kansas City has been called "an entrepreneur's dream" by *Inc.* magazine. One reason behind this accolade is the Kauffman Foundation Center for Entrepreneurial Leadership, a $1 billion organization that devotes its resources to training and nurturing young business builders.

The strong agribusiness sector in Kansas City supports farms in Missouri's northwest, northeast, and southeast regions, while the city's Board of Trade leads the nation in marketing hard winter wheat. Farmland Industries, the largest farm cooperative in the country, helps independent farmers compete with the industry giants.

City and business leaders are backing aggressive urban renewal efforts, earmarking $1 billion to give the city a facelift, with renovated skyscrapers, new federal office buildings, residential lofts, and a twenty-first-century science center inside the nineteenth-century Union Station.

In 1997, Kansas City played host to the conference Brownfields: Partnering for a Greener Tomorrow. Brownfields are former industrial or commercial properties that have been left idle because they need to be cleaned up. The brownfields movement aims to redevelop these unused or underused urban properties, thus revitalizing city centers and saving pristine areas on the outskirts from development. In 1998, the Environmental

Crown Center Square is a favorite gathering spot during spring and summer. Families enjoy the Friday Funfests, which offer food, activities, and live music. © Hallmark Cards, Inc.

This neon sign evokes the culinary delight of barbecue in Kansas City, which hosts the annual American Royal Barbecue contest. © David Morris/Midwestock

Protection Agency (EPA) designated Kansas City as one of sixteen Brownfields Showcase Communities in the nation.

As more people discover this midwestern gem, Kansas City continues to grow. Between 1980 and 1990, the Kansas City metropolitan area, spanning the Missouri-Kansas border, grew 8.2 percent from 1.4 million people to 1.5 million. By 2000, the city and its environs are expected to support more than 1.9 million residents.

Kansas City has many attributes that make it an exciting and pleasant place to live. Reflecting Missouri's characteristic diversity, Kansas City is as cosmopolitan as any great U.S. metropolis, and its low cost of living affords residents a chance to get ahead. In fact, "KC," as natives call it, was one of only two cities of more than one million residents to make the National Association of Home Builders' list of twenty-five most affordable housing areas in 1996. It was also the first major metro area to be designated a "clean air city" by the EPA. And several of its school districts—in Independence, Blue Springs, Warrensburg, and Grandview—have earned awards for educational excellence.

When the day is done, Kansas Citians unwind in style, especially in nightclubs that carry on the city's jazz and blues legacy. Gustatory delights also await. The more than seventy barbecue establishments, each with its own secret sauce and smoking rituals, deservedly place Kansas City as the capital of the barbecue aficionado's world. As *New Yorker* columnist and K.C. native Calvin Trillin writes: "Not all the best restaurants are in Kansas City—just the top four or five."

Kansas City has more fountains than any other U.S. city. © Bruce Mathews/Midwestock

TOP: *These sailboats are anchored in Sailboat Cove at Fleming Park in Jackson County, whose several lakes are favorite weekend destinations.* © *Susan Pfannmuller/Midwestock.* BOTTOM: *The bronze sculpture* Spider *by Louise Bourgeois greets visitors to the Kemper Museum of Contemporary Art & Design, part of the Kansas City Art Institute.* © *The Kemper Museum of Contemporary Art & Design*

TOP: *Kansas City is home to almost two hundred of the country's largest industrial firms, including car manufacturers, steel and metal fabricators, and food processors.* © Kevin Sink/Midwestock. BOTTOM: *The Jazz Museum highlights the careers of trumpeter Louis Armstrong, saxophonist Charlie Parker, singer Ella Fitzgerald, and pianist, composer, and band leader Duke Ellington.* © Bruce Mathews/Midwestock

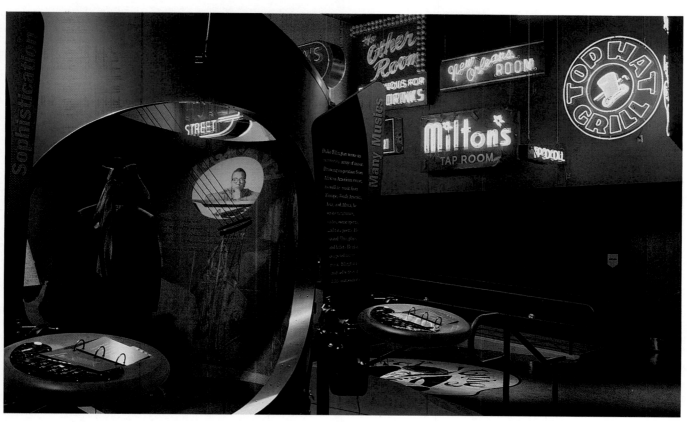

CHAPTER EIGHT

CENTRAL MISSOURI
POLITICAL, INTELLECTUAL HUB

Ah, to be in the midst of it all: bustling Jefferson City, vibrant Columbia, and heavenly Lake of the Ozarks are just some of the stellar facts of life in Missouri's central region. The area's three hundred thousand residents enjoy such easy access to the state's political, cultural, educational, and recreational hot spots that they don't need anyone to show them they have the best of all worlds. These homegrown attributes, along with the amenities reached through a relatively short drive to Kansas City and St. Louis, inspire central-Missouri natives to stay generation after generation.

STATE CAPITOL

White-collar employment, especially in government and academic jobs, drives the economy in this area of the state. Work in construction, insurance, and medical services is also important. The area can boast a low threat of unemployment, with the number of jobs expected to grow 3.6 percent by 2000. Of the numerous industries contributing to the region's economic stability, wine-making stands out not only as a profitable enterprise but also as a tourist attraction. A weekend getaway brings many a Missourian to picturesque Hermann, home of the state's oldest wineries. Its German heritage is reflected in the 1800s-style architecture of homes, churches, museums, and bed-and-breakfast inns. Residents of this town of 2,800 also find employment in area metal-working, plastics, and shoe factories.

Adding to the region's livability are some of the best-rated health care facilities and educational institutions in the nation. In Columbia, Columbia College, Stephens College, and the University of Missouri–Columbia together help give the region its deserved reputation for excellence in higher education.

When it comes to outdoor pursuits, the central region's forests, rivers, lakes, and trails provide countless ways to exercise one's body and reconnect with the spirit of the land. Rock Bridge Memorial State Park, Katy Trail State Park, which follows the former route of the Missouri-Kansas-Texas Railroad, and the Mark Twain National Forest give area residents plenty of reasons to stay close to home, even while getting away from it all.

This bed-and-breakfast adds to the charm of Hermann, which was founded by German immigrants in 1836. German heritage is preserved at the German School of Arts and Crafts, the Deutschheim State Historic Site, and area wineries. © David Morris/Midwestock

TOP LEFT: *Designed by George Ingham Barnett, the Governor's Mansion was built in 1871. © Lewis Portnoy/Spectra-Action, Inc.* TOP RIGHT: *The Katy Trail winds through some breathtaking scenery, including this spot along the Missouri River near Rocheport. © Frank Oberle/ Tony Stone Images.* BOTTOM: *A day of classes begins at the University of Missouri–Columbia. © Lewis Portnoy/Spectra-Action, Inc.*

CHAPTER NINE
ST. LOUIS
GATEWAY TO THE WEST

Nearly one hundred years after Lewis and Clark pushed off from the banks of the Missouri River in 1804, St. Louis jumped into the twentieth century with both feet and never looked back. St. Louis placed itself firmly on the map as a world-class city in 1904 when it hosted both the first U.S.–based Olympic Games and the Louisiana Purchase Exposition. Today, with more than 2.5 million people in six counties, the St. Louis metropolitan area is Missouri's largest economic hub and one of the top industrial corridors in the nation.

ST. LOUIS AND GATEWAY ARCH

Outstanding highway, rail, air, and barge facilities help make St. Louis a prospering distribution center, as well as a locus for banking, retail, manufacturing, telecommunications, construction, and tourism. Emerson Electric, Southwestern Bell, Anheuser-Busch, May Department Stores, and The Boeing Company are a few of the region's largest employers. St. Louis ranks among the top five cities nationally for creating new jobs, about 52,700 between January 1995 and April 1997. New facilities by MCI Communications, Southwestern Bell, and the Union Pacific Service Center added many more new jobs in the late 1990s.

The city's solid economy, combined with the second-lowest cost of living among the nation's top twenty metropolitan areas, helps promote population growth in the region. St. Louis's current population is expected to reach 2.67 million by the year 2000.

The population of St. Louis is as diverse as any metropolis, where the blend of people from many cultural backgrounds helps create an exciting environment. African Americans, people of Latin American origins, Italian and German Americans, as well as Asian people have all established thriving communities, enhancing the city's richness with their arts, cuisines, and entrepreneurial spirits.

Area residents have many outstanding educational options to choose from. Twelve universities, eight professional schools, seven graduate schools, eight two-year colleges and more than one hundred vocational schools provide myriad opportunities for students. Several school

Union Station no longer caters to trains, but it bustles with the activity of thousands of shoppers and diners. Restored as a downtown landmark, Union Station now houses markets, a hotel, and 125 shops and restaurants. © Lewis Portnoy/Spectra-Action, Inc.

districts have earned awards for excellence, and many of the programs within the city's colleges and universities are recognized as among the best in the nation.

When it comes to recreational or cultural pursuits, area residents have a plethora of parks and sports facilities, theaters and restaurants to choose from. The city has also revitalized key parts of its urban core, increasing civic pride and attracting tourists and new businesses downtown.

RIGHT: *Cousins and siblings enjoy a family reunion in Forest Park, St. Louis's principal oasis for outdoor fun and cultural activities.* BOTTOM: *Busch Stadium has been the site of many memorable moments for the St. Louis Cardinals. Both photos © Lewis Portnoy/Spectra-Action, Inc.*

TOP LEFT: *Unlike similarly imposing projects, the Gateway Arch did not cost the life of one worker who helped construct it.* © UPI/Corbis-Bettmann. TOP RIGHT: *A horse-drawn carriage graces a cobblestone street at Laclede's Landing.* © Lewis Portnoy/Spectra-Action, Inc. BOTTOM: *The Missouri Botanical Garden features a two-level domed greenhouse.* © Gay Bumgarner/Tony Stone Images. OPPOSITE: *Twilight paints a warm backdrop for the silhouettes of downtown St. Louis.* © Lewis Portnoy/Spectra-Action, Inc.

CHAPTER TEN

THE SOUTHWEST
SPORTSMAN'S PARADISE

FISHING AND BOATING

Twenty-eight years ago, outdoor enthusiast and entrepreneur John L. Morris of Springfield envisioned a sportsmen's one-stop shop where they could find everything they needed under one roof. Morris launched Bass Pro Shops in 1971.

Since then, he has transformed the small Springfield sporting-goods setup from a couple of aisles in his father's local liquor store to a 300,000-square-foot mecca, complete with cascading waterfalls, fresh seafood, and thousands of retail sporting goods. Today, nearly four million people visit Morris's Bass Pro Shops Outdoor World, making it the number one tourist attraction in the Show Me State.

With more than 670,000 residents, the southwest region is one of the state's fastest-growing areas, and business opportunities abound. In Branson, Missouri's "best-known small town," three dozen music theaters offer more than sixty music shows, ranging from country and pop classics to New Age and classical sounds. Springfield, the state's third-largest city, has been called one of the ten "hottest" cities for small business in the United States.

Telecommunications, transportation, food service, health care, manufacturing, and warehousing are major local industries. Kraft Foods, MCI Corporation, Mid-America Dairymen, 3M Company, and Springfield Remanufacturing Corporation top the list of employers. In the late 1990s, the new manufacturing facilities of the American National Can Company in Joplin–Webb City and of Schreiber Foods in Mt. Vernon added many jobs to the region.

Tourism will continue to play a principal role in the local economy for decades to come. Each year, thousands of outdoor enthusiasts visit Lake Taneycomo, Bull Shoals Lake, Norfork Lake, and Table Rock Lake for swimming, boating, fishing, scuba diving, and water skiing. They do so rarely without stopping by Morris's shop first.

Bass Pro Shops opened its second Outdoor World store in Gurnee, Illinois (shown here), in 1997. It was the first Outdoor World in the upper Midwest and the first to anchor a mall, the Gurnee Mills Mall. Through April 2000, six Outdoor World Showrooms were being planned in the South and Midwest. © Bass Pro Shops

 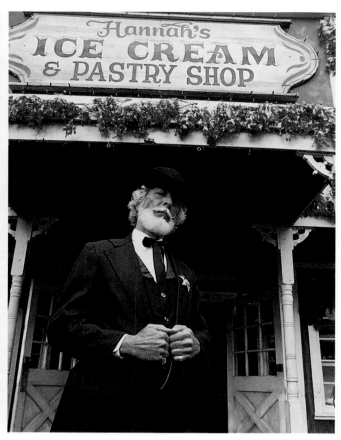

Top LEFT: *Roy Clark opened his Celebrity Theatre in 1983 on 76 Country Boulevard, also known as "the Strip." © Andre Jenny/International Stock.* Top RIGHT: *This "sheriff" gets into the spirit of authenticity at the Silver Dollar City theme park, which was opened in 1960 by Mary Herschend and her sons. © Dave G. Houser.* BOTTOM: *The Glade Top Trail in the Mark Twain National Forest offers a palette of warm colors for hikers to behold. Citizens from nearby Ava organize the Glade Top Trail Flaming Fall Revue every year. © Kevin Sink/Midwestock*

CHAPTER ELEVEN
SOUTH CENTRAL
MISSOURI'S PLAYGROUND

Missourians know that the word *vacation* is just about synonymous with "the Lake," shorthand for Lake of the Ozarks. Known for its canoe-and-camp industry, the south-central region is the state's playground, drawing thousands of canoers, campers, fishers, and floaters each year from throughout the state and beyond. They flock to such resort communities as Osage Beach and Camdenton, where visitors enjoy water sports and also golf, tour caves, dine, and shop.

With its nearly 380,000 residents, the Ozarks are also a favorite retirement destination, drawing people to the area's scenic beauty, four distinct seasons, recreational opportunities, and low cost of living. Other area waterways, state parks, and woodlands add to the region's appeal.

The area supports many thriving industries besides tourism. With its dense expanses of wooded land, the Ozark Plateau is the center of Missouri's eight hundred wood-using industries. As a whole, about 29 percent of the state's total area is forested.

Regional businesses include producers of baby foods and frozen foods, as well as manufacturers of equipment and boats. New plants for Caterpillar, Inc., Copeland Corporation, and Barber Foods, as well as a new men's prison in Licking, have added to area job growth. Well-established companies include Lee Apparel Company in Houston, Fasco Industries in Eldon, Systems & Electronics, Inc., in West Plains, and Detroit Tool & Engineering in Lebanon. Since the 1950s, Fort Leonard Wood has been one of the region's largest employers. When a chemical-weapons training facility relocates to the fort in 1999, 6,600 people are expected to migrate to the area.

Educational options rate high. Rolla is home to seven colleges and universities, and several regional school districts have earned awards for excellence.

At day's end, students, families, and workers all have something exceptional to look forward to: the region's beauty, serenity, and open spaces.

LAKE OF THE OZARKS

Valleys and hollows, streams and rivers, hills, caves, and glades mark the Ozarks, among the world's most scenic karst landscapes. Their shape derives from the uplifting, folding, faulting, and erosion of limestone and dolomite slabs. © Kevin Sink/Midwestock

TOP: *Southern Missouri's fantastical landscape is a rock climber's dream. With boulders and cliffs galore of rock at many climbable angles, the Ozarks have added yet another activity to their long list of outdoor opportunities.* © Rick Adair/Midwestock. BOTTOM: *Created in 1964, the Ozark National Scenic Riverways preserve 134 miles of the Current and Jacks Fork Rivers, as well as beautiful public lands on either side, such as this forest showing signs of early spring.* © Kevin Sink/Midwestock

CHAPTER TWELVE
THE SOUTHEAST
LAND OF BEGINNINGS

French and Spanish explorers tenaciously sought riches up and down the Mississippi River. They weren't disappointed when they chose the site of Ste. Genevieve as the first Missouri settlement, establishing a launching point for further inspection of the region. By the early 1700s, area mineral ore, especially lead veins, had inspired the construction of several mines, and Ste. Genevieve earned its permanent place as a trading post on the Mississippi.

The "Lead Belt" has been mined ever since, and the St. Joseph Lead Company, in operation since 1864, is Missouri's largest lead-mining concern. Missouri, in fact, has been the primary producer of lead in the United States since 1906, accounting for 75 percent of the nation's output. Other major mineral products mined and quarried from the southeastern region include stone (especially limestone, marble, and granite), coal, cement, zinc, sand and gravel, and barite. The St. Francois Mountains supply lead, zinc, and barite, and bituminous coal deposits lie north of there.

The Mississippi creates a constant flow of activities—touring in steamboats, gaming in riverboat casinos, fishing, boating, swimming, and hiking. The Corps of Engineers recently gave Cape

SHIPPING INDUSTRY

Girardeau's harbor a facelift, making the region's largest city a shipping and business hub. Levees and drainage systems have transformed Pemiscot County in Missouri's Bootheel from swamplands (*Pemiscot* is a Native American word for "liquid mud") into some of the world's best farmlands. Today, the Bootheel's fertile farms produce more than 14 percent of Missouri's cash crops, including corn, grain sorghum, cotton, rice, and soybeans, Missouri's premier cash crop.

The natural beauty of the Show Me State extends to the southeast, where the 21,676-acre Mingo National Wildlife Refuge in Puxico harbors the largest hardwoods swamp in the state. At Bonne Terre, the wide passageways of the world's most spacious man-made caverns and the billion-gallon underground lake offer ample opportunities for walking or scuba diving. To the south, people yearning for perspective can hike to the peak of 1,772-foot Taum Sauk Mountain. From the state's highest point, they can survey the southeast region, the place where Missouri began.

The official animal of the Show Me State since 1995, the hardy Missouri Mule is known for its strength, intelligence, and temper. Most are now bred for show. © Lewis Portnoy/Spectra-Action, Inc.

TOP: *While cruising along the Mississippi River, passengers may enjoy a game of craps or poker, or partake of many amenities aboard the* Casino Queen *riverboat. © Lewis Portnoy/Spectra-Action, Inc.* BOTTOM: *The dance between water and stone roars and rushes at the Castor River Shut-Ins in the Amidon Conservation Area on the border of Madison and Bollinger Counties. © Kevin Sink/Midwestock*

A CENTURY OF PROGRESS

PART THREE

BY ROBERT L. DYER

The 1904 St. Louis World's Fair encapsulated Missouri's intention to remain at the vanguard of industrial and technological innovation. Missouri succeeded in doing just that as the twentieth century progressed. Now, as the new millennium begins, the Show Me State is a leading producer of lead, transportation equipment, food products, chemicals, and defense and aerospace technology. Other industries have also stepped up to the forefront, contributing to a dynamic economy.

In the late 1990s, 28 percent of Missouri's nonagricultural workers are employed in the service industries, the most robust and rapidly growing segment of the economy; about 16 percent are government employees; and 6 percent work in transportation and public utilities. About 24 percent make their livelihoods in wholesale and retail trade, while about 16 percent are employed in manufacturing.

This diverse economy helps make Missouri an ideal place in which to live and work. The state's urban and rural markets are well balanced, and the cost of doing business is low. Since the early eighties, Missouri's per capita income has steadily increased while the cost of living has remained below the national average. The state supports business expansion with generous tax credit, incentive, and abatement programs. These motivators add to the many attributes that persuade people and companies to relocate to Missouri. And once they have settled in, they can count on the state to show them many reasons to stay.

Built in the nineteenth century, the Eads Bridge symbolizes the technological know-how that made Missouri a great state in its early days and that continues to move the state forward into the twenty-first century. © James Blank

LAND OF PLENTY

CHAPTER THIRTEEN

YOU DON'T NEED TO TELL THE EMPLOYEES OF THE DOE RUN COMPANY TO GET THE LEAD OUT, BECAUSE THAT'S WHAT THEY AND THEIR PREDECESSORS IN THE OLD ST. JOE LEAD COMPANY HAVE BEEN DOING IN SOUTHEAST MISSOURI SINCE 1864. INDEED, AS EARLY AS 1690 FRENCH EXPLORERS AND ENTREPRENEURS WERE GETTING THE LEAD OUT OF THE LAND THAT WOULD BECOME MISSOURI. THEY CAME LOOKING FOR GOLD AND

silver, but the lead they found proved to be a valuable commodity in and of itself, drawing the first capital investments and settlers into the region.

Lead mining, as well as the mining of zinc, copper, and iron in the vicinity of the St. Francois Mountains in southeast Missouri, continued throughout the nineteenth century and into the twentieth, supplemented by the opening of a similar mining area in southwest Missouri near Joplin. The zinc and lead deposits around Joplin, however, played out by

the 1950s just as the southeast Missouri lead-mining area was infused with new life by the discovery of richer deposits, known as the Viburnum Trend, about fifty miles west of the old lead belt. This deposit continues to be profitably worked by Missouri's main lead-producing concern, The Doe Run Company.

Doe Run is, in fact, the world's largest producer of lead metal from the ground and the world's second-largest total lead producer. In 1998, with sales of $717 million, it ranked among the top twenty-five largest privately held companies based in the St. Louis area. The company employs 6,500 people worldwide, 1,900 in Missouri. Within the state Doe Run operates eight underground mines, six milling units, two primary smelters, and a recycling smelter. Doe Run also conducts lead fabrication activities in Texas, Arizona, and Washington. In South America Doe Run Peru operates the La Oroya metallurgical complex, which produces eleven metals ranging from lead to gold, and an underground copper mine with surface milling.

Although iron mining is not nearly as significant as lead mining in Missouri, geologists estimate that as much

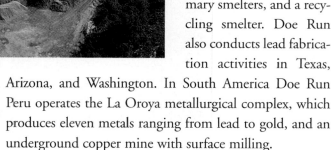

FACING PAGE: *A worker manipulates bands of steel at a mill. Steel is a commercial iron whose malleability makes it useful for thousands of applications. Iron ore is mined in the St. Francois Mountains region of Missouri. © Kevin Cruff/FPG International LLC.* THIS PAGE: *Limestone, showing its whitish-blue hue in this mine, is found in significant quantities throughout Missouri, which is the third-largest producer of commercial limestone in the country. Ozark quarries supply commercial lime plants and cement mills. © John Mutrux/Midwestock*

ANHEUSER-BUSCH, ESTABLISHED IN ST. LOUIS IN 1852, IS THE WORLD'S LARGEST BREWING OPERATION AND THE SECOND-LARGEST U.S. MANUFACTURER OF ALUMINUM BEVERAGE CONTAINERS. IT ALSO OPERATES THE LARGEST ALUMINUM RECYCLING BUSINESS IN THE WORLD. THE COMPANY'S MOST SUCCESSFUL BEER BRAND, BUDWEISER, WAS CREATED IN 1876. IT OUTSELLS ALL OTHER BRANDS IN THE WORLD.

as one billion tons of iron ore are scattered throughout south-central and southeast Missouri and could be available for future development. At present, the one major iron-mining company in the state is the Pea Ridge Iron Ore Company, established in 1964 as a division of Big River Mineral Corporation in Clayton. As of 1998, its mine just south of Sullivan in Washington County employed about 150 people and in 1994 produced more than three hundred thousand long tons of iron ore. The mine has the distinction of being the only operating underground iron-ore mine in the United States.

Limestone is the second-leading mineral commodity in Missouri. In fact, 88 of Missouri's 114 counties produce limestone. The Mississippi Lime Company, established in Ste. Genevieve in 1907, is the largest independent lime producer in the nation, processing and shipping more than one million tons of high-calcium lime per year.

Among Missouri's other valuable mineral resources are coal, clay, shale, silica sand, and granite. Associated Electric Corporation and Pittsburgh & Midway Coal Company account for most of the three million tons of coal produced annually in the state, while A. P. Green, Lowe's Southern Clay, and River Cement account for two-thirds of the 925,000 tons of clay processed annually. Nearly one million tons of shale are quarried every year by Dundee Cement and Buildex, Inc., while the leading producers of silica sand are U.S. Silica and the Unimin Corporation. G. A. F. Chemicals Corporation is responsible for most of the four hundred thousand tons of granite produced annually in the state. Taken together, these rich mineral resources make Missouri the tenth-leading producer of crushed stone, lead, cement, and lime in the United States. These four commodities alone are valued at more than $1.1 billion annually.

In 1951, these cattlemen examine the Livestock Receipts Board at the Kansas City stockyards. For most of the twentieth century, Kansas City was the primary cattle-trading center in the nation.
© UPI/Corbis-Bettmann

This decorative façade welcomes visitors to a Missouri winery and harks back to the owners' Bavarian origins. © Dave G. Houser

FROM MINES TO FIELDS

Although mining was an important early source of Missouri's wealth, agriculture was the driving force in the state's economy. Prior to the Civil War, hemp and tobacco farming were vital agricultural pursuits in the fertile Missouri and Mississippi River valleys, along with grape cultivation introduced by German immigrants in towns like Hermann, Augusta, Washington, and Westphalia. These German settlers established numerous wineries and breweries, several of which still operate in the state despite a major setback brought on by Prohibition in the 1920s. But the real foundation of the agricultural economy in the Show Me State has always been crop and livestock farming, supplemented by the breeding of fine horses, purebred livestock, and mules. (In 1995, the Missouri Mule was chosen as the official state animal by the eighty-eighth General Assembly.)

Missouri's fertile soils lend themselves to the successful production of a variety of agricultural products. Although corn was the state's leading crop for more than one hundred years, its place has been usurped since the late 1950s by soybeans. Missouri is a leading producer of soybeans nationwide while remaining among the top ten states in corn,

A verdant latticework of cropland, vineyards, and woods colors the fertile wine region along the Missouri River west of St. Louis. © Randall Hyman

winter wheat, and hay production. The Missouri Bootheel continues to be the only region of the state where cotton and rice are grown, and increasing attention is being given in this region to corn, wheat, soybean, and grain sorghum production. Seven counties in the Bootheel are responsible for nearly one-third of all crop production in the state. Missouri is also a principal producer of beef cows, hogs, and poultry. Cattle and hog farming are most prevalent north of the Missouri River, and poultry production, along with some dairy farming, are more heavily concentrated in southwestern Missouri.

During the twentieth century, Missouri agriculture followed the national trend toward fewer and larger farms as mechanization, technology, and growing consumer demands made it difficult for the small family farm to compete with corporate-owned "megafarms." Among the few independent farmer co-ops left in the state, the Missouri Farmers Association is the oldest and most respected of the statewide co-ops, while Mid-America

© Corbis Digital Stock

Dairymen, located in Springfield, is the main voice for
dairy farmers in the state. Co-ops have traditionally given
the smaller farmers a more direct role in controlling the
quality, pricing, and distribution of their seed stock, chemicals, fertilizers, feed, and other necessities, as well as in the
marketing of their products.

The tendency toward corporate centralization has had
its effect on the marketing of seed, chemicals, and fertilizer.
A few large corporations such as ADM, ConAgra, and
Monsanto have come to control these key agricultural
necessities. Although some observers decry this corporate
control and the genetic tampering with seed stock, others
point out the positive effects, such as the development of
improved and more insect- and disease-resistant seed
stocks; chemical herbicides and insecticides with less environmentally damaging side effects; and more cost-effective
planting and harvesting methods.

*Near Chillicothe, farmer Bill Christenson shovels soybeans while
a combine pours them into his truck. The fifth leading producer
of soybeans in the country, Missouri harvested more than 4.8
million acres of the versatile legume in 1997. © Randall Hyman*

Corporate centralization is also the major theme in
Missouri's food-processing industry. While the state's giant
in this field—St. Louis–based Anheuser-Busch—has dominated the beer-brewing industry for
more than one hundred years, St.
Louis is also the home of the famous
red-and-white "checkerboard square"
company, Ralston Purina Company,
as well as the wholesale grocery distributor Wetterau, Inc. Kansas City, on
the other hand, is the headquarters for
two of the state's other food-processing giants, Farmland Industries and
Interstate Bakeries. Missouri also has
major divisions of national corporate

*A stone eagle greets visitors to the head-
quarters of Anheuser-Busch Companies,
founded in 1852 in St. Louis. © Doug
McKay/HMS Group/Tony Stone Images*

Missouri timber makes the state a leader in the production of charcoal, walnut logs and lumber, red cedar, and barrel staves. © Larry Stanley/Unicorn Stock Photos

conglomerates, such as Arkansas-based Tyson Foods (which recently merged with Hudson Foods), Omaha-based ConAgra (which markets the Butterball Turkey and Chicken line), and national food giant Kraft. The aggressive marketing and technological advances promoted by these corporations have placed Missouri among the top fifteen states nationwide in food processing.

THE FOREST FOR THE TREES

The end of the Civil War initiated a seventy-year period of exploitation of Missouri's abundant timber resources. During this time some fifteen million acres of forest land, most of which lay south of the Missouri River, were decimated. The denuding of Missouri's forest lands and careless land cultivation practices by farmers in the late nineteenth and early twentieth centuries created massive soil erosion. To remedy the environmental disaster, state laws were passed in the 1930s to establish a system of national forests and promote soil and timber conservation. Missouri's subsequent efforts in this field, spearheaded by the Missouri Conservation Commission since 1937, have been recognized and imitated nationwide. The increasingly widespread acceptance among Missouri's farmers of terracing and no-till farming methods has restored much of the state's prime farm land, while the restoration of Missouri's forest lands has sparked the develop-

ment of several thriving forest-related industries.

Wood-using industries contribute about $3 billion a year to Missouri's economy and employ more than 34,600 people, with an annual payroll of about $500 million. Approximately 2,600 firms are involved, including loggers, sawmills, paper-product manufacturers, and makers of chairs, bowls, gift items, and log homes. Several of the largest pallet makers in the state are sheltered workshops, which employ nearly 1,000 handicapped workers. Among the

MULE-TEAM SPIRIT

MISSOURI MULES ARE KNOWN FOR THEIR STRENGTH, INTELLIGENCE, AND HARDINESS. MULES FROM MISSOURI HAVE HELPED BUILD RAILROADS, LOG FORESTS, PLOW FIELDS, AND MINE COAL. THEY'VE ALSO BEEN EMPLOYED ON THE BATTLEFIELD—DURING WORLD WAR I, THE UNITED STATES EXPORTED ABOUT 232,000 MULES, MANY COMING FROM MISSOURI. NOWADAYS, THE MAJORITY OF MISSOURI'S MULES ARE BRED FOR SHOW.

These Holstein and Hereford dairy cows are two of the nearly 180,000 animals that place Missouri fifteenth in U.S. milk production. © Rick Adair/Midwestock

ness. Increasingly, consumers are becoming more concerned with quality rather than quantity of the product, and environmental issues connected with exploitation of the state's dwindling natural resources.

Anheuser-Busch has been addressing environmental matters for a number of years, including the implementation and operation of its major aluminum can recycling endeavor. And Doe Run, whose lead-mining operation was once considered a principal environmental polluter, has engaged in an environmental clean-up effort in recent years. In addition to land reclamation and revegetation of abandoned mining sites, the company has also replaced dust-generating driers in its mills with more efficient vacuum filters and equipped its smelter with an acid-recovery unit, a major baghouse system, and dust scrubbers. Doe Run has also established a technologically advanced resource recycling facility that reclaims ninety thousand tons of refined lead from spent lead-acid batteries and other lead-bearing waste. The efforts of Anheuser-Busch and The Doe Run Company, along with other like-minded actions on the part of other companies profiting from the riches of Missouri's land, illustrate that profit and productivity can go hand in hand with responsible environmental stewardship.

largest charcoal manufacturers are Imperial Products, employing about 200 people, with sales in the $10 million to $25 million range; Kingsford Products, employing about 120 people and having sales in the $10 million to $25 million range; and West Plains Charcoal, a division of Kindred, Inc., employing about 150 people, with sales in the $25 million to $50 million range.

A unique forest products industry has also arisen in the south-central Missouri town of Stockton. Established in the 1940s, family-owned Hammons Products has grown into a highly profitable and multifaceted business that markets a wide variety of products from nearly every part of the fruit of the black walnut tree. This innovative company also conducts continuing research into the replenishing of the walnut tree in Missouri's forests, working closely with the agroforestry research program at the University of Missouri.

As Missouri enters the twenty-first century, the realities of the global marketplace are already changing the way government officials, farmers, mining executives, timber products manufacturers, and agribusiness leaders do busi-

FACING PAGE: *Fields of winter wheat hug the contour of the land along the Missouri River. Wheat is grown throughout the state, especially in the southeastern lowland and northern plains. Missouri ranks fourteenth in U.S. wheat harvest. © Randall Hyman*

THE WIZARD OF TUSKEGEE

GEORGE WASHINGTON CARVER WAS A SUPERIOR INNOVATOR IN THE AGRICULTURAL SCIENCES. HIS RESEARCH AT THE TUSKEGEE (ALABAMA) NORMAL AND INDUSTRIAL INSTITUTE LED TO THE DEVELOPMENT OF MANY PRODUCTS MADE FROM COTTONSEED, PEANUTS, SOYBEANS, SWEET POTATOES, AND SEVERAL OTHER CROPS. IN 1953 THE 210-ACRE FARM ON WHICH HE WAS BORN NEAR DIAMOND, MISSOURI, IN 1864 WAS DEDICATED AS THE GEORGE WASHINGTON CARVER NATIONAL MONUMENT.

This humorous fellow welcomes visitors to the Schlup Farm pumpkin stand, near Defiance. © Randall Hyman

LAND OF PLENTY

THE DOE RUN COMPANY

THE DOE RUN
COMPANY,
THE WORLD'S
LARGEST PRIMARY
PRODUCER OF LEAD,
IS COMMITTED
TO EMPLOYEE
SAFETY, SOUND
ENVIRONMENTAL
PRACTICES, CLIENT
SATISFACTION, QUALITY,
AND EFFICIENCY

From its modest beginnings near Bonne Terre, Missouri, nearly 130 years ago, the St. Louis–based Doe Run Company has grown into a world-class mining and mineral-processing operation. Its mining, milling, and recycling facilities are situated 100 miles southwest of St. Louis near Viburnum, Missouri, the heart of what has become known as the New Lead Belt. Near the town are six hard-rock underground mines, four mills, and one of the country's newest state-of-the-art lead-recycling plants. Located about fifty miles south of

The St. Joseph Lead Company, The Doe Run Company's parent organization, established its first smelter complex at Bonne Terre, Missouri, in 1864.

St. Louis, in Herculaneum, is Doe Run's primary lead smelter, the largest of its type in the world.

Doe Run is the single-largest primary producer of lead in the world, with milling capacities of 30,000 tons of ore daily. Its 1,308 United States employees produce more than half of all lead mined in the nation. Doe Run's operations in the United States generate more than $200 million in annual sales.

The company integrates its mining, milling, smelting, alloying, fabrication, and recycling into the largest array of both primary and secondary lead products available. Doe Run leads the industry not only in production but also in environmental responsiveness and innovation, while maintaining unrivaled employee safety. The company has been recognized for outstanding safety more times than any other United States mining company.

Today's Doe Run Company can trace its roots to the St. Joseph Lead Company (known colloquially as St. Joe), which was organized in 1864 by a group of investors who bought a large tract of Missouri land that was noted for lead deposits.

Doe Run's primary lead smelter, located about fifty miles south of St. Louis, in Herculaneum, is the largest of its type in the world.

The company's first mine was established at Bonne Terre. The going was tough at first, but by the end of 1866, the company had produced and sold 260,126 pounds of lead. Today The Doe Run Company can produce the same amount in about four and a half hours.

By 1869, St. Joe's progressive management had brought in a diamond core drill, which soon revealed tremendous lead ore reserves. Its use marked the beginning of underground mining in place of the previous open trench and surface "gophering." The diamond drill was the first of many St. Joe innovations and inventions that have kept the company at the forefront of lead mining throughout its history.

In 1886 St. Joe trustees granted local management approval to form a small company, The Doe Run Lead Company, primarily to acquire a tract of 150 mining acres on Doe Run Creek.

Around 1890 St. Joe took options on several tracts of land in the vicinity of Flat River and began an extensive drilling campaign. The company hit a rich deposit of ore 150 feet below its older mines. With the courage of its convictions, St. Joe proceeded further with its enterprise, identifying all the great lead-bearing lands of the Flat River District to become one of the largest lead producers in the world.

The La Oroya metallurgical complex, in Peru, sits on a 12,500-foot-high plateau, surrounded by the natural beauty of the Andes.

St. Joe also constructed a lead smelter in Herculaneum, Missouri, in the 1890s. It took two years to build and began operating in 1892. While the smelter has been substantially reconstructed, it has been in continuous operation since that time, processing lead-ore concentrates from mining properties owned by the company.

By 1922 the famous St. Joe Shovel, a mechanical loader on crawler treads, began its fifty-year career as the main underground extraction and loading tool. In 1923 a 250-mile underground railroad was completed, linking most of the company's mining properties, boosting efficiency by eliminating expensive surface hauls, and centralizing hoist operations. Subsequently, St. Joe introduced the roof bolt, still the mining industry's standard method of securing overhead rock.

By the 1950s diamond drilling to locate more favorable deposits was intensified, culminating in the outlining

The Fletcher Mine/Mill Complex is one of Doe Run's six underground mines located 100 miles southwest of St. Louis.

THE DOE RUN COMPANY (CONTINUED)

The Buick recycling facility processes spent lead-acid batteries and other lead-bearing waste. This state-of-the-art facility has proved itself to be one of the most advanced, environmentally sound, and safest of its kind in the world.

of the Viburnum Trend, which is one of the most productive deposits today. This area, about fifty miles southwest of Bonne Terre, gave birth to the "New Lead Belt" that grew around it. The ore bodies in the New Lead Belt are one to five miles long, average about 1,000 feet in depth, and vary in width up to 2,000 feet.

In 1986 The Doe Run Company was formed as a partnership between St. Joe Minerals and Homestake Mining Company, 100 years after the formation of the original Doe Run Lead Company. Homestake was then the owner of the Buick mine, mill, and smelter located in the New Lead Belt. The assets of both St. Joe and Homestake were joined in this partnership. In 1990 Homestake exited the partnership and in 1994 The Renco Group, Inc., a private New York firm, acquired Doe Run.

In 1996 Doe Run established its Fabricated Products division by acquiring Lone Star Lead, in Texas, and Seafab Metals, now located in Casa Grande, Arizona, and Vancouver, Washington. This division produces variously shaped lead items, lead-oxide powders, and radiation-shielding products.

The Doe Run Company's first acquisition outside the United States was the purchase of the Metaloroya smelter and refinery in La Oroya, Peru. The deal was completed in October 1997 and more than doubled the size of the company. Adding the La Oroya complex to its operations not only increased Doe Run's lead production but also expanded its product line beyond lead metal for the first time, to include copper, silver, zinc, gold, and several other metals.

With a strong commitment to the future, Doe Run continues to emphasize efficient production. In the United States today, the company's six mines and four mills deliver ore and concentrates at efficiencies second to none in the world. The concentrates are shipped to the company's primary smelter in Herculaneum, which ranks as one of the most productive facilities in the world.

As part of its commitment to the future, Doe Run has built a world-class lead recovery facility in Boss, Missouri. Lead-acid batteries and other lead waste materials are recycled at this safe, environmentally sound, and highly efficient plant. And Doe Run's commitment to its people and its communities continues to grow. New, more effective safety measures are instituted in all operations as they become available, and lands are returned as close to their original state as possible when operations end.

Doe Run's ultimate objective is to keep its customers supplied with high-purity, consistent-quality lead products at competitive prices, while maintaining a good-neighbor status.

"Most people simply don't recognize the many ways lead is used in their everyday lives," says president and CEO Jeffrey L. Zelms. "Car batteries, emergency-power batteries, television and computer screens, radiation shielding involved with every X ray, lead oxides in light bulbs, counterweights in golf clubs, and piano keys are just a few of the uses for this essential and highly recyclable metal."

Doe Run and its predecessors are proud to have been serving Missouri and the nation for 134 years.

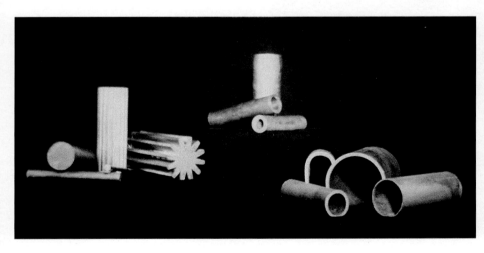

Seafab Metals Company, part of Doe Run's Fabricated Products division, produces extruded lead shapes used for roofing, plating, and pollution control.

HOLNAM INC

NATIONWIDE

CEMENT-MAKER

HOLNAM INC HAS A

SALES AND MINERAL

COMPONENTS DIVISION

IN CHESTERFIELD AND

A WET-PROCESS

CEMENT PLANT IN

CLARKSVILLE WHERE

ITS WET KILN—THE

LARGEST ON EARTH—

MAKES 1,400,000

TONS OF CEMENT

EACH YEAR

Cement is the key ingredient or "glue" in concrete used to construct buildings, bridges, streets, and sidewalks—concrete structures that touch everybody's daily lives. Holnam INC is the largest cement manufacturer in the United States. It is part of Holderbank Financière Glaris Ltd. of Switzerland, the world's largest producer of cement.

Holnam has a nationwide presence in the United States cement industry with fourteen manufacturing facilities and more than seventy distribution terminals. As the nation's market share leader, Holnam has the ability to manufacture more than twelve million tons of cement and mineral components annually. Holnam markets cement through three geographical divisions, which are further subdivided into fourteen marketing regions, each with its own office, staff, and knowledge of the market it serves. These offices include facilities in Chesterfield and Clarksville.

The company maintains its Central Sales Division and its Mineral Components Division in Chesterfield. The Mineral Components Division promotes the use of fly ash from coal combustion in electric power generation and granulated blast furnace slag from steel production as additives in making special types of cement.

The Clarksville plant is the largest and one of the most modern wet-process cement-making plants in the world. It is located on the Mississippi River near Clarksville, Missouri, approximately seventy miles north of St. Louis. The plant's acreage is underlain with a prime deposit of limestone and shale, the principal ingredients used to manufacture cement.

The plant began production in 1967 with some of the largest cement-making equipment in

The cement kiln at Holnam's Clarksville plant is the largest wet kiln on Earth. An engineering masterpiece, it is 25 feet across its core and extends 760 feet in length. Each day, the rotary kiln processes 10,000 tons of slurry feed (pulverized limestone and shale with 33 percent water) and produces 4,000 tons of cement clinker.

the world. Its cement kiln—the rotating, cylindrical furnace that is the heart of the cement-making process—is an engineering masterpiece 760 feet in length and 25 feet in diameter. It is still the largest wet-process cement kiln in existence. The kiln produces more than 4,000 tons of cement clinker per day, which, when pulverized in a ball mill with 5 percent gypsum, makes approximately 1,400,000 tons of cement every year.

The Clarksville plant provides high-quality jobs and makes significant contributions to the local economy. It employs 200 people and puts more than $7 million in payroll and more than $2 million in local goods and services into the economy as well as more than $700,000 into local taxes. The plant is the largest employer in Pike County, Missouri.

Holnam takes its environmental responsibility seriously, working closely with local, state, and federal authorities to conserve and protect natural resources. The company also supports the efforts of its employees who are active in youth organizations, schools, clubs, and churches within the community.

Holnam INC's Clarksville wet-process cement plant is situated in Little Calumet Valley along the Mississippi River.

THE FABICK COMPANIES

THE FABICK COMPANIES BRING CATERPILLAR CONSTRUCTION MACHINERY SALES AND SERVICE TO WORK SITES AROUND THE WORLD— WHEREVER THINGS ARE BEING IMPROVED

As it marks more than eighty years in business, the John Fabick Tractor Company looks back and thanks its customers for the support that helped Fabick become one of the oldest, largest, and most experienced Caterpillar dealers in the United States. The company sells and services construction and agricultural equipment in a territory of seventy-three counties and is a major supplier of pipeline equipment worldwide.

Machinery from The Fabick Companies can be found at work in nearly every sector of the economy— building roads, bridges, and dams; excavating basements; moving coal, rock, metal ore, sand, and gravel; clearing land—wherever things are being improved. And behind these machines are the total support capabilities of the Fabick organization.

John Fabick Sr. founded the John Fabick Tractor Company in 1917, merchandising Cletrac Crawler Tractors and John Deere farm implements. With only three employees and a small store in St. Louis, Mr. Fabick set out to "build the greatest sales and service organization of its kind."

A CAT 5130 front shovel removes overburden at a limestone quarry set alongside the Mississippi River near Ste. Genevieve, Missouri.

To achieve this goal, he adopted as his company creed, "to ever serve our customers better." That creed still guides the company's efforts today.

In 1921 Fabick expanded his business by including the Model A and Model S Crawler Tractors manufactured by C. L. Best. Four years later, C. L. Best and Holt Manufacturing merged to form what is known today as Caterpillar, Inc., the world's leading manufacturer of construction machinery. From this early beginning, the association between Fabick and Caterpillar has grown hand in hand and continues to thrive.

Today, under the active leadership of the founder's great-grandson, Douglas Fabick, executive vice president, and his father, Harry Fabick,

The corporate headquarters of The Fabick Companies is located in Fenton, Missouri.

Caterpillar's parts network and linked to Caterpillar dealers around the world.

Fabick service has been keyed to the pace of United States and international pipeline construction since 1920. It has been involved with every major pipeline constructed throughout the free world; one of its largest projects was the Trans-Alaska pipeline. In addition, Fabick has provided special pipeline equipment all over the world for such entities as the Mojave Pipeline Operating Company, Iroquois Gas Transmission System L.P., and El Paso Natural Gas.

In recognition of outstanding contributions to the Export Expansion Program of the United States of America, Fabick was given the President's "E" Award in 1964. In 1972 Fabick received the President's "E Star" Award for continued superior performance.

Caterpillar's full product line of more than 300 models, which is represented by Fabick, is continuously improved and regularly updated to respond to customers' changing needs.

John Fabick Sr., in photograph at right, founded The Fabick Companies as the John Fabick Tractor Company in 1917. Above, the founder's sons (from left), Joseph Fabick, John Fabick II (deceased), and Francis Fabick (deceased), and their families have carried on John Fabick Sr.'s dream of producing a customer-oriented sales and service company.

"Fabick joins Caterpillar in entering the twenty-first century with the most extensive lineup of machines ever—from the entirely new family of Challenger agriculture tractors to the most recently announced Compact Construction Equipment line of products," says Harry Fabick.

Since 1995 Caterpillar has introduced the improved H-series motor grader family and the new R-series of large track-type tractors and has made many improvements to its already-industry-leading

president and CEO, there are currently eight Fabick Companies (at twelve facility locations) and more than 400 employees, including members of the Fabick family's fifth generation, working together. What makes Fabick unique is not only its size, but its outstanding people, support, and facilities bound together by the single concept of total service capability for the equipment owner.

Fabick service departments have more than 160,000-square-feet of under-roof service area. Each service department is equipped with the very latest in tooling and diagnostic equipment. Fabick field service is provided through forty-one radio-dispatched, fully equipped service vehicles operated by master mechanics. In addition to these, there are eighty-three radio-dispatched support vehicles that also serve to provide quick response to customer requirements. Fabick's computerized inventory of more than 90,000 different types of replacement parts and components is backed by

The most recent addition to the Caterpillar line of agricultural equipment is the Lexion Combine. This machine takes crop harvesting to a higher level of productivity.

THE FABICK COMPANIES (CONTINUED)

The new Challenger 35 row-crop tractor shows Caterpillar's renewed commitment to the agricultural market.

product lines. In the agricultural market, three new row-crop tractors were introduced, the Challenger 35, 45 and 55, along with the new line of Caterpillar Lexion Combines.

Additionally, Fabick is proud to provide its customers with the Caterpillar line of power-generation equipment. Caterpillar systems are engineered for power and built for reliability. The lineup of Caterpillar generators spans applications from standby to prime power.

The product line represented by Fabick sets a standard for its industry—one that is increasingly customer focused. These products have distribution and product support systems that are state of the art in the capital goods industry.

The Fabick family and the construction machinery sales and service business they have built have played a vital role in Missouri's economic progress since 1917. As the industry has evolved, so has Fabick. Throughout the years, the company has been governed by the single purpose expressed in the founder's motto, "to ever serve its customers better." Harry Fabick, the founder's grandson, vows this motto will continue to be the guiding principle for the company as it moves toward the twenty-first century.

Shown below, the Caterpillar Pipelayer is used around the world in the construction of pipelines for oil and gas. Below right, the Mini-Excavator is a part of the Caterpillar line of compact construction equipment designed for use on smaller jobs and in tight spaces.

THE FABICK COMPANIES

- *John Fabick Tractor Company*, Fenton and Wentzville, Missouri; Troy, Illinois
- *Fabick Power Systems*, Fenton, Missouri
- *Fabick and Company*, Jefferson City and Columbia, Missouri
- *Fabick Machinery Company*, Marion, Illinois
- *Fabick Tractor Company*, Salem, Illinois
- *Fabick Brothers Equipment Company*, Sikeston and Cape Girardeau, Missouri
- *Fabick Rental Services*, St. Charles, Missouri
- *Gateway Machinery Company/Fabick Rental Services*, Arnold, Missouri

BOEHRINGER INGELHEIM VETMEDICA, INC.

BOEHRINGER

INGELHEIM

VETMEDICA, INC.,

CONDUCTS LEADING

RESEARCH TO

ADVANCE THE

DEVELOPMENT OF

SAFE AND EFFECTIVE

THERAPIES FOR

THE HEALTH CARE OF

ANIMALS

Searching for better ways to do things is how innovators such as Boehringer Ingelheim Vetmedica, Inc., in the United States become industry leaders. The company has long been one of the trusted top suppliers of livestock biological products in North America. With the banner Change Is Our Opportunity and an aggressive operating philosophy, Value through Innovation, the employees of St. Joseph–based Boehringer Ingelheim Vetmedica are striving to take their company, an energetic supplier of animal health products, to the level of world leader in animal health care research and development.

As a member of the global Boehringer Ingelheim Animal Health family, the St. Joseph firm is respected as an international center for the discovery, development, and manufacture of safe and effective health care products for the world's livestock and horses.

Founded in 1930 as the Anchor Serum Company, Boehringer Ingelheim Vetmedica has a history of expansion. Since the early 1990s, its facilities have tripled in size.

The company is continuing to make major investments to dramatically increase its production capacity and enhance its cutting-edge research capabilities. In mid-1998 it added a $50 million global Biological Manufacturing facility to its St. Joseph campus.

Research and development play a key role in Boehringer Ingelheim Vetmedica's industry leadership. In addition to its powerful in-house capabilities, researchers also manage programs in collaboration with leading independent biotechnology centers throughout the world. Boehringer Ingelheim Vetmedica's forward-thinking scientists are helping to define the practice of animal

Boehringer Ingelheim Vetmedica, Inc.'s new Biological Manufacturing facility in St. Joseph allows the company to manufacture products to global standards. These products will be sold by Boehringer Ingelheim Vetmedica Operating Units around the world.

health care for the next century through the development of important new products and technologies in biological preventative and pharmaceutical therapies.

Boehringer Ingelheim Vetmedica's product advances include its proprietary EDGE (Electronically Defined Growth Environment) BioGrowth vaccine technology, which reduces by 200 times the risk of contamination to vaccines and eliminates the risk to operators. EDGE has profound implications for the manufacturing of vaccines in the future. Boehringer Ingelheim Vetmedica's Porcine Reproductive and Respiratory Syndrome (PRRS) vaccine was introduced in 1994 and quickly became the leading vaccine for this important indication.

Boehringer Ingelheim Vetmedica, Inc., in the United States is guided not only by its commitment to ensuring good health for animals but also by its belief in the importance of its work for the good of humanity. "The ultimate goal of our research and development work is to deliver safe and effective therapies for the use of veterinarians, farmers, and breeders around the world," says Fintan Molloy, president and COO of Boehringer Ingelheim Vetmedica, Inc., in the United States.

Boehringer Ingelheim Vetmedica, Inc., strives to improve the health of animals around the world.

Boehringer
Ingelheim

LAND OF PLENTY

73

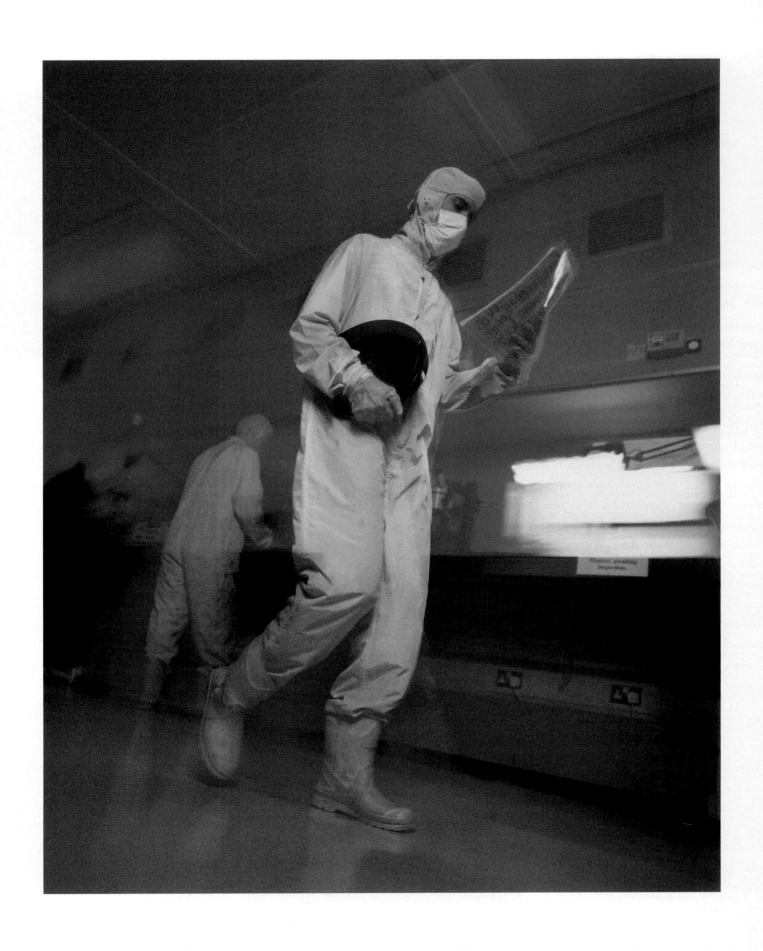

GATEWAY TO HIGH TECH

CHAPTER FOURTEEN

PROVING THE SKEPTICS OF HIS DAY WRONG, ENGINEER CAPTAIN JAMES B. EADS AND HIS WORK CREWS COMPLETED THE CONSTRUCTION OF THE WORLD'S FIRST STEEL-TRUSS BRIDGE IN 1874. THE FACT THAT IT SPANNED THE MIGHTY MISSISSIPPI RIVER IN ST. LOUIS GAVE MISSOURIANS PLENTY TO CHEER ABOUT. MANY PEOPLE THOUGHT AT THE TIME THAT NO MAJOR BRIDGE WOULD EVER JOIN THE BANKS OF THE GREAT WATERWAY. EADS, WHOSE

confidence was surely boosted by his earlier successful innovations for the steamboat trade, knew otherwise. His greatest engineering achievement, representing the most advanced technology of his time, still stands today.

Closed in 1990 to vehicular traffic, the Eads Bridge is the subject of a $25 million resurfacing project that calls for the fifty-foot-wide deck to have four traffic lanes and a pedestrian thoroughfare. The two-deck bridge is scheduled to reopen to traffic in 2000.

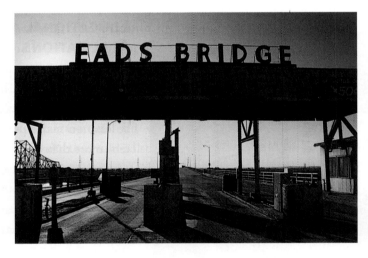

Eads's engineering feats contributed prominently to Missouri's nineteenth-century technological achievements, many of which were heralded at the great Louisiana Purchase Exposition (also known as the St. Louis World's Fair) of 1904. The fair also gave glimpses of incipient technologies that would come to change the way the world lived in the twentieth century and beyond. Along with impressive displays of the latest in steam-powered machinery were awe-inspiring demonstrations of electric lighting and power, the telephone, the automobile, and many other inventions and devices that would be steadily refined over the next one hundred years.

But few people at the turn of the last century could have predicted the phenomenal variety of technological developments that would affect almost every facet of human life by the end of the twentieth century. Missouri has kept itself abreast of these changes, remaining on the cutting edge of developing technologies. The demands of the global marketplace on Missouri's economy have sparked robust statewide growth over the last twenty-five years in telecommunications, microelectronics, aerospace manufacturing, and other high-tech fields. From research and development to manufacturing and implementation, Missouri features a long list of companies, organizations,

FACING PAGE: *Missouri is home to a growing number of technology-based companies attracted by the state's many programs that offer a variety of financial incentives; educational programs in technological disciplines; consultation, relocation, and research services; and more.* © Telegraph Colour Library/FPG International LLC. THIS PAGE: *Completed in 1874 and one of the great technological wonders of its day, historic Eads Bridge has undergone a ten-year, $25 million renovation and will reopen to traffic in 2000.* © Bob Barrett

end of the company, in the Seattle facility. Boeing will, however, remain one of the most important giants in the aerospace and aircraft industries for many years to come.

ON THE CUTTING EDGE

More than 1,200 high-tech companies employ 150,000 workers in the St. Louis metropolitan region. For much of the twentieth century, the most prominent high-tech leader in the area was McDonnell Douglas. This company, originally known as the McDonnell Aircraft Corporation, was established in St. Louis in 1939 and produced many firsts in the aircraft and aerospace industries. In 1946, McDonnell Aircraft manufactured the FH-1 Phantom, the first combat jet to operate from the flight deck of a U.S. aircraft carrier. Other military fighter aircraft built in St. Louis include the F-4 Phantom, the F-15 Eagle, and the F/A-18 Hornet. McDonnell built all of the Mercury and Gemini spacecraft that catapulted the American space program to the forefront. The Mercury spacecraft in 1961 carried the first American, Alan Shepard, into space. Less than a year later, John Glenn, in a Mercury craft, became the first American to orbit the earth. In 1965 and 1966, Gemini spacecraft also set records: the first American to walk in space, the first rendezvous of two orbiting spacecraft, and the first docking of two spacecraft in orbit. In 1967 McDonnell merged with the Douglas Aircraft Company to form McDonnell Douglas.

Most recently the long-familiar name of McDonnell Douglas was subsumed when the company merged with the Seattle-based Boeing Company to become the world's largest maker of aircraft. Boeing's Military Aircraft and Missile Systems unit in St. Louis employs thousands of people. At the end of 1998, the company announced it would lay off up to 20 percent of its workforce over the following two years because of fallout from the Asian economic crisis. Most of the layoffs will be on the commercial

Other prominent high-tech companies in Missouri include St. Louis–based Monsanto, which has long been one of the nation's leaders in the research and development of plastics and other chemical technology and continues to be an innovator in this field, and MEMC Electronic Materials, Inc., the second-largest producer of silicon wafers in the world and the leading worldwide supplier of silicon wafers outside of Japan. MEMC began operations in 1959 in St. Peters, Missouri, the site of the company's corporate headquarters as well as its largest U.S. plant. And in the St. Louis County community of Clayton is the corporate headquarters of Graybar Electric, the nation's largest independent distributor of electrical and communications data products.

On the western frontier of the state, the Kansas City metropolitan area (which includes Johnson County across the state line in Kansas) can boast of three important high-technology research organizations: the Midwest Research Institute (MRI); AlliedSignal, Inc.; and the Agricultural Technology Application Center (ATAC). MRI provides scientific and technology-based solutions to industry and government clients around the world in association with the National Renewable Energy Lab in Colorado. Established in 1944 as an independent not-for-profit research organization, MRI leads the world in thermoelectric technology, which provides cooling without the use of conventional cooling chemicals. (Space shuttle astronauts, for example, are cooled during launch and reentry by per-

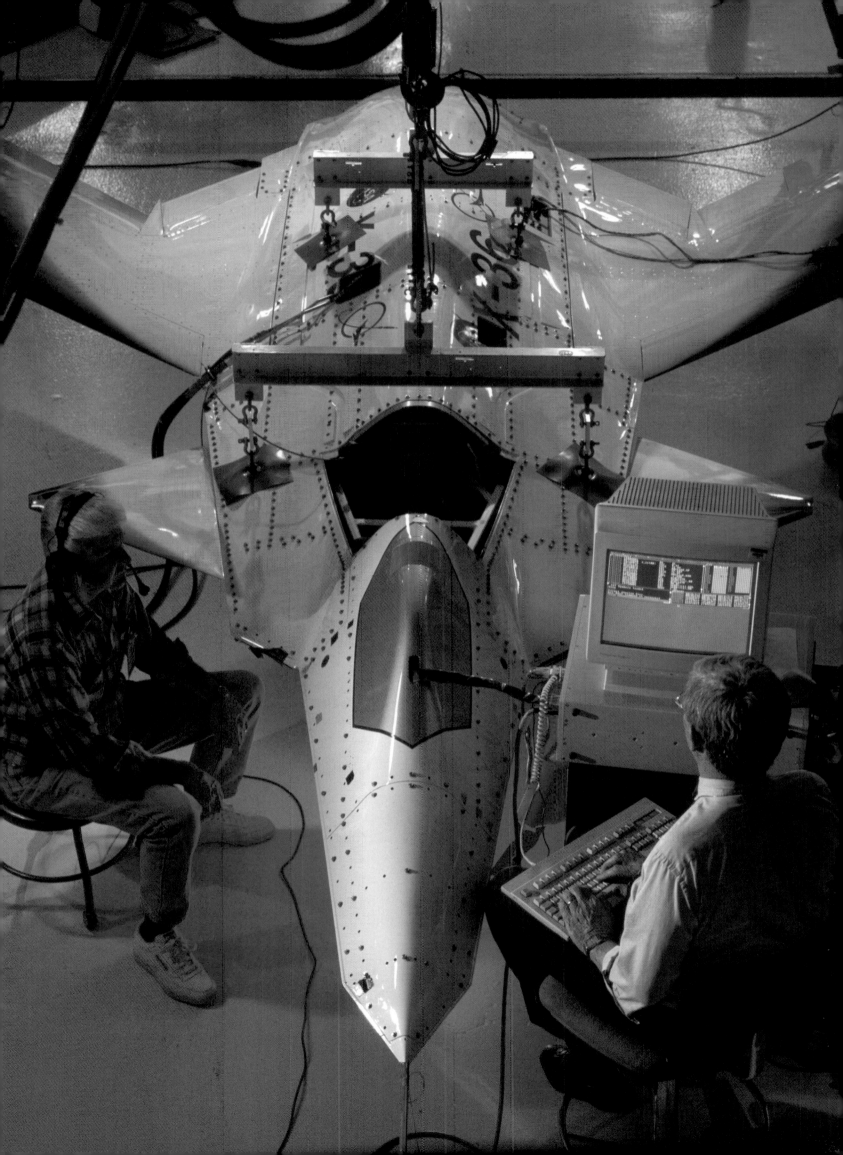

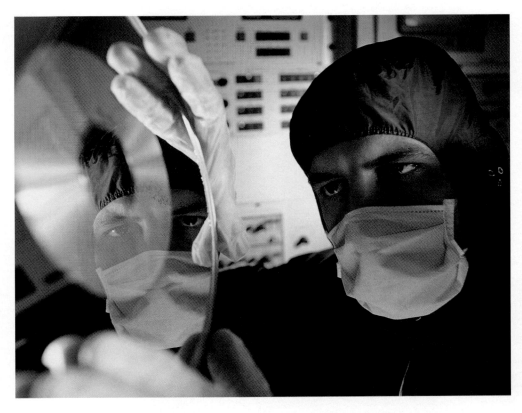

sonal thermoelectric cooling units developed by MRI.) AlliedSignal, one of the largest employers in the state, has produced high-quality electrical, mechanical, and engineered materials for the U.S. Department of Defense since 1944. AlliedSignal now offers world-class technological assistance to industry and to other government entities.

ATAC, at the Department of Energy (DOE)'s Kansas City plant (operated by AlliedSignal), serves as a gateway for a network of laboratories and facilities for the DOE and the National Council of Farmer Cooperatives. ATAC aims to develop technologies applicable to such agricultural areas as crop and livestock production and food processing, marketing, and distribution. ATAC focuses especially on the use of seed, fuel, feed, fertilizers, and chemicals; the management of waste; techniques for food packaging, preservation, and processing; and practices affecting food safety and quality.

Other important high-tech companies in the Kansas City area include Sprint, the national and international telecommunications giant; Harmon Industries, which manufactures high-tech transportation control systems; the Cerner Corporation, a producer of software technology for hospitals and clinics; the international pharmaceutical giant Hoechst Marion Roussel USA, the manufacturer of a wide variety of prescription medicines for the treatment of cardiovascular disease, infectious disease, allergies, cancer, and diabetes; and Gateway, a leading manufacturer of computers, computer systems, and computer-related products.

One of the many exciting high-tech projects under way in Missouri is the joint effort to develop the dielectric wall accelerator (DWA), a potentially revolutionary microelectronics manufacturing process using X-ray lithography to inscribe smaller lines on microchips than is now possible using ultraviolet lithography. DWA allows more information to be put on each chip at a fraction of typical production costs. The attempt to develop DWA in Missouri is being directed through a group of state and private entities known as the Missouri Silicon River Consortium. Among others, the group includes AlliedSignal, the University of Missouri–Rolla, MEMC, and The Boeing Company.

BUILDING A BETTER BOAT

IN THE 1840S CAPTAIN JAMES B. EADS INVENTED EQUIPMENT TO SALVAGE STEAMBOAT WRECKS AND TO CLEAR THE MISSISSIPPI RIVER OF DANGEROUS SNAGS. DURING THE CIVIL WAR HE CONSTRUCTED A NUMBER OF "IRONCLAD" STEAM GUNBOATS FOR THE FEDERAL GOVERNMENT THAT GREATLY ENHANCED THE UNION ARMY'S ABILITY TO CONTROL THE MISSISSIPPI RIVER. THE TECHNOLOGY INVOLVED IN CONSTRUCTING THESE IRONCLADS WAS EXPANDED IN THE YEARS AFTER THE WAR TO DEVELOP IRON-HULLED BOATS AND BARGES, STRONGER VESSELS THAN VULNERABLE WOODEN-HULLED STEAMBOATS. IN 1881, SIX YEARS BEFORE HIS DEATH, EADS WAS HONORED BY THE BRITISH ASSOCIATION FOR THE ADVANCEMENT OF SCIENCE AS ONE OF THE GREAT CIVIL ENGINEERS OF HIS GENERATION.

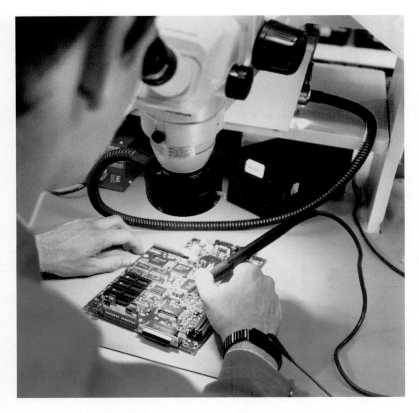

In addition to the corporate giants, a number of smaller high-tech research and electronics manufacturers show great potential for growth. One such company, Brewer Science, Inc., based in Rolla, has received the DED's backing and has become a leading producer in the advanced field of lithography-coated filter plates and products for flat panel displays. Brewer Science is the sole producer of this innovative electronics technology outside of Japan.

STATE-OF-THE-ART TELECOMMUNICATIONS

In 1996, with an investment of $14 million, Southwestern Bell opened the doors on its *TeleCommunity* Center Program. Forging a team of educational institutions, architects, and computer companies, Southwestern Bell created user-friendly centers where individuals, small-business owners, local government officials, health care professionals, law enforcement officials, and others could learn how to apply the latest computer technologies in their private and professional endeavors. The facilities provide not only a learning environment but also the resources with which to conduct research, prepare business documents and newsletters, and hold teleconferencing sessions with business associates or prospective clients. In its first phase, use of the centers was free of charge to registered members who completed the basic orientation session.

Trained staff members offer assistance. Seven of the centers are based at colleges throughout the state: one at the University of Missouri–St. Louis, three on the campuses of the Metropolitan Community College system in the Kansas City area, one at Three Rivers Community College in Poplar Bluff, Missouri, one at Longview Community College in Lee's Summit, and one on the campus of Central Methodist College in Fayette. Since the centers began operating in 1996, more than 2,700 courses have been offered and over 27,000 people have become members.

Investment in Missouri telecommunications encompasses much more than these state-of-the-art programs to educate the public. By 1998, for instance, Missouri had more than five thousand miles of fiber-optic cable in place and an ambitious program to install more along the state's major highways. And more than four hundred international, national, regional, and local communications companies in Missouri make the state one of the principal communications hubs in the country.

The energy with which Missouri's high-tech leaders continue to explore and invest in new technologies has taken businesses in the Show Me State far beyond the wildest dreams of anyone who attended the St. Louis World's Fair in 1904. Almost one hundred years later, the fruits of that early display of potential for innovation are plain to all who view Missouri's achievements as the new millennium dawns.

REVOLUTIONARY TECHNOLOGY

IN 1998 ALLIEDSIGNAL RESEARCHERS RECEIVED A PRESTIGIOUS RESEARCH AND DEVELOPMENT "TOP 100" AWARD FROM *R&D* MAGAZINE FOR THEIR WORK ON DEVELOPING THE ULTRA-HIGH GRADIENT INSULATOR (UHGI). THE UHGI COULD REVOLUTIONIZE THE USE OF INSULATORS FOR SEMICONDUCTOR FABRICATION, MEDICAL IMAGING, ELECTRICAL POWER TRANSMISSION, AND OTHER USES WHERE SPACE IS AT A PREMIUM.

Compact disks contain millions of data. © David McGlynn/FPG International LLC

TECHNOLOGY

MEMC ELECTRONIC MATERIALS, INC.

THE SECOND-

LARGEST PRODUCER

OF SILICON WAFERS

IN THE WORLD,

MEMC ELECTRONIC

MATERIALS, INC.,

DEVELOPS NEW

TECHNOLOGIES THAT

ADVANCE THE

CAPABILITIES OF

SEMICONDUCTOR

DEVICES

The silicon wafer is the fundamental building block of the semiconductors found in every type of microelectronic application. MEMC Electronic Materials, Inc., manufactures silicon wafers that are used to make semiconductor devices, which are redefining the way people live and work. MEMC is the second-largest producer of silicon wafers in the world.

MEMC works on the leading edge of silicon wafer technology. It is moving forward with the development of 300-millimeter wafers, and is the first to have introduced a new class of high-yielding wafers called "perfect silicon." MEMC partners with leaders in the semiconductor industry for the development of new technologies and forms strategic alliances with companies such as IBM, Samsung, and Texas Instruments, among others.

MEMC's operations originated in 1959 in St. Peters, Missouri, which remains the site of the company's corporate headquarters as well as the location of its largest United States plant.

The St. Peters plant is the company's largest manufacturing and research and development facility. This plant provides advance-specification, large-diameter polished and epitaxial silicon wafer products for the industry's most sophisticated integrated circuit applications. MEMC also operates manufacturing facilities, directly or through joint ventures, in Italy, Japan, Malaysia, South Korea, Taiwan, and the United States.

One of the semiconductor industry's next significant technological changes will be the transition to 300-millimeter silicon wafers. This transition

The St. Peters, Missouri, plant of MEMC Electronic Materials houses the company's largest manufacturing and research and development facility as well as its corporate headquarters. The site covers 185 acres and employs more than 2,000 people.

is driven by the industry's need to produce more overall wafer output at a lower cost; a wafer-diameter increase achieves this by improving factory capacity and producing cost economies. At the company's St. Peters plant, state-of-the-art facilities enable process and product research as well as development of the 300-millimeter line by MEMC's technologists.

MEMC's customers include many of the twenty-six leading makers of semiconductor devices, who have pooled resources to speed the transition to the new larger wafers for their next generation of memory and microprocessor products.

The company has received more than forty awards and commendations from its customers during the last four years. In addition, all of MEMC's manufacturing facilities have received the ISO-9001 or ISO-9002 certification, the internationally recognized manufacturing quality rating. The company also received the 1994 Missouri Quality Award, which recognizes management and quality excellence. The MEMC St. Peters facility was selected in 1995 by *Industry Week* magazine as one of "America's 10 Best Plants."

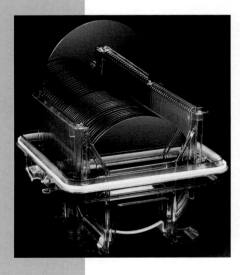

The silicon wafers manufactured by MEMC are the foundation for integrated circuits and computer chips used in all aspects of daily life. At left is a cassette of 200-millimeter (8-inch) wafers, the current industry standard. MEMC also is leading the industry in the development of 300-millimeter (12-inch) wafers.

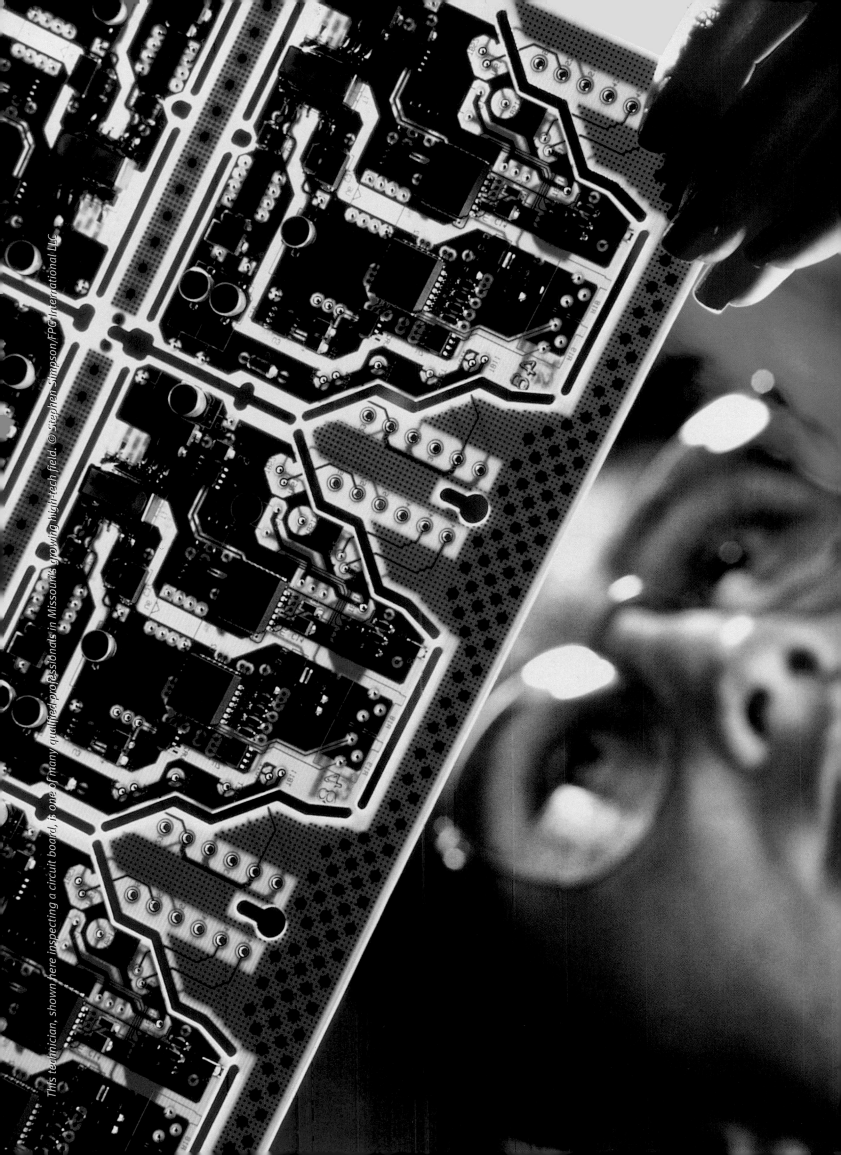

The F/A-18, the mainstay fighter of the U.S. Navy and Marine Corps, is built in St. Louis. Courtesy, The Boeing Company

AEROSPACE

THE BOEING COMPANY

THE HISTORIC

BOEING–MCDONNELL

DOUGLAS MERGER

CREATED THE

WORLD'S LARGEST

AEROSPACE

COMPANY—A GLOBAL

ENTERPRISE THAT

DESIGNS, PRODUCES,

AND SUPPORTS

COMMERCIAL

JETLINERS, DEFENSE

SYSTEMS, AND

CIVIL AND DEFENSE

SPACE SYSTEMS

In August 1997 two aerospace giants, The Boeing Company of Seattle and McDonnell Douglas Corporation of St. Louis, merged. They formed a single company to more successfully compete in a high-stakes, rapidly consolidating industry and to capitalize on the promise of advancing technology and new markets in the twenty-first century.

With a strong balance of commercial, defense, and space capabilities, the new Boeing is now the largest aerospace company in the world. It has customers in 145 countries, operations in 33 states, and ranks among the nation's top-fifteen Fortune 500 companies.

The people of Boeing own a rich history. The now-combined companies of Boeing and McDonnell Douglas, along with units of North American Rockwell, separately gave shape to aviation.

In the twentieth century's first half, Boeing built seaplanes and profit-making mail planes. The Douglas DC-3 popularized commercial passenger travel. During World War II, North American Rockwell produced the legendary P-51 Mustang; Boeing contributed the B-17 Flying Fortress and B-29 Superfortress.

The early jet age of the 1940s and 1950s saw Boeing introduce swept-wing B-47 and B-52 bombers. North American F-86 Sabre Jets became aces over Korea. Then came the Boeing 707, the world's first successful passenger jet. Later,

Boeing employs more than 20,000 people in St. Louis to produce and support fighter aircraft, such as the F-15E Eagle, shown above, and tactical missiles, and to manufacture parts and subassemblies for Boeing's other products.

stretched Douglas DC-8s were the largest jetliners flying.

In the 1960s Boeing introduced the 727 trijet and the twin-engine 737—the best-selling jetliner in history. McDonnell Douglas made DC-9s, which introduced jet service to small cities. Its F-4 Phantom became the mainstay of United States forces in Vietnam.

The high-capacity jumbo jets of the 1970s—the Boeing 747 and the McDonnell Douglas DC-10—made long-range air travel more affordable. The McDonnell Douglas F-15 Eagle became the world's preeminent air-supremacy fighter.

McDonnell's Mercury and Gemini capsules carried the first Americans into space. North American Rockwell's Apollo capsule and the Boeing lunar orbiter carried them to the moon. A Boeing lunar rover transported the astronauts across the moon's surface. They had traveled there aboard a Saturn V rocket, its second stage and many of its engines built by North American Rockwell. All three companies collaborated to build today's space shuttle.

The Boeing F/A-18 Super Hornet, larger and more powerful than previous Hornets, is designed to serve as the backbone of U.S. Naval aviation into the next century.

For more than thirty years, Boeing has been the world's leader in commercial flight. The company now has more than 9,000 jetliners in service worldwide. Market projections show a demand for 16,000 new passenger jets over the next twenty years. Boeing will compete in this trillion-dollar-plus market with a flexible family of jetliners ranging from its newest, the 717, 777, and next-generation 737, to its present 747, 757, and 767 aircraft.

As a leading NASA contractor, Boeing's future is linked to space flight and exploration and to the burgeoning commercial use of space. The company is the prime contractor on the International Space Station. Boeing and Teledesic Corporation are teamed to create a satellite network that will provide an "Internet-in-the-sky." Sea Launch, a Boeing joint venture with Norway, Russia, and Ukraine, will put satellites into orbit from a mobile platform in the Pacific Ocean. The company is developing advanced versions of its highly reliable Delta rocket to provide commercial and military customers with larger, more economical payload launch capability. Boeing also provides systems integration and operations support for the space shuttle and prepares the payloads the shuttle carries into space.

Today's Boeing is the world's largest military aircraft manufacturer. It builds the U.S. Air Force's C-17 Globemaster III airlifter, a 767 Airborne Warning and Control System, and the

A technician inspects a one-piece aircraft structure produced with high-speed machining. Pioneered at the Boeing Phantom Works, in St. Louis, these structures are stronger, lighter weight, and less expensive than multipiece structures.

U.S. Marines' V-22 Osprey tilt-rotor aircraft. For the U.S. Army it builds the CH-47 Chinook heavy-lift helicopter, the RAH-66 Comanche reconnaissance helicopter, and the AH-64D Apache Longbow anti-armor helicopter. Boeing is teamed with Lockheed Martin to build the nation's next-generation air-dominance fighter, the U.S. Air Force F-22 Raptor. And it is developing prototypes in a competition to build as many as 3,000 multiservice Joint Strike Fighters in the next century.

In St. Louis more than 20,000 people are employed at the company's Military Aircraft and Missile Systems Group. The F-15E Eagle, the most able fighter-bomber in the U.S. Air Force, is built at this site. The U.S. Marines' unique AV-8B Harrier II, capable of vertical takeoff and landing, is assembled alongside the T-45 Goshawk Trainer, part of the U.S. Navy's newest aviator-training system.

The new centerpiece of U.S. Naval aviation, the F/A-18 Super Hornet strike/fighter, is now in low-rate production and will join the fleet in 2001. Designed to perform both air-to-air and air-to-surface missions, the Super Hornet is a more advanced version of its Hornet predecessors, which serve with the U.S. Navy and Marine Corps and the air forces of seven nations.

The Harpoon antiship missile and its advanced derivative, the U.S. Navy's new SLAM ER precision-guided standoff missile, are built in St. Charles, Missouri.

St. Louis is headquarters for the Phantom Works, the Boeing advanced research and development unit. This group pursues breakthrough improvements in design and manufacturing with innovations such as 3-D modeling, high-speed machining, and composite structures. Its mandate is to improve the quality, performance, and affordability of all Boeing aerospace systems—to help Boeing and the communities in which it operates thrive in the twenty-first century.

Boeing tactical aircraft produced in St. Louis are (from top) the F-15E Strike Eagle, F/A-18C/D Hornet, AV-8B Harrier II Plus, and T-45C Goshawk Trainer.

BY ALL MEANS, COMMUNICATE

CHAPTER FIFTEEN

OVER THE LAST CENTURY THE ORGANIZATION OF THE COMMUNICATIONS INDUSTRY IN MISSOURI HAS GONE THE WAY OF NEARLY ALL OF THE STATE'S OTHER INDUSTRIES: SMALLER INDEPENDENT COMPANIES EVENTUALLY MERGE WITH OR ARE SUBSUMED BY LARGE CORPORATE ENTITIES. WHEN TELEPHONE SERVICE WAS FIRST INTRODUCED IN THE 1880S, MOST OF THE PROVIDERS WERE SMALL LOCAL OR REGIONAL COMPANIES. AS TIME PASSED,

many of these smaller companies were absorbed by the monolithic Bell Telephone system's American Telephone and Telegraph Company (AT&T). In 1984, however, AT&T was forced to divest its regional "Baby Bell" subsidiaries. One of these subsidiaries, Southwestern Bell, then became the provider of much of the local telephone service in the five-state region of Arkansas, Kansas, Missouri, Oklahoma, and Texas. Some smaller independent companies, however, continued to compete with Southwestern Bell. In 1995, AT&T dominated long-distance service in Missouri and had recently combined with Tele-Communications, Inc. (TCI), one of the nation's largest cable providers, to compete in local telephone markets throughout the country. Missouri now has more than three million telephone access lines and more than forty companies that provide local telephone service.

COMMUNICATIONS BREAKTHROUGHS

During the twentieth century, Southwestern Bell developed technological innovations that are now commonplace. In 1946, Southwestern Bell Telephone Company in St. Louis launched the first commercial mobile telephone service by installing mobile phones in the automobiles of two subscribers, a Monsanto Chemical Company executive and contractor Henry L. Perkinson. In 1966 Southwestern Bell developed the first single-slot pay phone that distinguished nickels, dimes, and quarters electronically. Now, as the twenty-first century dawns, ever more sophisticated technology changes the way and rate at which people communicate.

Computer, fiber-optic, and wireless communications technologies continue to push the Missouri communications industry into the next phase of its

FACING PAGE: *This woman holds a newspaper commemorating Kansas City Day in 1993. Kansas City has a proud tradition of excellence in journalism. Staff members of the* Kansas City Star *have been recipients of Pulitzer Prizes five times in the twentieth century. Reporting performed for the now-defunct* Kansas City Times *was awarded two Pulitzer Prizes in 1982. © Bruce Mathews/Midwestock.* THIS PAGE: *The tools of telemarketing and satellite communications make the world seem smaller every day. © Ron Chapple/FPG International LLC*

MISSOURI CAN TRACE ITS HISTORY AS A COMMUNICATIONS CENTER TO 1858 WHEN THE BUTTERFIELD STAGE LINE INAUGURATED THE FIRST OVERLAND MAIL SERVICE, FROM TIPTON, MISSOURI, TO SAN FRANCISCO. LATER, ON APRIL 3, 1860, THE SPEED OF MAIL DELIVERY BY STAGECOACH WAS CUT IN HALF WITH THE INCEPTION OF THE PONY EXPRESS FROM ST. JOSEPH TO SACRAMENTO. ITS SERIES OF EIGHTY RIDERS CARRIED MAIL TWO THOUSAND MILES IN AN AVERAGE OF TEN DAYS. AFTER ONE AND A HALF YEARS, THE PONY EXPRESS WAS MADE OBSOLETE BY THE COMPLETION OF THE FIRST TRANSCONTINENTAL TELEGRAPH LINE.

© Dave G. Houser

A technician pulls a circuit card from a switching terminal bank at the Southwestern Bell facility in St. Louis. © Randall Hyman

evolution. Southwestern Bell has carved its own niche in the telecommunications field by establishing several telecommunications centers at educational institutions around the state. It is also seeking to expand its control of the local service market. A strong competitor is the telecommunications giant Sprint, based in the Kansas City metropolitan area. In 1987, Sprint became the country's first 100 percent digital, wireless phone service. By the end of the 1990s, Sprint's network covered thirty-three major trading areas, serving a population of 190 million people. Sprint's partnership with two large cable television companies—Comcast Corporation and Cox Communications—will allow it to compete more effectively with AT&T and other long-distance telephone companies in the region. All of these growing networks rely on communications satellites, which are increasingly being launched into orbit around the planet. Forming a net of transmission and reception signals around the globe, these state-of-the-art satellites are key to the building of telecommunications empires.

A STRONG NEWSPAPERING TRADITION

Before there were satellites and telephones receiving invisible transmissions, there was the tangible

WDAF began as a radio station in 1922, when it was established by the Kansas City Star. In 1949 WDAF added TV broadcasting to its media capabilities. WDAF-TV is now a Fox affiliate. © Bob Barrett

One of the largest communications companies in the world, Sprint has its headquarters in Kansas City. At the time this photo was taken, the company was expanding its campus. © Bob Barrett

© Museum of the City of New York/Archive Photos

communication tool called the newspaper. And in Missouri, the history of the newspaper is unquestionably among the strongest in the country.

Missouri's journalistic traditions date back to the days before statehood was achieved. In 1808, the *Missouri Gazette* was established in St. Louis, and in 1819 in the frontier town of Franklin the *Missouri Intelligencer* became the first newspaper west of St. Louis. As the nineteenth century unfolded, the number of newspapers proliferated, many of them operated by a succession of partisan, colorful, and fiercely independent editor-

The Kansas City Star *building is a downtown landmark. Ernest Hemingway was a reporter at the* Star. *And Walter Cronkite, at the age of nine, sold newspapers for the daily.* © Bob Barrett

publishers. In the 1830s Elijah Lovejoy edited the weekly *St. Louis Observer* and agitated outspokenly against slavery, intemperance, and "popery." Eventually he was driven out of St. Louis and was later killed by a pro-slavery mob in nearby Alton, Illinois. Orion Clemens, older brother of Samuel Clemens, edited the *Hannibal Journal* in the 1850s. He hired his younger brother as an assistant editor, who enlivened the paper with entertaining articles about local people and happenings.

In 1867 a group of editors who hoped not only to promote fraternity among newspapermen but also to break down personal animosities among them established the Missouri Press Association in St. Louis. By the late nineteenth and early twentieth centuries many of the

As they do today—with more advanced technology—these early-twentieth-century reporters and editors lived and breathed their journalist craft at the Kansas City Star. *Courtesy, the* Kansas City Star. *Reprinted by permission.*

smaller newspapers, especially in the principal cities, were absorbed into larger and larger entities controlled by a few strong and influential men. In 1908, the national importance of Missouri journalism received a significant boost when Walter Williams, who began his career as a small-town journalist in the central-Missouri town of Boonville, established the first degree-granting school of journalism in the world at the University of Missouri in Columbia. This school of journalism continues to enjoy a reputation as one of the best in the country.

Although enough small local newspapers still exist in the state to rank Missouri ninth in the nation in total number of newspapers (about 250 weekly and semi-weekly newspapers in the state exist as well as about 50 community dailies), many of these smaller papers are owned by a few large, often out-of-state, syndicates.

In St. Louis and Kansas City, publishers founded newspapers large enough to cover the issues of the cities' growing population and influence. In 1875, William M. Grosvenor, a Yale-educated easterner, and Walter Barlow Stevens paved the way for the emergence of one of the two great St. Louis newspapers, the *Globe-Democrat.* In 1878 Hungarian-born journalist Joseph Pulitzer established the other great St. Louis newspaper, the *Post-Dispatch,* which eventually outlasted the *Globe-Democrat* to become the highest-circulation newspaper in the state. As of 1998, its Sunday circulation was more than 530,000. St. Louis is also home to several influential special-interest periodicals, including the *St. Louis Business Journal* (with a sister publication in Kansas City) and the venerable *Waterways*

Journal, founded in 1887 to cover news relating to the Mississippi-Missouri-Ohio-Illinois river trade.

Kansas City's strong journalistic presence was established immediately before and after the Civil War. There, the story was much the same as in St. Louis. Among several major dailies published at one time in Kansas City, the only survivor today is the *Kansas City Star,* founded in 1880 by William Rockhill Nelson, the most distinguished of all the early Kansas City journalists and a powerful force in the development of Kansas City's cultural environment. Nelson energetically promoted the public park system in Kansas City, and the Nelson-Atkins Museum of Art was established on the site of his Oak Hall mansion in the years after his death in 1915. In 1911 the *Star* moved to its current location, a historic Italian Renaissance–style building at Eighteenth Street and Grand Avenue. Ernest Hemingway was an eighteen-year-old cub reporter at the *Star* from October 1917 to April 1918, when he left to join an ambulance unit in Italy during World War I. In later years Hemingway credited his immediate supervisor at the *Star,* C. G. "Pete" Wellington, and the *Star* Copy Style Sheet as having a major influence on his writing style. Walter Cronkite, the revered American journalist and CBS news commentator, who was born in St.

Walter Cronkite, the foremost 20th-century fixture of U.S. broadcast journalism, is a Missouri native. © Peter Borsari/ FPG International LLC

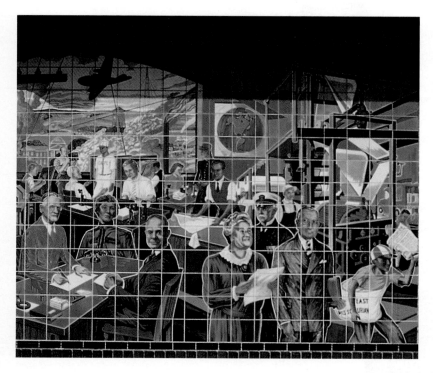

a year after the first regularly scheduled broadcast in Pittsburgh, Pennsylvania, in 1920. In 1921, radio station WEW in St. Louis, the first radio station to operate in Missouri, transmitted the first weather radio broadcasts for the U.S. government. That same year, WIL in St. Louis transmitted the first police broadcast. In addition, Missouri has several other firsts in radio broadcasting. On Christmas Eve, 1922, KSD in St. Louis was the first radio station to broadcast a midnight Mass, and on June 21, 1923, the voice of a president of

Joseph, Missouri, also worked briefly for the *Kansas City Star* in his early career.

HOT OFF THE PRESSES

In the nineteenth and early twentieth centuries, newspaper publishers did most of the commercial printing and book publishing in Missouri, but of the 1,500 printing and publishing establishments currently in the state, only a few are also newspaper publishers. Missouri ranks eleventh in the nation in the total number of commercial printing and publishing establishments. One of the largest and most successful book-publishing companies in the state, family-owned Walsworth, is located in Marceline, with a large prepress plant in nearby Brookfield and a sales and marketing office in Kansas City. The company started printing playbills in 1937 and began producing school yearbooks in 1947 for schools in Missouri and throughout the nation; although yearbooks are still the foundation of the business, the company expanded into book and other commercial printing in 1970 and has gained a national reputation in the printing and publishing field.

OVER THE AIRWAVES

Radio broadcasting was pioneered in Missouri less than

Of the many types of sophisticated printing presses in use today, this one hot stamps printed information onto labels. © Lonnie Duka/Tony Stone Images

WORDS AND PICTURES

IN 1914 THE *ST. LOUIS POST-DISPATCH* PUBLISHED ONE OF THE FIRST NEWSPAPER ROTOGRAVURE SECTIONS IN THE COUNTRY. ROTOGRAVURE IS AN INTAGLIO PRINTING PROCESS THAT USES LARGE ROLLS OF PAPER.

This radio tower traces a lean silhouette against a midsummer sky at sunset. © Scott Cook/Midwestock

the United States was heard over the air for the first time when Warren G. Harding delivered a speech in St. Louis. KSD also participated in the first broadcast from a moving train, as well as in the establishment of two-way transmission between a dirigible and a radio station.

The early popularity of this new medium offered serious competition to newspapers, spurring two of the state's largest to add radio broadcasting to their media holdings. KSD in St. Louis was established by the *St. Louis Post-Dispatch* in 1922, and the *Kansas City Star* established one of the first radio stations in Kansas City, WDAF, in 1922 and operated it until the 1950s, when it was forced to divest itself of the station in an antitrust suit. WDAF attracted a national audience with its *Nighthawks Frolic* broadcasts from Kansas City jazz clubs and the Muehlebach Hotel. Thanks to WDAF's signal and its late-night hours, people from as far away as London, Hawaii, and Panama could hear the program. Both KSD in St. Louis and WDAF in Kansas City participated in one of the most momentous early radio broadcasts when they carried the address of President Coolidge to Congress on December 6, 1924. This broadcast was heard by more listeners than had ever before heard a single individual.

When the National Broadcasting Company organized the first major radio network in the nation in 1926, KSD and WDAF were among the twenty original stations that signed on. The first NBC broadcast on November 15, 1926, originated from the Waldorf-Astoria Hotel in New York and featured such luminary future radio talents as Walter Damrosch and the New York Symphony Orchestra, as well as the vaudeville comedians Weber and Fields. In the fall of 1924 radio station WOS in Jefferson City became one of the first in the nation to broadcast a college football game, when a local sports announcer delivered an exciting play-by-play description of a University of Missouri contest in nearby Columbia. By the fall of 1949 the Missouri Sports Network was founded to bring all sections of the state coverage of collegiate sports activities.

THEY CAN'T TAKE THEIR EYES OFF OF IT

When radios became a part of more than 35 percent of Missouri homes in the first decade of broadcasting, the number of newspapers in the state dropped from about 720 to 575. But the popularity of radio was, itself, over-shadowed in the late 1940s by the introduction of tele-

Inside a radio broadcast studio, announcers must master many controls to provide seamless sound to their listeners. © Jay Thomas/International Stock/Photo Network

vision. At the time, Missouri's two largest and most popular radio stations, KSD and WDAF, led the way in this new technology when they established their own television stations in 1947 and 1949, respectively. By the 1950s television was becoming a fact of life in Missouri homes, which no doubt played a part in the development of a common piece of television paraphernalia by Lamar, Missouri, resident Thomas O'Sullivan. At a Fourth of July cookout in 1954, he overheard his host griping about how hard it was to move his so-called portable television. That off-hand remark led O'Sullivan to create and manufacture the first TV cart. (Now, O'Sullivan Industries Holdings, Inc., is a leading manufacturer of ready-to-assemble furniture.)

Some 275 radio stations and about thirty television stations (five of which are noncommercial, public stations) now operate in the state. St. Louis has twenty radio stations and seven television stations, while Springfield has thirteen radio and five television stations. Kansas City, Missouri, ranks third in the state with ten radio and three television stations. Cable television is also available statewide, from companies such as Multivision Cable (serving forty-three cities), Cencom of Missouri (covering the St. Louis area), and Kansas City Cable Partners, doing business as American Cablevision of Kansas City.

The leaders of Missouri's communications and media industries continue to consolidate their power and resources, develop and adapt new technologies, and provide their customers with the tools and information necessary to unravel the complexities of the next century. These new technologies include more sophisticated versions of cable television and satellite dishes, as well as the burgeoning fiber-optics technology. All of these make it possible not only for urban but also for rural residents to be kept in almost instantaneous touch with local, regional, national, and world events and to have access to a stunning array of cultural and educational resources. Rural isolation, which was commonplace throughout the Midwest at the beginning of the twentieth century, is rapidly becoming a thing of the past, thanks to the wide availability of state-of-the art communications.

BROADCAST NEWS

In 1949, KSD-TV was still the only television station in St. Louis. That's why the programs of the four existing TV networks—NBC, CBS, ABC, and DuMont—were all broadcast by the station. At the time, the KSD-TV studio was housed in the *St. Louis Post-Dispatch* building.

Color separations are prepared for printing. © Vic Bider/Photo Network

PRINTING AND PUBLISHING

GOSPEL PUBLISHING HOUSE

GOSPEL PUBLISHING HOUSE, THE PRINTING FACILITY OF THE GENERAL COUNCIL OF THE ASSEMBLIES OF GOD, PRODUCES TWENTY TONS OF PRINTED MATERIALS EVERY DAY, SERVING MISSIONS AND MINISTRIES WORLDWIDE

The rich historic past of White City Park includes a St. Louis Cardinals baseball farm team where the great Stan Musial once made appearances. Today the Springfield, Missouri, park is gone, but the site is home to another historic organization, The General Council of the Assemblies of God.

Springfield has been home to the General Council throughout most of the Assemblies of God's history. The church was established in 1914 in Findlay, Ohio. It was moved to St. Louis in 1915 and was relocated to Springfield in 1918.

The national, multifaceted nonprofit organization serves some 12,000 churches across the United States and interacts with nearly 160 nations. Worldwide, an estimated thirty million people are affiliated with an Assemblies of God church.

The General Council employs more than 1,100 men and women who have a variety of skills. Within its building complex is Gospel Publishing House (GPH), which has a fully equipped printing plant and bindery and a complete array of supporting departments. The company produces as much as twenty tons of printed materials daily, ranging from single-color pamphlets to hardcover and softcover books, to full-color magazines with international

Gospel Publishing House, built in 1949, is in the center of the office buildings of The General Council of the Assemblies of God national headquarters in Springfield, Missouri.

Among the presses at Gospel Publishing House is the five-unit Harris M-200, at left, which runs five days a week, twenty-four hours a day. Other presses include a Miller four-color sheetfed press and several smaller presses.

subscription lists, to a full line of Christian education curricula.

Gospel Publishing House's more than 300 employees represent a major portion of the General Council workforce. As the publishing industry converts to electronic publishing to meet current demands for speed and professionalism, so do the various departments within GPH. Many printing jobs now travel completely in electronic format from concept to completion.

The *Pentecostal Evangel*, the church's official weekly magazine, is the largest Pentecostal magazine in the world. With a circulation of more than 250,000, the *Evangel* must be produced and shipped efficiently. GPH's web press runs the *Evangel* quickly, and its state-of-the-art packaging equipment creates personalized bundling shipments for churches. Through the pages of the *Evangel*, Foreign and Home Missions programs and many other ministries are profiled in vivid color and compelling narrative, drawing the fellowship together in the local community and worldwide.

From its Missouri home base, the Assemblies of God is moving forward into the twenty-first century.

TRANSPORT AND ENERGY HUB

CHAPTER SIXTEEN

THE FIRST MISSOURIANS, ADVANCED MOUND-BUILDING PEOPLES WHO CRE-
ATED PERMANENT SETTLEMENTS IN THE FERTILE HEART OF THE CONTINENT,
FISHED THE BOUNTIFUL WATERS OF THE REGION AND TRAVELED THEM IN
CANOES. IMPORTANT TO THESE CIVILIZATIONS AND TO THE EUROPEANS WHO
CAME AFTER THEM, MISSOURI RIVERS SHAPED THE HISTORY OF THE STATE,
AND THE NATION THAT WAS BEING BORN. THE MISSOURI RIVER IN PARTICULAR

became the great water "highway" for Virginians Meriwether Lewis and William Clark as they launched the first exploratory expedition into the Louisiana Territory from St. Louis in 1804.

The Missouri forms the northern part of the western boundary of the state, bends eastward at Kansas City, and divides the state almost in half before emptying into the Mississippi River just above St. Louis. The Mississippi River forms the entire eastern boundary of the state; from the east the Illinois and Ohio Rivers empty into it.

The convergence of these great rivers has made Missouri a trade center and a transportation crossroads and hub for well over two hundred years. The rivers were, in effect, the superhighways of their time and not only brought many of the first white settlers to the state but also provided them with their main avenues of trade.

Throughout the nineteenth century, the rivers saw a succession of ever-more efficient means of transport ply their waters—first canoes, then keelboats and flatboats, then steamboats, and finally diesel-powered towboats pushing huge "tows" of lashed-together barges. Steamboat traffic on the Mississippi was immortalized by the tall tales of Mark Twain, who worked as a steamboat pilot from Hannibal before he became a renowned writer.

Although river traffic has declined on the Missouri River over the last half of the twentieth century, traffic on the Mississippi River has increased—St. Louis can boast of being one of the largest and busiest of the major river ports on the nation's inland waterways. In 1990 about 475 million tons of freight (about 60 percent of all the tonnage transported on U.S. inland waterways) were car-

FACING PAGE: *Tow barges, steamboats, and myriad other craft ply the Mississippi River at St. Louis, one of the largest and busiest river ports in the nation. Each year, nearly 500 million tons of freight are carried along the Mississippi.* © James Blank. THIS PAGE: *Kansas City's Union Station, once a hub for passengers heading to Chicago and other major cities, will attract new generations of visitors when it reopens in 1999 as Science City, a world-class education and entertainment center.* © Alpha Photo Associates/FPG International LLC

ried on the Mississippi, while about 1.3 million tons were carried on the Missouri. The two main Missouri barge lines on the Missouri River are Sun D Transportation and Phoenix Towing Company. The four main Missouri companies operating on the Mississippi are American River Transportation Company (ARTCO, a subsidiary of ADM), Marine Equipment Management Company (MEMCO), Marquette Towing, and Missouri Barge Lines.

The confluence of riverways engendered the birth of roadways. In the nineteenth century, Missouri emerged as the meeting point of several of the most important roads in the country's early history: the National Road from the east; the Boonslick Road from St. Charles to the state's interior; the Santa Fe Trail from the interior to the important trading center at Santa Fe, New Mexico; and the Oregon-California Trail from Independence to the Pacific Ocean. These early trails formed the foundation for the later system of highways that crisscrossed the state in all directions, including Route 66 (later replaced by I-44), running southwest from St. Louis through Springfield and

FACING PAGE: A barge hauls grain grown in Missouri along the Mississippi River. © Kevin Horan/Tony Stone Images. BOTTOM: The town of Arrow Rock, settled in 1810, was a major trading center along the Santa Fe Trail. © Bruce Mathews/Midwestock

Joplin, and Route 40 (later replaced by I-70), crossing the state from St. Louis to Kansas City. Currently, eight other interstate highways help give Missouri the sixth-largest highway system in the nation, with 120,000 miles of urban and rural roads, streets, and highways. These roads have seen much traffic since their beginnings. The first automobile was brought into Missouri in 1891, and one of the nation's first automobile manufacturers—the St. Louis Motor Carriage Company—turned out sixty-five cars at $1,200 each in 1901.

ALL ABOARD!

Railroads also converged on Missouri in the years after the Civil War. Union Pacific, the first great cross-country railroad, passed through the center of the state and was soon

THE FIRST COMMERCIALLY SUCCESSFUL OVERLAND EXPEDITION TO SANTA FE WAS LAUNCHED FROM FRANKLIN, MISSOURI, IN 1821 AND MARKED THE BEGINNING OF THE SANTA FE TRAIL. THE FIRST OVERLAND WAGON ROAD FROM MISSOURI, ACROSS THE ROCKY MOUNTAINS, TO VANCOUVER, WASHINGTON, WAS OPENED IN 1842.

followed by railroads radiating outward from St. Louis and Kansas City to Texas, Chicago, Memphis, and New Orleans. Union Pacific was taken over by an investor group in 1876 and renamed the Missouri Pacific. After a series of mergers it became one of the four major railroads in Missouri throughout much of the twentieth century, the others being the "Frisco" (St. Louis and San Francisco Railway Company); the Burlington Northern; and the "Katy" (Missouri, Kansas, and Texas Railway Company).

With so much rail activity taking place in the Show Me State, it's only natural that Missouri inventors would

ABOVE: *This motel stands on old Route 66 near Carthage, testimony to the highway's colorful past. © Bob Greenspan/ Midwestock.* LEFT: *Route 66 is today the I-44, seen here at the interchange with U.S. 65 in Springfield. © James Blank*

soon make welcome improvements to railroad transportation. The General Pershing Zephyr, the first train with fluorescent lights, made its first run between St. Louis and Kansas City on April 30, 1939. Coaches, parlor-lounge, dining car, rear car, dressing rooms, and lavatories were all equipped with the lights. And the first all-electric railroad dining car, the Café St. Louis, started service on March 9, 1949, between St. Louis and Chicago. Its self-contained electric power unit generated fifty thousand watts to

Lambert—St. Louis International Airport is one of two United States hubs for Trans World Airlines, whose headquarters are in St. Louis. © Randall Hyman

of the largest rail terminals in the United States, with another line running northeastward from Kansas City into Iowa and a line running south from St. Louis to Poplar Bluff.

UP, UP, AND AWAY

Missouri has had a love affair with air transportation since the early years of commercial airline service. A group of St. Louis businessmen, in fact, financed Charles

power two broilers and ranges, a hot-food table, a coffee urn, plate and cup warmers, a deep-fry kettle, dish and glass washers, mixers and juicers, refrigerators, and a garbage disposal.

As the century progressed, the railroads experienced further reorganization and renaming. In the early 1980s the Missouri Pacific was once again subsumed by the Union Pacific; and by the 1990s, Burlington Northern had become the chief competitor with Union Pacific after absorbing both the Frisco and the Katy. Although half a dozen other railroads still operate in Missouri, Union Pacific and Burlington Northern account for about 4,600 miles of the 6,500 miles of railroad track in the state, more than 60 percent of the total freight tonnage hauled in Missouri, and the lion's share of railroad revenues.

While railway freight traffic has remained fairly strong over the years, there has been a reduction of more than two thousand miles of track since the 1940s due to mergers and cost-cutting measures; passenger traffic has dropped off drastically. As Missouri enters the twenty-first century, Amtrak (established by Congress in 1971 to provide cost- and energy-efficient rail passenger transportation throughout the country) is the only provider of railway passenger service. Amtrak service in Missouri runs between St. Louis and Kansas City, two

ALTERING NATURE'S FLOW

BETWEEN 1879 AND 1972 THE U.S. ARMY CORPS OF ENGINEERS' CHANNELIZATION WORK ON THE MISSOURI RIVER FROM RULO, NEBRASKA, TO THE RIVER'S MOUTH ABOVE ST. LOUIS SHORTENED THE RIVER BY MORE THAN FORTY-FIVE MILES AND REDUCED ITS SURFACE AREA BY 50 PERCENT.

Situated seventeen miles north of downtown, Kansas City International Airport sits amid a patchwork of lush fields, scattered woods, and isolated roads. © Eric Berndt/Midwestock

THE AVERAGE REVENUE PER KILOWATT-HOUR OF COMMERCIAL ELECTRIC POWER IN MISSOURI IS 6.4 CENTS, NEARLY 22 PERCENT LESS THAN THE NATIONAL AVERAGE. THE AVERAGE GAS PRICE PER MILLION BTUS FOR INDUSTRIAL CUSTOMERS IN MISSOURI IS $3.72, FIFTY CENTS TO ONE DOLLAR LESS THAN IN THE NORTHEASTERN UNITED STATES.

Smoke rises from a coal-fired electrical power plant in Kansas City. High-sulfur coal is the source of more than 80 percent of the state's electricity. © Eric Berndt/Midwestock

Lindbergh's successful nonstop flight from New York to Paris—the world's first—in 1927 in the *Spirit of St. Louis,* a single-engine Ryan monoplane made in San Diego. Missouri's two principal centers of airline transportation are Lambert–St. Louis International (established in 1923 and now the third-fastest-growing airport in the world) and Kansas City International (established in 1972 to replace the old Kansas City Municipal Airport). These two airports serve nine major airlines, including American, Continental, Delta, Northwest, Southwest, Trans World, United, US Airways, and America West, as well as half a dozen commuter airlines and a number of charter and cargo operators.

Six regional airports also serve the state—in Springfield/Branson, Columbia, Joplin, Cape Girardeau, Kirksville, and Jefferson City. In addition, there are about 130 smaller public-use airports and about six thousand registered aircraft in the state. The only major airline with a corporate headquarters in Missouri is Trans World Airlines (TWA), which has had its corporate headquarters in St. Louis since 1994 and one of its two U.S. hubs at Lambert–St. Louis International Airport. Vanguard Airlines, a low-fare passenger airline, is based in Kansas City.

UTILITIES POWER UP

Missouri's central geographic location, which makes it an important transportation hub, is one of the features of the state that make it an attractive location for business and industry. Another factor that entices new business and industry is the availability of cost-effective electrical power, natural gas, and water supplies. The history of regulated public utilities in Missouri dates to 1913 when the Missouri Public Service Commission was established. At the end of the twentieth century, electricity is supplied to the state by forty-nine electric cooperatives along with ten investor-owned and ninety-two municipal electric systems. The investor-owned companies serve a majority of the state and include Arkansas Power and Light, Citizens Electric Corporation, Empire District Electric Company, Kansas City Power and Light, Missouri Public Service Company, St. Joseph Power and Light Company, AmerenUE (formerly Union Electric),

and Central Illinois Public Service Company. These companies maintain a generating capacity 20 percent to 30 percent over anticipated peak load. More than 80 percent of the state's electricity comes from high-sulfur coal, though two nuclear power plants—one in Callaway County and the other partially owned by Kansas City Power and Light in Emporia, Kansas—provide about 13 percent of the state's electrical power.

Missouri's abundant supply of natural gas is distributed by eight investor-owned gas companies (the largest being Laclede Gas Company and Missouri Gas Energy) and thirty-four municipal gas systems. With nearly twenty-five thousand miles of pipeline, Missouri ranks nineteenth among the fifty states in natural gas distribution. Missouri also has vast underground and surface water sources; about 85 percent of housing units in Missouri have a public system or private company as a source of water, while about 75 percent have a public sewer system.

Missouri's full range of transportation services along with its ample power and energy resources and competitive energy costs should continue to attract wholesale and retail trade, manufacturers, technology, and people well into the twenty-first century.

Cost-effective electrical power, natural gas, and water supplies make Missouri attractive to business and industry. One such source of power is the Table Rock Dam and hydroelectric plant, situated southwest of Branson. © Eric Berndt/Midwestock

THERE'S NOTHING LIKE A CHILLED BEER ON A HOT DAY. ADOLPHUS BUSCH, THE PRIMARY FOUNDER OF ANHEUSER-BUSCH BREWING COMPANY, KNEW THIS WELL. IN THE 1890s HE CREATED A NETWORK OF RAILSIDE ICEHOUSES TO COOL CARS OF BEER BEING SHIPPED LONG DISTANCES, THUS LAUNCHING THE INDUSTRY'S FIRST FLEET OF REFRIGERATED RAIL CARS. THE FIRST DIESEL ENGINE INTENDED FOR COM-

MERCIAL SERVICE WAS BUILT AT THE ST. LOUIS IRON AND MARINE WORKS IN 1898 AND WAS PUT IN OPERATION AS PART OF THIS FLEET.

MetroLink provides service from downtown St. Louis to the airport. © Lewis Portnoy/Spectra-Action, Inc.

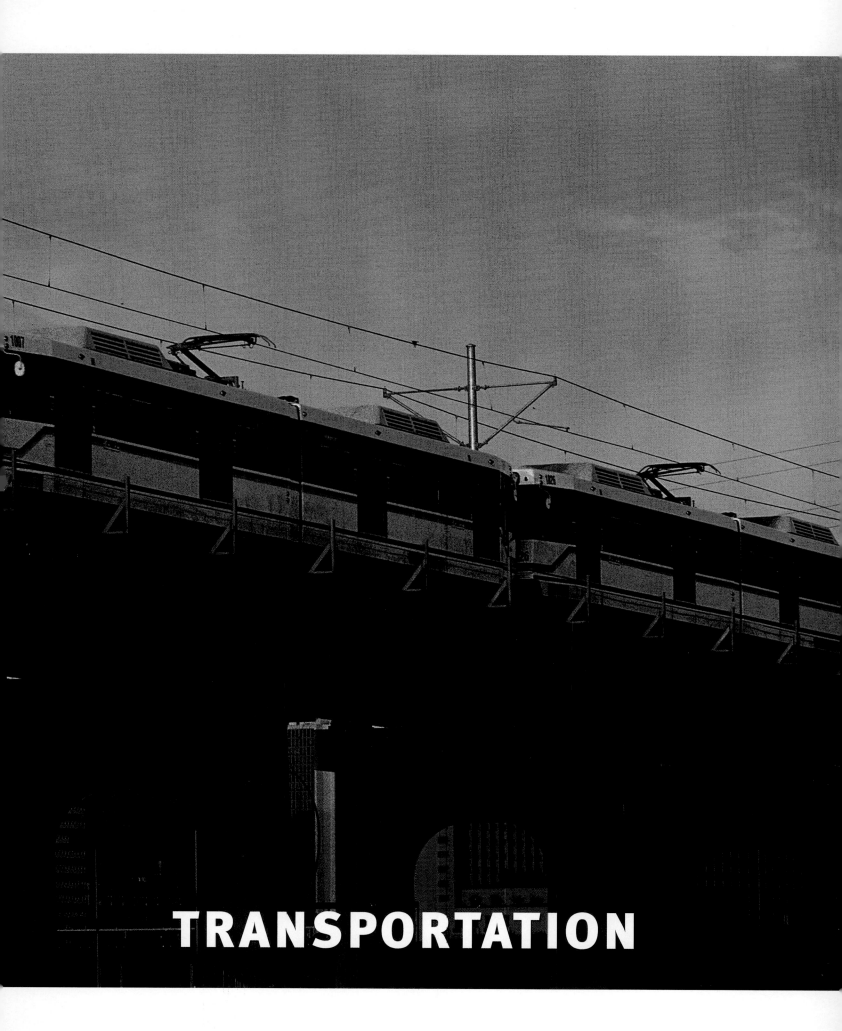

TRANSPORTATION

UNIGROUP, INC.

UNIGROUP, INC.,

TOGETHER WITH

UNITED VAN LINES,

MAYFLOWER

TRANSIT, AND ITS

OTHER SUBSIDIARIES,

BRINGS TOGETHER

AND COORDINATES

ALL THE SERVICES

INVOLVED IN MOVING

GOODS TO A

NEW PLACE

With a core business handling 600,000 shipments of household and other goods every year through its United Van Lines and Mayflower Transit subsidiaries, UniGroup, Inc., ranks as one of the nation's largest transportation companies. From its thirty-nine-acre headquarters in the St. Louis suburb of Fenton, UniGroup coordinates the transportation activities of an international network of independent agent affiliates which, in turn, look to UniGroup's other operating companies for needed goods and services.

UniGroup's roots extend back to the 1920s and the creation of a predecessor of United Van Lines, called "Return Loads Service," formed as the household goods moving business began to shift from railroads to over-the-road transportation. After delivering goods, movers needed return tonnage to haul back to their base cities in order to make the round trip profitable for their trucks. Return Loads Service offered a way for movers to share business with each other for mutual benefit.

After undergoing several changes in ownership and name, the company was reorganized in 1947 into United Van Lines, owned by and operated for the benefit of its agent affiliates. The same ownership structure was retained when, in 1987, corporate reorganization created UniGroup, Inc., as the parent holding company of United Van Lines and other operating subsidiaries.

UniGroup, Inc.'s thirty-nine-acre headquarters campus in Fenton is home base for the 1,600 professionals who support the operations of United Van Lines, Mayflower Transit, and other operating subsidiaries.

A small business in the 1940s, with annual revenues of less than $4 million, United grew steadily through the years. In 1963 it moved its offices to Fenton, Missouri, becoming one of the first companies to locate in what is now a major office and industrial center for the region. By the mid-1970s United had become the fourth-largest mover in the nation.

Federal regulatory reform in 1980 represented a turning point for the entire trucking industry. The removal of many regulatory limitations prompted carriers to actively compete with one another for the first time, both in price and in services offered.

Regulatory reform also led to a dramatic restructuring of the household goods moving industry, with all major van lines except United undergoing ownership changes in the ensuing years. Unburdened by such internal disruptions, United saw its market share climb from 16 percent in 1979 to 24 percent in 1998. It became the nation's largest household goods mover in 1992, according to data from the American Moving and Storage Association, the moving industry's trade organization.

In 1995 UniGroup made transportation history when it acquired Indianapolis, Indiana–based Mayflower Transit, Inc., a household goods van

The careful handling of household goods is a specialty of the more than 400 agent affiliates of Mayflower Transit located throughout the United States.

ranked by *Forbes* magazine as the ninety-third-largest privately owned company in the nation. It is also the ninth-largest private company based in the greater St. Louis area.

Today, the UniGroup companies consist of United Van Lines; Mayflower Transit; Total Transportation Services, Inc., which supplies trucks, equipment, and apparel for movers; Vanliner Group, Inc., one of the largest specialty insurers serving the moving and storage industry; UniGroup Worldwide, Inc., a global-mobility management company; and Pinnacle Group Associates, Inc., a relocation management company.

With the completion of an $18.2 million building addition in late 1998, the UniGroup campus is now home to 1,600 transportation and financial services professionals who support the operating companies. UniGroup itself supplies commonly needed services, including information technology; corporate finance; legal services; human resources; creative art and printing services; facilities management; mail and supply centers; purchasing; food services; corporate travel; advertising; corporate communications; and public relations.

UniGroup is owned exclusively by active agents and senior corporate management of United Van Lines and Mayflower Transit. Maurice Greenblatt, who owns United and Mayflower agencies, is chairman of the UniGroup, Inc., board of directors and of subsidiary boards. Robert J. Baer is president and chief operating officer of UniGroup, as well as chief executive officer of the operating subsidiaries.

line founded in 1927. Mayflower, which has the highest unaided brand name recognition in the moving industry, according to the 1997 Gallup Moving Company Index, had experienced difficulties in the post-deregulation 1980s. After resisting a hostile takeover, Mayflower underwent a leveraged buyout, which took the then publicly held company private. Six years later, it was taken public once more, and in March 1995 it became part of UniGroup. In 1997 Mayflower Transit's corporate headquarters was relocated from Indiana to St. Louis.

United Van Lines and Mayflower Transit, while sister companies, are active competitors in the marketplace, with separate sales and operational activities. Between them, the two carriers handle approximately one in every three professional interstate relocations in the United States. Actual moving services are provided by the employees of the 900 United and Mayflower agencies located in cities throughout the country. An additional 500 representatives are located in Canada and other countries around the globe.

The agencies are all independent businesses that maintain their own offices, warehouses, and fleets, relying on Fenton headquarters to coordinate shipment handling through the United and Mayflower systems.

UniGroup's combined revenues ($1.8 billion in 1998) make it the largest privately owned trucking group in the United States, according to *Transport Topics* magazine. It is

Gas and electric company linemen make repairs. © Stephen Simpson/FPG International LLC

UTILITIES

UTILICORP UNITED

UtiliCorp United, an international, growth-oriented energy company based in Kansas City, Missouri, provides electricity, natural gas, and related products and services to more than three million direct and indirect customers. The company operates utilities in eight states, one Canadian province, Australia, and New Zealand. It also markets wholesale energy across North America and in the United Kingdom.

As the deregulation of utilities transforms the industry, UtiliCorp stays at the leading edge of change and innovation in the face of a newly competitive marketplace by finding new ways to structure its operations and services to meet customers' needs.

"We believe it's important to be a first mover, to step forward with bold strategies and to execute them," says Richard C. Green Jr., UtiliCorp's CEO and the fourth generation of his family to head the company. "The prospect of deregulation makes us more creative, more customer focused, and more cost conscious. We have completely transformed this company by consolidating our operations to meet the challenges and seize new markets around the world created by privatization, deregulation, and new technology."

To compete in a deregulated environment, Green's vision of UtiliCorp's future is to completely redefine what a utility company is by introducing the concept of branding, adding new products, increasing emphasis on customer service, and expanding nationally and internationally. The company's goal is to increase its presence as a national and multinational provider of total energy solutions.

Towering above the Missouri River east of Kansas City, the Sibley Generating Station is UtiliCorp United's largest power facility and the primary source of electricity for the company's Missouri Public Service division.

That goal was the reason behind UtiliCorp's launch of the utility industry's first national brand, EnergyOne℠ and the first nationally branded line of products and services for electric and gas customers. Perhaps ahead of its time, part of the EnergyOne concept was to provide a single source for the sale of branded nonenergy products and services such as long-distance telephone service and home security, along with traditional energy offerings by electric and gas utilities. That extension of the brand could eventually be implemented when deregulated energy markets eventually open up on a state-by-state basis.

UtiliCorp subsidiary Aquila Energy is one of the country's highest-volume wholesale merchants of natural gas and electricity. It is the nation's second-largest wholesaler of natural gas and third-largest wholesaler of electric power. Through Aquila Energy, UtiliCorp has long been a model of wholesale energy sales and trading, initially in natural gas and today also in electricity. The scope of the company's wholesale operations is enormous; it has trading relationships with more than 700 gas producers, local distributors, and financial intermediaries throughout the United States.

UtiliCorp launched a whole new concept in 1995 with the creation of EnergyOne, the first national brand to serve electric and gas utility customers.

Aquila also gathers, transports, and processes natural gas and sells natural gas liquids. In 1995 the company began to market electricity to large-volume wholesale customers. It was one of the first utility affiliates authorized to enter this new type of business. The company was a first mover in providing energy on a national basis to commercial customers, including supplying natural gas to a number of large national restaurant chains, merchandisers, hotels, and school systems.

"Aquila has earned a leadership position in gas and electricity markets that have become extremely competitive due to continuing deregulation," says Charles K. Dempster, chairman and CEO of Aquila Energy and a senior vice president of its parent company, UtiliCorp United.

Aquila has grown by providing sophisticated products that essentially help customers buy, transport, and use natural gas and electricity; and a wide range of financial instruments, including management tools for credit control and price-risk control.

In 1997 Aquila introduced a breakthrough line of new products, called GuaranteedWeather®. GuaranteedWeather products allow customers to manage the volumetric risk associated with weather that impacts weather-sensitive industries

such as agriculture, travel and leisure, construction, and utilities. GuaranteedWeather gives customers the ability to manage the financial risk associated with temperature, rain, snow, or wind. UtiliCorp's Aquila Energy pioneered the development of weather-based financial hedges. Unlike insurance, which pays based on actual damages, the Guaranteed-Weather hedges pay based on the difference

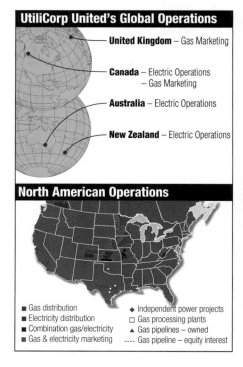

between a negotiated "strike price" and the actual weather as determined by the National Weather Service. Aquila's weather-related products are available for 2,000 locations throughout the United States. In addition, Aquila has sold several GuaranteedWeather products in Australia.

"The weather affects the earnings of countless companies across the United States, and we believe weather hedging will become an important part of every viable risk management portfolio," says Green. "Any company whose earnings can be affected by weather volatility now has the mechanism to mitigate that risk."

UtiliCorp's energy delivery networks include electric and gas distribution utilities in Colorado, Iowa, Kansas, Michigan, Minnesota, Missouri, Nebraska, and West Virginia. In addition to Aquila Energy, the company's nonregulated businesses include independent power production, energy management services, and appliance repairs and servicing.

The company was named 1997 Utility of the Year by a leading energy trade publication and ranked 176th on the Fortune 500 list. In 1998 UtiliCorp had record sales of $12.6 billion and the second consecutive year of 8 percent earnings growth. These accomplishments are just the beginning of a successful and enduring future for UtiliCorp as it continues its industry leadership to achieve growth, expansion, and innovation.

The restoration of 20 West Ninth Street, UtiliCorp's world headquarters in Kansas City, Missouri, received honors from the National Trust for Historic Preservation for its innovative combining of state-of-the-art technology and environmental awareness with meticulous attention to architectural detail.

TRIGEN ENERGY CORPORATION

AS ONE OF THE

WORLD'S LEADING

THERMAL SCIENCES

COMPANIES,

TRIGEN ENERGY

CORPORATION

IS DEVELOPING

NEW TECHNOLOGIES

TO PROVIDE

ENERGY-EFFICIENT

HEATING, COOLING,

AND ELECTRICITY AT

SIGNIFICANT SAVINGS

Trigen Energy Corporation's mission is to provide heating, cooling, and electricity with half the fossil fuel and half the pollution of conventional generation. This mission has guided Trigen Energy to become a thermal sciences company on the leading edge of mitigating global climate change while remaining committed to customer satisfaction and financial growth. It is a company focused on new products and services to promote energy efficiency in an increasingly competitive industry.

Trigen serves more than 1,500 customers at its twenty-two locations throughout North America. Customers include industrial plants, electric utilities, commercial and office buildings, government buildings, colleges and universities, hospitals, residential complexes, and hotels. In each location, Trigen has a team of energy professionals committed to providing a reliable source of energy.

Trigen's approach to energy services involves the sequential production of steam, chilled water, and electricity from a central plant. This method offers customers the most efficiently produced energy available along with the significant capital and operating savings that result. Trigen patents cover an array of innovations designed to convert fuel to energy more efficiently, with less pollution. As the leading thermal sciences company, Trigen

Trigen–Kansas City's Grand Avenue plant features electric generation, high-pressure steam distribution, chilled-water generation, and a state-of-the-art boiler-automation system to deliver reliable sources of energy to its customers.

continues to develop new technologies as well as integrate and optimize existing power plant assets.

Trigen is investing heavily in its plants in order to meet customer needs into the twenty-first century. In Kansas City, Trigen has installed a new district chilled-water system to serve its district heating customers downtown. In St. Louis, Trigen is bringing the latest power-generation technology to the downtown area by investing in a high-efficiency, combined heat and power facility. These two projects are exemplary of the way Trigen employs state-of-the-art technology to improve reliability for customers and financial return for shareholders; and to improve efficiency in a manner that reduces greenhouse gas emissions into the environment.

Traded under the symbol TGN, Trigen is listed on the New York Stock Exchange. With its strong emphasis on the development of new projects, the company is positioned to continue and improve upon its history of growth.

Trigen–St. Louis's Ashley plant is in the process of constructing a high-efficiency combined heat and power facility that utilizes clean-burning natural gas.

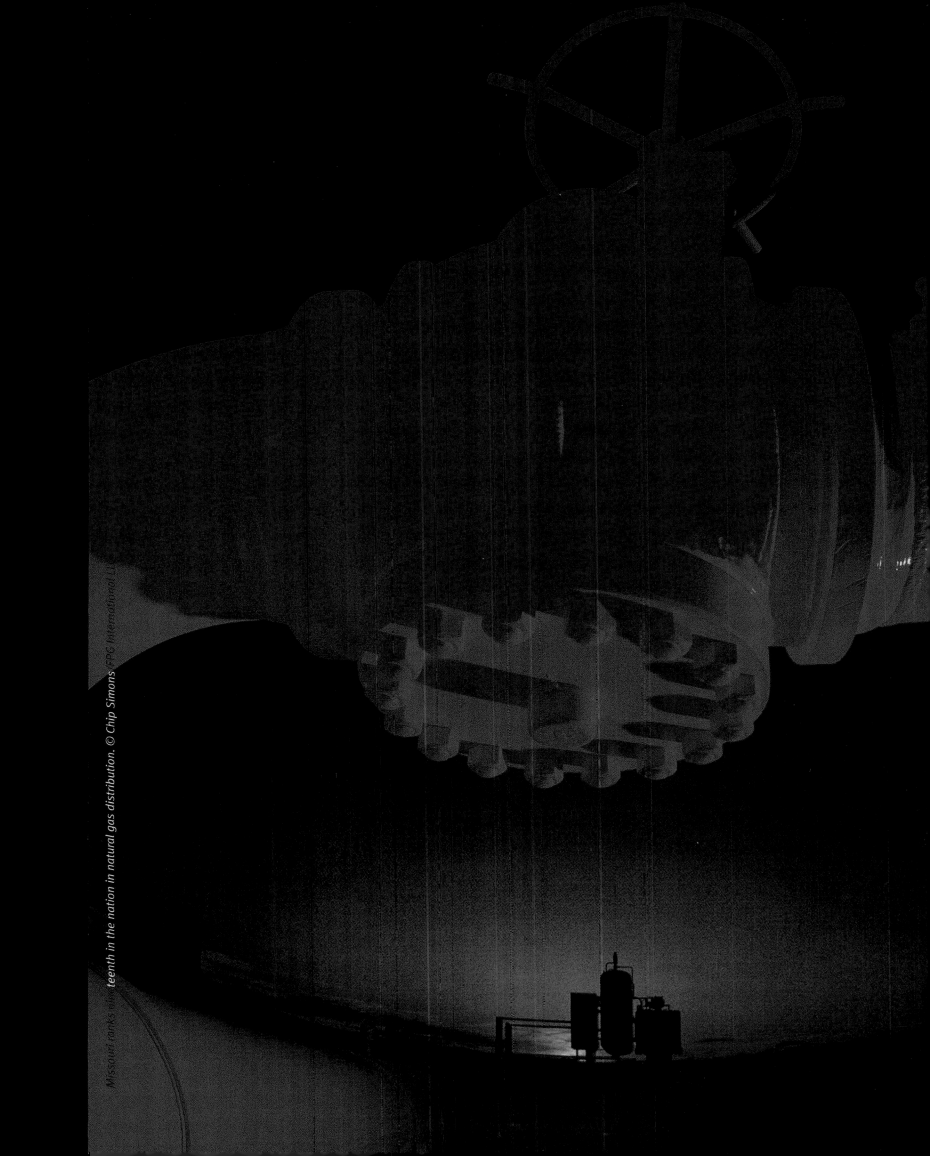

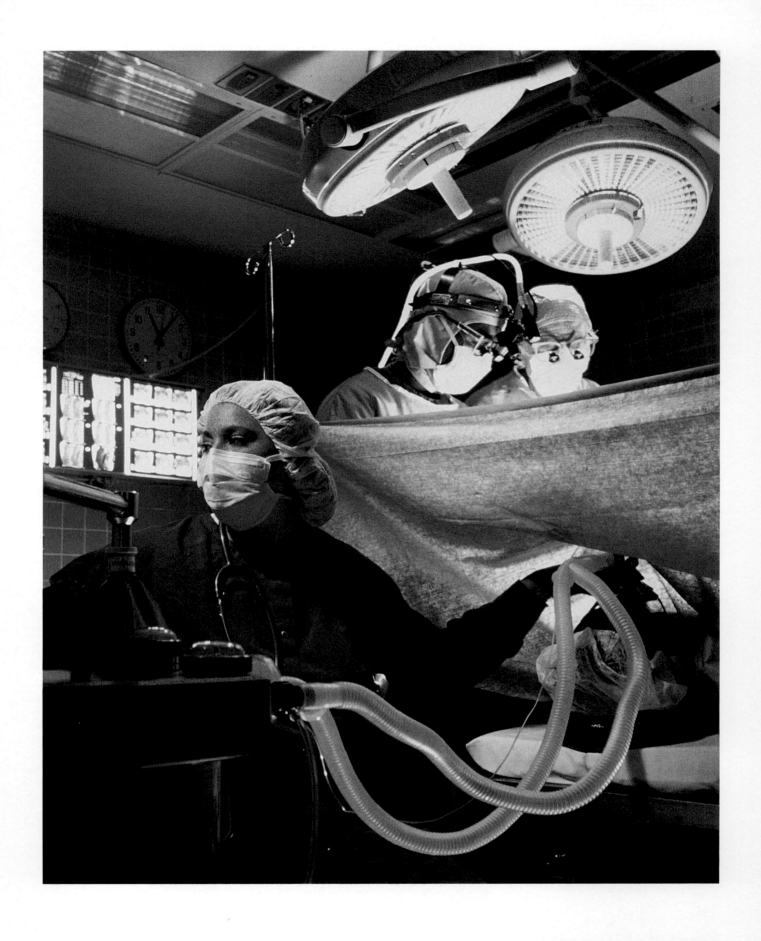

A HEALTHY STATE TO BE IN

CHAPTER SEVENTEEN

THE SIMPLER DAYS OF HEALTH CARE DELIVERY, WHEN A DOCTOR'S HOUSE CALL WAS STILL THE NORM, HAVE LONG PASSED. MODERN-DAY HEALTH CARE HAS EVOLVED INTO A COMPLEX AND EXPENSIVE BEHEMOTH, WHOSE PRACTITIONERS ARE INCREASINGLY SPECIALIZED. SPRAWLING HOSPITALS AND OTHER TREATMENT CENTERS, PHARMACIES DISPENSING A CORNUCOPIA OF PRESCRIPTION DRUGS, AND A WIDE VARIETY OF HEALTH MAINTENANCE

organizations now serve the health care needs of Missouri's citizens. The state has more than eight thousand health care facilities, which together employ 175,000 people. Their total annual income is more than $3.5 billion.

The evolution of health care from simpler methods to the now dizzying array of choices has brought with it technological innovations that cure diseases, treat acute and chronic conditions, and contribute to further research at levels not known at the beginning of the twentieth century. The main centers of medical research and treatment in Missouri are in St. Louis, Kansas City, and Columbia. St. Louis has two major medical schools, one associated with Washington University and the other with St. Louis University. St. Louis also has one of the largest research and medical treatment hospitals in the state, Barnes-

Jewish Hospital, a major Veterans Administration medical center, and three important children's hospitals, St. Louis Children's Hospital, Cardinal Glennon Children's Hospital, and Shriners Hospital for Crippled Children.

In Kansas City, two medical schools enhance the quality of health care in the region. One is associated with the University of Missouri–Kansas City (UMKC) and the other with the University of Kansas (KU). The primary teaching hospitals connected with UMKC are St. Luke's, Children's Mercy, and the two Truman Medical Centers. The latter have served the area since the mid-1800s and are the largest health care providers for the medically indigent population of Kansas City and Jackson County. The main treatment facilities associated with the KU Medical School are located at the University of Kansas Medical

FACING PAGE: *Missouri's health care facilities use the most technologically advanced methods available. Here an anesthetist monitors a patient during microsurgery.* © Charles Thatcher/Tony Stone Images. THIS PAGE: *Trinity Lutheran Hospital, a 731-bed medical campus in Kansas City, offers patients comprehensive medical services. The hospital is also the site of the Infectious Disease Unit and the Limb Preservation Institute, both firsts for the region.* © Wally Emerson/Midwestock

form the third-largest teaching and medical care facility in the state. Columbia can also boast of several other major medical facilities: Boone Hospital Center, Columbia Regional Hospital, Ellis-Fischel Cancer Center, Rusk Rehabilitation Center, Charter Behavioral Health Center, and the Veterans Administration Hospital. Major regional hospitals are also located in Springfield, Joplin, Cape Girardeau, St. Joseph, and Rolla. Numerous smaller hospitals serve many of the smaller communities and rural areas of the state.

Center in Kansas City, Kansas. This multidimensional institution has an eighty-five-year tradition in health care, teaching, and research and contains more than forty buildings on a fifty-acre campus.

Kansas City is also home to Health Midwest, which encompasses fourteen general acute care, rehabilitation, and mental health centers in the Kansas City metropolitan area; Healthsouth Corporation, the nation's largest provider of comprehensive outpatient and rehabilitative services, with five branch offices in Kansas City and St. Joseph; Baptist Medical Center; the Department of Veterans Affairs Medical Center of Kansas City; Mid-America Rehabilitation Hospital, the area's largest comprehensive facility dedicated solely to physical rehabilitation and located in Overland Park, Kansas; Kansas City Hospice (established in 1980, it is the largest hospice in the Kansas City area); and Trinity Lutheran Hospital (founded in 1906, it is known today for its specialty programs). Kansas City, as well as western Missouri and the entire state of Kansas, is also served by the Midwest Organ Bank, Inc., a federally designated organ-procurement organization in Westwood, Kansas.

The University of Missouri Medical School and the hospital associated with it in Columbia

Health maintenance organizations (HMOs) and other managed health care insurers have become increasingly consolidated in Missouri since the mid-1930s. At that time, the first health care insurers, Blue Cross and Blue Shield, pioneered prepayment for health care expenses. The first Missouri Blue Cross plan was organized in St. Louis in 1936, followed by the Kansas City Blue Cross plan in 1938. The first Missouri Blue Shield plan was organized in Kansas City in 1943 followed by the St. Louis plan in 1945. Blue Cross and Blue Shield is

A pharmacist serves a patient at Trinity Lutheran Hospital. The facility is one of the largest health care providers in Kansas City. © Wally Emerson/Midwestock

PRESIDENT LYNDON B. JOHNSON PRE-
SENTED THE FIRST MEDICARE IDENTIFI-
CATION CARD TO FORMER PRESIDENT
HARRY S. TRUMAN (SHOWN) ON
JANUARY 20, 1966, AT THE TRUMAN
LIBRARY IN INDEPENDENCE, MISSOURI.

This nurse practitioner is one of the 175,000 people employed in one of the more than eight thousand health care facilities throughout the state. © Corbis Digital Stock

the largest health insurance organization in Missouri. In 1994 it got into trouble with the Missouri Director of Insurance when it directed $434 million of assets into a for-profit subsidiary, RightCHOICE Care, Inc. This move compromised the organization's not-for-profit status, and after considerable wrangling in the courts, Blue Cross and Blue Shield agreed to settle the conflict of interest by establishing one of the largest charitable health care organizations in Missouri.

The move from not-for-profit to for-profit status has been a trend among the

The University of Kansas Medical Center in Kansas City has provided health care to Missourians for more than eighty-five years. © Bob Barrett

state's larger health maintenance organizations, raising a number of issues among consumer health care watchdog groups about the health care industry in general. Nevertheless, organizations like United Health Care of the Midwest, Inc., in St. Louis (Missouri's largest HMO); Humana Health Care Plans of Kansas City (offering HMO and PPO plans through offices in Springfield, Jefferson City, St. Louis, and Cape Girardeau); and Kaiser Permanente of Overland Park, Kansas (the largest HMO in the United States and the Kansas City area's largest group-practice HMO), continue to provide the majority of health insurance in Missouri.

LEADING INNOVATORS IN MEDICINE

Missouri's physicians, health care professionals, medical researchers, and health care facilities continue to offer some of the most technologically advanced medical care in the country. This isn't surprising, considering that Missouri has a long tradition of medical innovation. One early innovator was Dr. John Sappington of Arrow Rock,

THE FIRST OPEN-HEART SURGERY IN THE KANSAS CITY AREA WAS PERFORMED AT TRINITY LUTHERAN HOSPITAL IN KANSAS CITY. TRINITY LUTHERAN ALSO INITIATED THE FIRST COMPREHENSIVE CANCER PROGRAM IN A PRIVATE HOSPITAL IN THE KANSAS CITY AREA.

whose quinine pills, introduced in the 1830s, did much to eliminate the worst effects of the deadly malarial fevers that afflicted many of the settlers along the Mississippi and Missouri Rivers. In the 1860s, Dr. Margaret Ruck de Schell Schmidt, the first licensed woman doctor in Missouri, practiced medicine in Hannibal.

Missouri also has the distinction of being the birthplace of the osteopathic profession. Having formulated the fundamental principles of osteopathic medicine in 1874, Dr. Andrew Taylor Still founded the Kirksville College of Osteopathic Medicine (KCOM) in 1892. The college has been the seedbed for eighteen additional colleges of osteopathic medicine in the United States as well as more than one hundred accredited osteopathic hospitals and over forty thousand practicing osteopathic physicians

TOP: *The School of Medicine at the University of Missouri–Kansas City opened in 1971.* © *Jeff Morgan/Midwestock.* BOTTOM: *A technician carries on Missouri's long history of medical research.* © *Telegraph Colour Library/FPG International LLC*

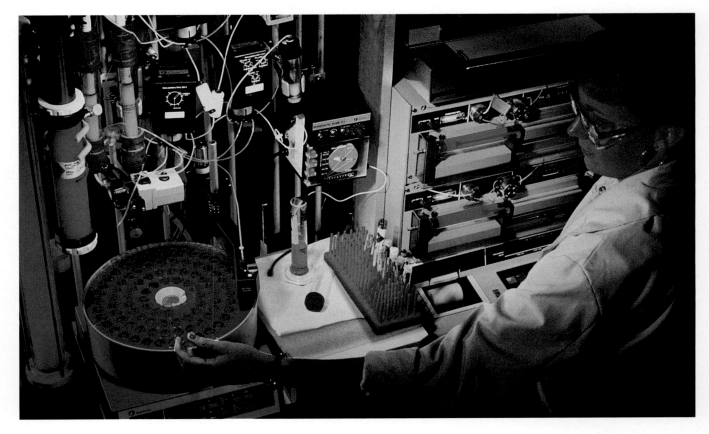

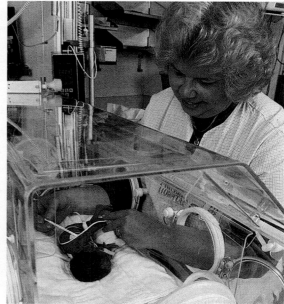

TOP LEFT: *The Children's Mercy Hospital serves as a teaching facility for the University of Missouri–Kansas City.* © *Bruce Mathews/Midwestock.* TOP RIGHT: *At St. Louis Children's Hospital a nurse takes a premature infant's temperature.* © *Randall Hyman*

nationwide. KCOM occupies twenty-one buildings on a sixty-acre campus in Kirksville and has a faculty of basic scientists and full-time and adjunct osteopathic and allopathic general practice and specialty physicians, who instruct more than 550 students from the United States and around the world. KCOM is associated with other osteopathic medicine sites in Arizona and Missouri. KCOM annually receives more than $4 million from the National Institutes of Health, the Health Resources and Service Administration, and other governmental and private agencies. The college uses these funds for the Missouri Rural Area Health Education Center Program and for research in such areas as hypertension, cancer, cataract formation, and fetal alcohol syndrome.

The first orthodontists society, the American Society of Orthodontists, was founded in St. Louis in 1900. And in January 1915 the *International Journal of Orthodontia,* the first magazine dedicated to orthodontia, was published in St. Louis. In

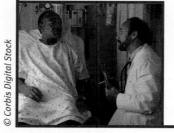

© Corbis Digital Stock

IN 1993 THERE WERE MORE THAN 10,600 LICENSED PHYSICIANS IN ACTIVE PRACTICE IN MISSOURI (TWENTY PER TEN THOUSAND POPULATION), A 23 PERCENT INCREASE SINCE 1982. ALTHOUGH MOST PHYSICIANS IN THE STATE ARE MALE, OVER 16 PERCENT OF ALL PHYSICIANS ARE FEMALE. THIS REPRESENTS A 109 PERCENT INCREASE OVER 1982. ABOUT 86 PERCENT OF THE STATE'S PHYSICIANS ARE WHITE, WHILE APPROXIMATELY 11 PERCENT ARE ASIAN AND ABOUT 3 PERCENT ARE BLACK.

A doctor reviews a patient's chart with interns at Northeast Regional Medical Center. Courtesy, Kirksville College of Osteopathic Medicine

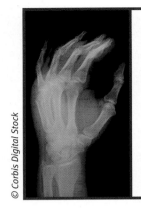

DOCTORS OF OSTEOPATHY ARE MORE WIDELY DISPERSED THROUGHOUT THE STATE THAN ARE DOCTORS OF MEDICINE AND ARE MORE LIKELY TO PRACTICE IN RURAL MISSOURI. ONE-THIRD OF DOCTORS OF OSTEOPATHY PRACTICE IN NON-METROPOLITAN AREAS AS COMPARED TO 9 PERCENT OF DOCTORS OF MEDICINE.

The Stowers Institute for Medical Research in Kansas City, expected to open in January 2000, will be one of the world's largest centers for cancer and biomedical research. © Bob Barrett

1929 the *Journal of Allergy*, the first magazine in the United States dedicated to the study of allergies, was published in St. Louis. In 1933 in St. Louis, at least two medical firsts occurred: the first medical fiberglass sutures were used (in a mastoid operation), and Dr. Evarts Ambrose Graham performed the first lung removal in the country, at Barnes Hospital.

In the early decades of the twentieth century a determined woman from Gallatin, Missouri, Icie Gertrude (Macy) Hoobler, devoted herself to the study of physiological chemistry and nutrition. She received her Ph.D. from the Sheffield Scientific School in New Haven, Connecticut, in 1920 and went on to direct research at the Nutritional Research Laboratory of the Merrill-Palmer School in Detroit, Michigan. Her pioneering work in the field of nutritional requirements for women during pregnancy and their impact on pre- and post-natal child development led to her induction into the Michigan Women's Hall of Fame in 1975. A few years later she retired. Eighteen months before her death in 1984 at the age of 91 she returned to her hometown of Gallatin.

Surely one of the most inspirational of Missouri's distinguished pantheon of doctors was the unassuming Thomas Anthony Dooley. Born in St. Louis in 1927, he garnered media celebrity for his supervision of the treatment of Catholic North Vietnamese refugees in 1954 as they were being transplanted to a newly created state in South Vietnam. His reputation was further enhanced when he returned to Southeast Asia in 1956 to build a clinic in Laos financed in part by royalties from his best-selling book about his earlier experiences in that part of the world, *Deliver Us From*

A prosthetist at Shriners Hospital for Crippled Children, St. Louis, works on a prosthetic leg. Courtesy, Shriners Hospital for Crippled Children, St. Louis

St. Louis's Barnes-Jewish Hospital is ranked by U.S. News & World Report as one of the best hospitals in the nation. © Steve Frazier/Courtesy, Barnes-Jewish Hospital

January 2000. The Stowers have endowed the institute with $300 million and have vowed to bequeath their $1 billion estate to the institute. Initially, the research center will employ up to one hundred scientists, ultimately staffing about six hundred. Among the scientists who are on the advisory board are Dr. Leroy Hood, a professor at the University of Washington School of Medicine, and Dr. Eric H. Davidson of the California Institute of Technology.

Evil. Although Dooley died of cancer in 1961 at the age of 34, his humanitarian works lived on in the Medical International Corporation, which he founded to provide medical care in remote areas of the world. Since 1962, his group has been part of CARE, a program launched by President Kennedy in part to keep Dooley's spirit alive.

If James C. Stowers has his way, the Kansas City area will soon be known as one of the major medical research centers in the world. Stowers, who established one of the nation's largest mutual fund companies (American Century Companies) in 1958 in Kansas City, and who can trace his roots back to the founding fathers of Kansas City, became interested in medical research while both he and his wife were undergoing treatment for cancer in 1993. He decided to found a medical research institute in Kansas City to delve into cancer research as well as biomedical research. The institute, which will be housed in the old Menorah Medical Center in Kansas City, Missouri, is projected to open in

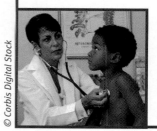

© Corbis Digital Stock

MORE THAN ONE-HALF OF MISSOURI'S 115 COUNTIES HAVE SHOWN A LOSS IN THE NUMBER OF PRIMARY CARE PHYSICIANS PER TEN THOUSAND POPULATION FROM THE LATE 1980S TO THE LATE 1990S. MOST OF THESE COUNTIES ARE RURAL.

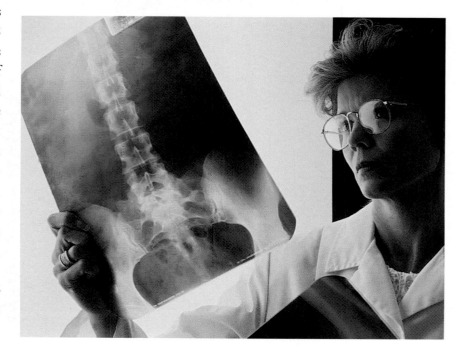

A doctor examines an X ray of a patient's lower back and prepares her diagnosis. © Dennis Hallinan/FPG International LLC

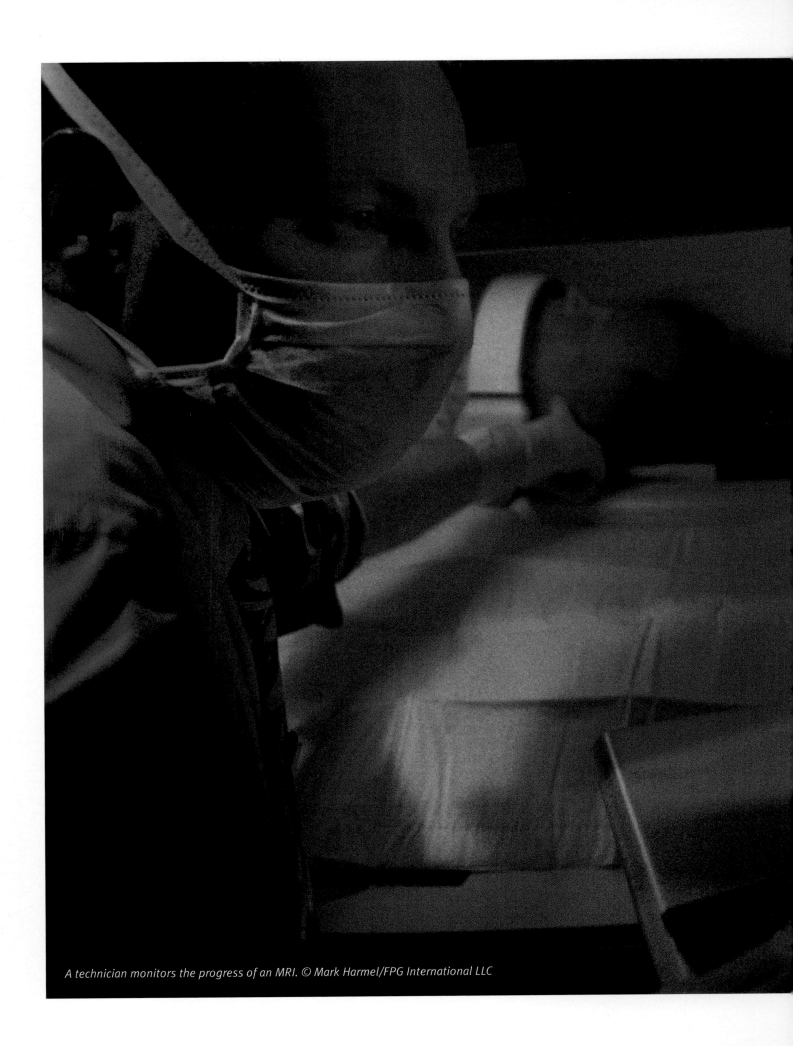

A technician monitors the progress of an MRI. © Mark Harmel/FPG International LLC

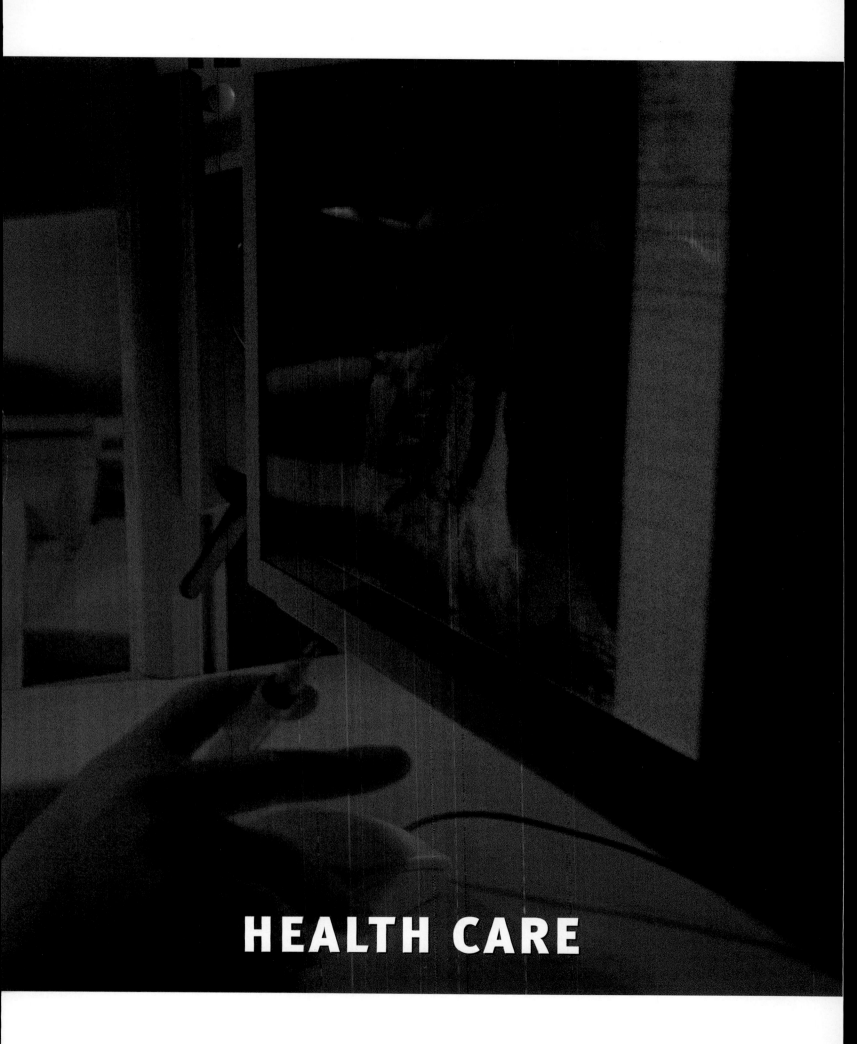

HEALTH CARE

FIRSTGUARD HEALTH PLAN, INC.

THE LOCALLY OWNED, COMMUNITY-FOCUSED HMO FIRSTGUARD HEALTH PLAN, INC., DEDICATED TO IMPROVING THE OVERALL HEALTH AND WELL-BEING OF THE CITIZENS OF KANSAS CITY, NOW OFFERS A PLAN FOR PRIVATE SECTOR AND PUBLIC EMPLOYERS

Like most successful HMOs, FirstGuard Health Plan, Inc., with corporate headquarters in Kansas City, offers outstanding customer service, affordable premiums, and an extensive network of high-quality primary care physicians, specialists, hospitals, other health care providers, and pharmacies.

But unlike most HMOs, FirstGuard is a locally owned community organization that lives by its motto, to provide The Heart and Soul of Healthcare. In this day of profit-driven corporate health care, FirstGuard is able to have a healthy business while emphasizing personal relationships and attention to the patient. With this community focus, FirstGuard Health Plan made history in Kansas City's competitive HMO marketplace when it began operations in January 1997.

After serving for a year as an HMO for 20,000 Medicaid-eligible Missourians living in a seven-county area, FirstGuard has recently broadened its scope. It now offers a commercial HMO plan for private sector and public employers. FirstGuard offers groups with two or more employees multiple plan designs for both its HMO and Point of Service health plans.

FirstGuard is a subsidiary of the Model Cities Health Corporation of Kansas City (known as the Swope Parkway Health Center), an

The FirstGuard staff of caring professionals is dedicated to the overall good health and well-being of the people in the community.

Locally owned FirstGuard Health Plan, Inc., committed to supporting its community, emphasizes the cultivation of personal relationships, as seen in this neighborhood event.

organization dedicated to community services and development for the past twenty-five years. FirstGuard operates as a for-profit corporation, with its earnings earmarked to support the health center.

"We formed FirstGuard as a part of our initiative to grow in the community," says E. Frank Ellis, chairman of FirstGuard. "Managed health care has become an integral part of government-sponsored health care. We began by becoming a provider for Missouri's managed care program for Medicaid. A natural continuation is to be a player in the employer-based commercial marketplace."

Those who were involved in the owner group—people at Swope Parkway and the leadership of FirstGuard—saw that the community could benefit from an HMO that understood and addressed the needs of the city's Medicaid patients.

"It is critical for us to look at improving the overall health and well-being of the community," Ellis says. "We have invested in overall community development and improvement. Our efforts to support the community—in a holistic way that goes beyond the traditional definition of health care—include providing preventative procedures and services, such as wellness exams, immunizations, prenatal care, and mammographies, as standard benefits for HMO members."

KANSAS CITY VETERANS AFFAIRS MEDICAL CENTER

A MAJOR TEACHING HOSPITAL, RESEARCH CENTER, AND PROVIDER OF SPECIALTY CARE IN MANY DISCIPLINES, THE KANSAS CITY VETERANS AFFAIRS MEDICAL CENTER IS DEDICATED TO KEEPING THE PROMISE TO AMERICA'S VETERANS

The dedicated staff and volunteers at the Kansas City Veterans Affairs Medical Center represent a large tertiary care and teaching hospital. It is part of VA Heartland Network (VISN 15), an integrated health care system dedicated to providing high-quality health care to the veterans of mid-America.

Through its half century of affiliation with the University of Kansas School of Medicine, the Veterans Affairs Medical Center is the principal teaching hospital for approximately 500 medical house staff and students annually. It maintains more than forty additional educational affiliations in thirty-one disciplines, including nursing, audiology and speech pathology, pharmacy, psychology, rehabilitation, prosthetics, and social work. It is the third-largest teaching hospital in Kansas City.

The center's humane and careful practice of the well-established principles of primary care rivals that of other health care organizations in the community. It provides a unique "one doctor–one patient" caregiver relationship for its veterans. Its practice of, and reputation for, excellence in customer service is unparalleled.

With two Nobel Laureates, a leading role in the development of the Computerized Tomography (CT) scanner, and many other medical innovations, the national VA is a world leader in research. The Kansas City VA Medical Center is known for its research in the use of aspirin for treating heart disease and alcohol and substance

Shown above is the main campus of the Kansas City Veterans Affairs Medical Center.

abuse, research in Alzheimer's Disease, and a host of other basic and clinical research studies.

As a tertiary care and referral center for eastern Kansas and western Missouri, the Kansas City center receives patients referred from throughout the Midwest. The center's award-winning eye programs attract patients from across the nation.

The national VA's reputation for the high-quality practice of medicine is reflected in its above-average scores from the Joint Commission on Accreditation of Health Care Organizations as well as in the national quality awards it receives from all over the United States.

The Kansas City Veterans Affairs Medical Center believes in its community. Through various partnerships, it shares its expertise, professionalism, and dedication to high-quality care of the whole person. The medical center operates in the belief that it must give something back to those who do so much for it.

Its dedicated and caring staff and volunteers are busily and enthusiastically engaged in the business conveyed in its motto, Keeping the Promise to America's Veterans.

"Like a beacon in the night..."

At the Kansas City VA Medical Center the staff and volunteers are dedicated to Keeping the Promise to America's Veterans.

SAINT LUKE'S–SHAWNEE MISSION HEALTH SYSTEM

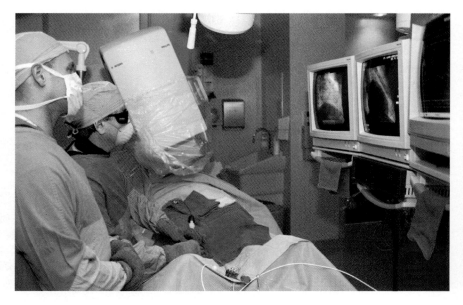

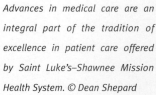

Advances in medical care are an integral part of the tradition of excellence in patient care offered by Saint Luke's–Shawnee Mission Health System. © Dean Shepard

"We are committed to bringing the quality and experience of our health system to as many people as possible," says Robert H. West, chairman of the system's board of trustees. "We now have the ability to handle nearly every kind of primary, acute, tertiary, and chronic health care service at multiple locations throughout the region. We've done that by looking realistically at the future and by expanding community access to our system."

From its renowned Mid-America Heart Institute to its primary care, behavioral health care, women's care, and perinatal, cancer, prevention, and emergency services, Saint Luke's–Shawnee Mission Health System supplies the Kansas City metropolitan area with high-quality health care services.

Saint Luke's–Shawnee Mission Health System treats approximately 50,000 inpatients and more than 500,000 outpatients each year from Kansas City and the surrounding Midwest region.

Although many of its principal facilities have a longer history, Saint Luke's–Shawnee Mission Health System began with the decision in 1989 to build a new Saint Luke's facility at Interstate 29 and Barry Road. The health system then further expanded by adding Crittenton; Wright Memorial Hospital, in Trenton, Missouri; and Anderson County Hospital, in Garnett, Kansas. When Saint Luke's and Shawnee Mission Medical Center merged in 1996, the present health system was formed.

Saint Luke's Hospital in midtown Kansas City, a 650-bed tertiary care hospital, was founded in 1885. The facility's network of 550 physicians represents more than 356 medical specialties. The hospital's special strengths include the highest standards in the state for trauma care at the Level I Trauma Center and for neonatal care in the Level II Intensive Care Nursery; comprehensive cardiac care in the Mid America Heart Institute; the regional Center of High Risk Maternity Care; the Ambulatory Surgery Center; the Cancer Center; the fifteen-bed dedicated Stroke Center; the Sexual Assault Treatment Center; and the Kidney Dialysis/Transplant Center.

In addition, Saint Luke's is a focal point for medical education, including a physician residency program and a College of Nursing program. The hospital is a primary teaching hospital for the University of Missouri–Kansas City School of Medicine, providing undergraduate, graduate, and continuing medical education. Saint Luke's is nationally accredited by the Accreditation Council for Continuing Medical Education (ACCME).

Saint Luke's Shawnee Mission Health System

Volunteers at Saint Luke's–Shawnee Mission Health System give the gift of time to patients and their families. © Clint Gillespie

The next largest component of the health system is **Shawnee Mission Medical Center**. Opened in 1962, the 383-bed acute care facility located in Merriam, Kansas, is a Seventh-Day Adventist community service. Within its fifty-four-acre campus, the medical center houses an outpatient surgery facility, a community health education facility, five medical office buildings, and a community fitness course.

Shawnee Mission Medical Center distinguishes itself through its specialties in cardiovascular services, behavioral health, outpatient care, and women's services. The Center for Women's Health at Shawnee Mission Medical Center is recognized as one of the top programs in the nation for women's care.

North of the Missouri River is **Saint Luke's Northland Hospital at Smithville**, which opened in 1938. This facility offers a ninety-two-bed hospital with skilled nursing care, inpatient rehabilitation services, mental health care for adults and seniors, home care, transportation services, emergency care, and urgent care services.

Saint Luke's Northland Hospital on Barry Road is a fifty-five-bed facility providing medical/surgical care, intensive care, maternity care with a Level II nursery, and radiology, surgical, cardiac catheterization, outpatient, and twenty-four-hour emergency services.

The reach of Saint Luke's–Shawnee Mission Health System extends further still. **Crittenton**, with roots going back to 1896, offers behavioral care for children and their families on its 156-acre campus in south Kansas City and through clinics in four metropolitan locations. Farther from the city center, **Anderson County Hospital**, in Garnett, Kansas, and **Wright Memorial Hospital**, in Trenton, Missouri, are part of the Saint Luke's–Shawnee Mission Health System.

Saint Luke's South, located in Overland Park, Kansas, is the newest facility in Saint Luke's–Shawnee Mission Health System.

Committed to children for more than 100 years, Crittenton (in Kansas City) offers comprehensive behavioral health care through a variety of inpatient and outpatient programs.
© Dean Shepard

SAINT LUKE'S–SHAWNEE MISSION HEALTH SYSTEM MISSION STATEMENT

Saint Luke's–Shawnee Mission Health System is a nonprofit integrated health system committed to enhancing the physical, mental, and spiritual health of the communities we serve. The system, supported by education and research, partners with others to achieve our goals.

It is a seventy-five-bed facility providing state-of-the-art patient care. Saint Luke's South has been designed to be patient friendly and operationally efficient. It also includes a 90,000-square-foot medical office building.

Saint Luke's–Shawnee Mission Health System prides itself on high-quality care and patient satisfaction. The organization has received local, state, and national citations for the level of care it delivers. Saint Luke's Hospital of Kansas City received the 1997 National Quality Health Care Award, the highest honor given to a hospital. The Voluntary Hospitals of America (VHA) bestowed St. Luke's Hospital with the Quality Leadership Award in Clinical Effectiveness in 1996. The hospital received the Missouri Quality Award in 1995, the first health care organization ever to receive this honor. Shawnee Mission Medical Center was selected by *Self* magazine in 1997 as one of the top-ten women's centers in the nation.

The **Mid-America Heart Institute** is widely recognized as one of the finest cardiac facilities in the world. For decades the institute has served as a major referral center for cardiac patients. Its Women's Cardiac Center was among the first programs in the nation to address specific cardiac health issues faced by women; its

offering a specialized center for the treatment of stroke. Trained to provide quick response, the multidisciplinary care team administers an aggressive treatment plan using the latest advances in stroke care. The Stroke Center participates in the research conducted by the National Institute of Health Studies on drug therapies and techniques.

Saint Luke's–Shawnee Mission Health System provides more than thirty primary care practices throughout the Kansas City region. Specialties include family practice, internal medicine, pediatrics, and obstetrics and gynecology. In addition, the health system provides occupational health services through its CorporateCare clinics. Comprehensive services include injury and disability management, work-related evaluations, drug and alcohol screenings, prevention services, and rehabilitation.

The Older Adult Services program complements the Saint Luke's–Shawnee Mission Health System mission by providing care and patient-support services to meet the growing needs of older adults. A comprehensive program of established services promotes healthy, more independent lifestyles.

Saint Luke's Hospital received national verification by the American College of Surgeons' Committee on Trauma, placing Saint Luke's Trauma Center among a leading group of trauma centers across the United States. A Level I Trauma Center, Saint Luke's Hospital cares for the most critically injured adult and pediatric trauma patients.

Shawnee Mission Medical Center's emergency department is one of the busiest in Johnson County, treating more than 30,000 patients a year. An important feature of this department is a seven-bed Chest Pain Emergency Center, providing early response for patients experiencing chest pain symptoms.

Cardiovascular Clinical Research Center conducts leading research into drugs and new medical equipment and techniques.

The services of Saint Luke's–Shawnee Mission Health System address the special needs of women with high-risk pregnancies. The system offers the most comprehensive obstetric services in greater Kansas City. The Center for Women's Health educates women about risk factors, stresses the importance of early detection, and encourages healthy lifestyles. More than 6,000 babies are delivered annually throughout Saint Luke's–Shawnee Mission Health System.

Saint Luke's–Shawnee Mission Health System offers comprehensive mental health and substance abuse programs. The system covers all levels of care including inpatient, outpatient, EAP (Employee Assistance Program), partial hospitalization, intensive outpatient, and in-home care. Wellness programs are available to the community, including screenings, fitness and exercise classes, a smoking cessation program, weight management programs, and a complete health management program.

Saint Luke's Hospital is the only hospital in Kansas City

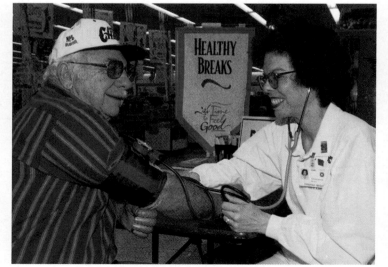

Health screening programs, such as "Healthy Breaks," presented at convenient community and workplace locations offer valuable health and wellness information. © Clint Gillespie

Emergency care service also is available at Saint Luke's Northland Hospital at Barry Road, which provides emergency care twenty-four hours a day, and at Smithville, which provides both urgent care and twenty-four-hour emergency care.

LifeFlight Eagle is an air ambulance service that operates twenty-four hours a day, seven days a week within a 150-mile radius of Kansas City. LifeFlight Eagle is staffed and equipped to treat and transport cardiac patients, critically ill neonatal infants, high-risk obstetrical patients, critical pediatric patients, and victims of life-threatening illnesses, injuries, and natural disasters.

Combining the latest in communications technology with the finest in medical care, the Saint Luke's–Shawnee Mission Health System has introduced telemedicine, giving physicians, nurses, and administrators access to a full complement of patient information from multiple locations throughout greater Kansas City and the Midwest. Patients in rural locations now can consult directly with physicians in Kansas City without the expense and time involved in travel. The Ask-A-Nurse Resource Center provides physician referrals and medical information through a twenty-four-hour access line. Staffed by registered nurses, Ask-A-Nurse has served more than one million callers since it was launched in 1986.

In addition to its fundamental connections with the University of Missouri–Kansas City, Saint Luke's–Shawnee Mission Health System emphasizes its commitment to the community through school partnerships and a rape crisis center. The system has also established an affiliation with the Cabot Westside Clinic, a provider of bilingual primary health care.

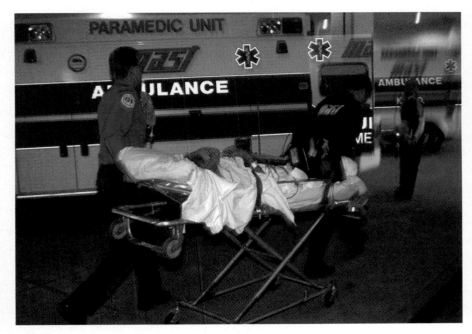

When moments count, Saint Luke's–Shawnee Mission Health System has the resources available for quick response. © Dean Shepard

Saint Luke's–Shawnee Mission Health System's Ask-A-Nurse Resource Center enables callers to make a doctor's appointment, register for a health event, or ask a nurse about a medical condition. © Clint Gillespie

"When I look to the future, I see a health system based on ideas as well as bricks and mortar," says G. Richard Hastings, Saint Luke's–Shawnee Mission Health System's president and CEO. "Saint Luke's–Shawnee Mission Health System is committed to enhancing the physical, mental, and spiritual health of the communities we serve. That means cutting-edge research and community education. That means matching our quality with our compassion.

"I am proud of our state-of-the-art facilities, but I am prouder still of the people who staff our facilities," Hastings says, "for it is they who create a place of caring and curing."

FACILITIES OF THE SAINT LUKE'S–SHAWNEE MISSION HEALTH SYSTEM

The Saint Luke's–Shawnee Mission Health System includes:
- Saint Luke's Hospital of Kansas City, 1885
- Shawnee Mission Medical Center, 1962
- Saint Luke's Northland Hospital at Barry Road, 1989
- Saint Luke's Northland Hospital at Smithville, 1938
- Crittenton, 1896
- Anderson County Hospital: Garnett, Kansas, 1951
- Wright Memorial Hospital: Trenton, Missouri, 1908
- Saint Luke's South, 1998
    . . . and more than thirty primary care physician practices

BJC HEALTH SYSTEM℠

BJC HEALTH SYSTEM℠,

ONE OF THE LARGEST

NONPROFIT HEALTH

CARE SYSTEMS IN THE

NATION, IS FORGING AN

INTEGRATED HEALTH

CARE DELIVERY AND

FINANCING SYSTEM

TO IMPROVE THE

HEALTH OF THE PEOPLE

AND COMMUNITIES

IT SERVES

Established in November 1992, BJC Health System℠ is committed to delivering new models of health care that enhance quality, increase access, and control costs. This commitment has led to national recognition of the system as a leader in integrated health care and research. Today BJC Health System ranks as one of the largest nonprofit health care systems in the United States.

The impetus for the founding of BJC Health System was the need to provide a regional, integrated health care delivery and financing system that would provide premier health care services, professional and community education, and health care research. The system serves two distinct geographic markets, mid-Missouri and the greater St. Louis region, which includes southern Illinois.

At its formation, BJC was the first health care system in the country to link urban, suburban, and rural health care facilities with an academic medical center, the renowned Washington University School of Medicine. BJC Health System is affiliated with Washington University through two of its member teaching hospitals, Barnes-Jewish Hospital and St. Louis Children's Hospital.

In partnership with its physicians, BJC provides a full continuum of services through an integrated network of more than 100 health care delivery settings including community health and wellness centers, physician offices, health clinics, ambulatory care facilities, hospitals, home health programs, skilled nursing services, retirement communities, rehabilitation programs, and hospice services.

BJC Health System employs more than 24,000 people who work to provide

Listening to patients' concerns is a first step for BJC professionals in providing high-quality care. BJC won the 1999 National Quality Health Care Award for its innovative quality improvement programs.

From home health care to a full continuum of medical services, BJC Health System strives to provide accessible, high-quality care.

exceptional health care service marked by quality, leadership, and compassion.

BJC Health System's specialties range from wellness initiatives, community lectures, screenings, and ambulatory care to urgent and trauma care, acclaimed transplantation services, and nationally recognized cancer treatments.

"Overall changes in the health care industry, shrinkages in Medicare/Medicaid reimbursements, increased penetration by managed care, and intensified competition from for-profit providers all mean that the way you receive health care has changed dramatically. One thing, however, will not change—our commitment to our mission, which is to improve the health of the people and communities we serve," says Edward B. Case, executive vice president and chief operating officer of BJC Health System.

To ensure that BJC fulfills its mission, it is looking in bold new directions, such as the integration of health care delivery and financing. BJC's long-term plan to bring together health care delivery and financing will assure patients that their doctors will make decisions about their medical care rather than third-party insurance carriers determining aspects of their treatment.

In 1992 Barnes Hospital and The Jewish Hospital of St. Louis affiliated to form Barnes-

Jewish, Inc. In 1993 Barnes-Jewish, Inc., and Christian Health Services came together under the name of BJC Health System.

In June 1994 Missouri Baptist Medical Center became a member of BJC Health System, followed by St. Louis Children's Hospital. In July 1995 BJC Health System established BJC^{SM} Medical Group, a system approach to developing an integrated group practice comprising primary care physicians, obstetricians, and pediatricians.

"Strong physician partnerships are a cornerstone of our strategy to be the region's leading health care provider, and physicians have taken leading roles on our strategic planning teams," Case says.

In January 1996 BJC Health System established BJC Home Care Services with the consolidation of administrative functions of nine certified home health agencies, four hospices, and private-duty nursing services. In February 1997 BJC Health System purchased the Group Health Plan's nine St. Louis area medical centers, strengthening the system's ability to deliver and finance primary care services across the community.

Since its inception, BJC has continued the traditions of its member hospitals in being highly responsive to the many communities it serves. In 1998, at the request of the City of St. Louis, BJC agreed to assist for five years with the management of ConnectCare, the metropolitan area's health care delivery program for those who are uninsured or underinsured.

On an ongoing basis, BJC Health System partners with community organizations as well as hospital-initiated child advocacy programs to promote health and wellness. The system conducts injury prevention programs for young people on topics

A member of BJC's health care team provides compassionate care for a young patient.

such as crib, gun, bicycle, and poison safety; provides immunizations; and offers vision, hearing, dental, and growth and development checkups in schools and at special events for low-income families.

Reaching into the classroom, BJC sponsors one of the largest school outreach programs in the St. Louis region. Further extending the system's helping hand to children, the BJC staff volunteers in an extensive youth mentoring network in Missouri and Illinois in an effort to positively influence students who are at risk. Further, it fosters and participates in school/business partnerships that enable employees of large and small businesses to bring their expertise into the classroom.

"BJC is committed to providing the highest quality services at the most appropriate cost," says Case. "We are achieving our goals by recruiting highly skilled, caring people who are dedicated to improving health services and outcomes. We are establishing meaningful relationships with physicians, employees, and the communities to continue our goal of being the region's leading health care provider."

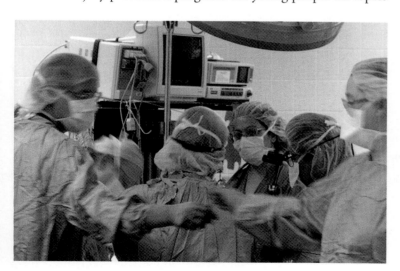

Physicians affiliated with BJC Health System and Washington University School of Medicine are known worldwide for innovative medical research that benefits the care of patients.

MONSANTO WAS THE LARGEST PRODUCER OF ASPIRIN FROM 1917 UNTIL THE 1980S.

tralized by forming two independent companies, Mallinckrodt Medical, Inc., and Mallinckrodt Specialty Chemicals Company. In 1991 the combined net sales of these two companies reached $1 billion. In 1997 the company acquired Nellcor Puritan Bennett, a worldwide leader in developing, manufacturing, and marketing respiratory products and a major supplier of nitrous oxide and other gas products for the health care industries. After this acquisition, Mallinckrodt divested its industrial chemicals businesses to concentrate exclusively on health care and specialty chemicals. Mallinckrodt Pharmaceuticals Group is the world's largest (and lowest-cost) producer of acetaminophen or APAP, the active ingredient in commonly used over-the-counter pain relievers. The company supplies roughly one-half of the U.S. market and more than one-third of the growing worldwide market. Mallinckrodt also produces a wide variety of both natural and synthetic narcotic products, as well as methadone, the most commonly used treatment in therapeutic maintenance programs for opiate and heroin addiction.

Monsanto has had a somewhat similar history. Established in St. Louis in 1901, the company has been involved over the years in a wide variety of chemical and medical products, including saccharin (Monsanto's first product, which it introduced in 1902), vanilla, caffeine, aspirin, soaps and detergents, plastics and resins, rubber

Scientists use small plant tissue to create crops that are more resistant to insects and that tolerate herbicides formulated to protect the environment. Courtesy, Monsanto Company

products, synthetic fibers, herbicides, food preservatives, pharmaceuticals, and sweeteners. In 1955, Monsanto became the first corporation in the world to install IBM electronic technology for data processing.

In July 1998, Monsanto CEO Robert Shapiro announced the company's intention to contribute more than $80 million to establish a major plant-science and biotechnology research center near Monsanto's Creve Coeur campus. This project is a joint venture between the Missouri Botanical Garden, Washington University, the University of Missouri at Columbia (UMC), and the University of Illinois at Champaign-Urbana.

Washington University and UMC's involvement in the proposed plant-science and biotechnology research center demonstrates one way in which Missouri's major educational institutions are committed to the fields of medical research and biotechnology. Washington University's School of Medicine is internationally known for research in neuroscience, genetics, diabetes, cardiovascular diseases, immunology, and diagnostic imaging. Medical research activities and achievements of Washington University in St. Louis include: establishing the effectiveness of taking aspirin to prevent heart attacks (in 1975); developing the PET scanner (in the early

FACING PAGE: *Missouri's pharmaceutical industry has provided treatment for allergies, cancers, arthritis, cardiovascular disease, AIDS, hypertension, and many more conditions and diseases. © Telegraph Colour Library/FPG International LLC*

ment pipeline, including innovative products for the treatment of rheumatoid arthritis, osteoporosis, Alzheimer's disease, schizophrenia, anemia, acute respiratory distress syndrome, and bacterial infections.

BLAZING A TRAIL IN DRUG RESEARCH

In the Kansas City metropolitan area, one of the small but growing biotechnology and pharmaceutical research companies is CyDex, Inc., based in suburban Overland Park, Kansas. In 1994 the company, which then had only twelve employees, won Kansas City's Silicon Prairie Technology Association Technology of the Year Award in the bioscience category. (As with many companies based on the Kansas side of Kansas City, the achievements of CyDex researchers are recognized by their counterparts across the state line, and their efforts bring prestige to the whole city, most of which lies in Missouri.) In 1998 CyDex signed a manufacturing agreement with the French pharmaceutical firm PPG-Sipsy to make Capistol, a compound CyDex

is bringing to the market that makes certain drugs water soluble. In addition, CyDex signed a cooperative agreement with Allergan, Inc., of Irvine, California, to provide it with Capistol for use in prescription eyedrops.

Located in Kansas City, Missouri, is the Midwest Research Institute (MRI), a pure and applied scientific research organization established in 1944. MRI medical technology scientists have done extensive research on cancer-fighting chemicals under contract to the National Cancer Institute. MRI has also assisted other companies in drug formulation development, toxicity testing, and preclinical studies related to the FDA approval process. In 1998 MRI was nearing completion of a new Health Assessment Research Center with state-of-the-art laboratories for research into the health effects of exposure to electrical and magnetic fields. More than 400 of MRI's 1,200 nationwide professional and support personnel are based in the Kansas City area. The other 750 are employed at satellite locations in North Carolina, Washington, D.C., California, Tennessee, and Colorado.

Missouri's reputation for innovative research and development of key pharmaceutical drugs was established early in the century by firms such as Monsanto and Mallinckrodt, along with educational institutions such as Washington University, St. Louis University, and the University of Missouri. Building on this solid foundation, these same firms and educational institutions continue to perform cutting-edge work in the state in the advanced fields of medical research, radiopharmaceuticals, and biotechnology. Missouri will undoubtedly remain at the forefront in these fields well into the twenty-first century.

Hoechst Marion Roussel USA, one of the world's leading pharmaceutical companies, has had its North American headquarters in Kansas City since 1995. © Bob Barrett

A lab technician adds a liquid catalyst to a reactivator vessel. © Telegraph Colour Library/FPG International LLC

BIOTECHNOLOGY

BIOKYOWA INC.

In 1982 when feed-supplement maker BioKyowa Inc. decided to locate its manufacturing operation in the Nash Road industrial park in Cape Girardeau, the project represented the first major plant investment by a Japanese company in the state of Missouri. Reflecting BioKyowa's success in the region, today its plant facilities are being expanded and a new sister company is being added nearby.

BioKyowa Inc. is a major supplier of the amino acid feed supplement L-lysine, serving the swine and poultry markets. It is in the process of adding feed-grade L-threonine and L-tryptophan to its product line.

BioKyowa produces feed supplements for the swine and poultry markets. It is a major supplier of the feed supplement L-lysine for livestock. BioKyowa is investing in the expansion of its Cape Girardeau L-lysine feed-supplement operation, bringing its capacity to 25,000 metric tons per year. It also is adding facilities where two other amino acids, L-threonine and L-tryptophan, will be made in feed grade.

BioKyowa's parent company, Kyowa Hakko Kogyo Co. Ltd., was founded in Tokyo in 1949 by Dr. Benzaburo Kato. The parent firm's many products include pharmaceuticals, biochemicals, food, liquor, chemicals, fermentation ingredients, and feed additives. It has 5,200 employees and $3.2 billion net sales worldwide.

In May 1998 Dr. Tadashi Hirata, president of Kyowa Hakko Kogyo, announced the incorporation of BioKyowa's new sister company, Kyowa Foods Inc., to be headquartered in Cape Girardeau. Facilities for the new firm will be designed and constructed to make full use of Kyowa Hakko Kogyo's well-established fermentation technology. Kyowa Foods will manufacture and sell nucleotide seasonings developed by Kyowa Hakko Kogyo.

Headquarters and manufacturing operations for BioKyowa Inc. are in the Nash Road industrial park in Cape Girardeau, Missouri.

The manufactured seasonings offer the four basic tastes—sweet, bitter, sour, and salty—plus a fifth taste, "umami," consisting of naturally occurring glutamic acids and nucleotides found in bonito, seaweed, and shiitake mushrooms.

"The establishment of this new company by Kyowa Hakko Kogyo represents a big investment by our parent company," says Kohta Fujiwara, president of BioKyowa and Kyowa Foods in Cape Girardeau. "The construction of the plant is projected for completion in summer 2000. It will be about 32,000 square feet, including processing space and warehouses."

Known as an exemplary corporate citizen, BioKyowa funds a scholarship program and supports other civic and charitable organizations. In conjunction with Southeast Missouri State University and the university's Center for Faulkner Studies, BioKyowa sponsors the Visiting Japanese Scholar Program. Through this program, one Japanese scholar per year is brought to the Southeast Missouri State University campus to conduct research and to participate in various types of cultural exchanges.

In 1991 BioKyowa was presented with the "Industry of the Year" award by the Cape Girardeau Chamber of Commerce.

IN THE HANDS OF PROFESSIONALS

CHAPTER NINETEEN

DURING THE STATE'S FIRST HUNDRED YEARS, MISSOURI'S ECONOMY WAS DOMINATED BY AGRICULTURE. FOR THE NEXT FOUR DECADES, MANUFACTURING DROVE THE ECONOMIC ENGINE. SINCE ABOUT 1970, HOWEVER, THE SERVICE INDUSTRIES HAVE GRADUALLY BECOME THE STATE'S ECONOMIC BREAD AND BUTTER. BY 1997, PROFESSIONAL SERVICES ACCOUNTED FOR APPROXIMATELY 28 PERCENT OF MISSOURI'S NONFARM WORKERS, LEADING ALL

categories of employment in the state. Among the more than seven hundred thousand Missourians engaged in the service industries, the greatest growth has occurred in professional services, including law and accounting, architecture and engineering, business management, data processing, and environmental services.

Legal services have the longest history in the state, dating to the period of early land-claim litigation. The legal profession also became heavily involved in the thorny legal issues connected with the spread of railroads in the last half of the nineteenth century. At present, many of the state's law firms are primarily engaged in corporate acquisitions, divestments, and mergers, as well as health care litigation. As Missouri enters the twenty-first century, almost fifteen thousand attorneys practice statewide, nearly two-thirds of them in either the St. Louis or Kansas City metropolitan areas.

Law firms are increasingly following the lead of their corporate clients by arranging mergers among themselves. In one of the biggest cross-state law-firm mergers to date, Kansas City–based Blackwell Sanders Matheny Weary & Lombardi (established in 1916) and St. Louis–based Peper Martin Jensen Maichel & Hetlage (founded in 1941) merged, creating a 312-lawyer powerhouse firm with nearly 700 employees. The combined law firm, called Blackwell Sanders Peper Martin, is the third largest in Missouri, behind St. Louis–based Bryan Cave, which has 550 lawyers, and Shook Hardy & Bacon in Kansas City. Blackwell Sanders Peper Martin's combined client list includes such blue-chip companies as Hallmark Cards, UtiliCorp United, Black & Veatch, Applebee's International, Monsanto, The Boeing Company, Planet Hollywood International, Hard Rock Café International, and St. Louis University. Two other significant mergers

FACING PAGE: *This statue in the United States Courthouse in St. Louis stands watch over the rights of Missouri citizens. Approximately 24,000 lawyers are currently practicing throughout the state. © Bob Barrett.* THIS PAGE: *The 1894 courthouse in Carthage, a town about one hundred miles northwest of Branson, is known for its beautiful Romanesque Revival architecture and is constructed of the area's famous white marble. The square on which it stands is on the National Historic Register. © Bob Barrett*

have taken place in Kansas City since 1995: Lathrop & Norquist and Gage & Tucker formed Lathrop & Gage L.C., and Bryan Cave absorbed Smith Gill Fisher & Butts.

Accounting services have proliferated primarily as a result of the 1913 introduction of the federal income tax.

One of Kansas City's greatest success stories, H&R Block has nearly ten thousand offices worldwide. The company was founded in 1955 by Richard and Henry Bloch (top photo). Courtesy, H&R Block. The firm's headquarters are shown above. © Bob Barrett

FACING PAGE: *Crown Center houses many of Kansas City's leading firms. Its original two million square feet of office space will grow considerably with the planned expansion. © James Blank*

One of the best-known tax preparation firms in the world is H&R Block, founded in 1955 in Kansas City. In 1997, the company served more than 18 million taxpayers in nearly ten thousand offices worldwide. About 450 employees work for H&R Block in the Kansas City area.

Both Kansas City and St. Louis can also boast regional offices of some of the nation's largest accounting firms, like Ernst & Young or Deloitte & Touche. And both cities have large local firms, like Mayer Hoffman McCann, one of Kansas City's largest public accounting firms, and Rubin Brown Gornstein & Company, the fifth largest firm in St. Louis.

BUILD IT AND THEY WILL COME

Another professional service well represented in Missouri is architectural design. Both Kansas City and St. Louis have a reputation for unique architectural landmarks. St. Louis has its soaring Gateway Arch, designed by Eero Saarinen; its Eads Bridge, envisioned by Captain James B. Eads; and its Wainwright Building, created by the Chicago architect Louis Sullivan. Kansas City can boast about its Country Club Plaza shopping district and its art deco architecture, the most prominent example of which is the downtown Kansas City Power & Light Building.

Most of the state's principal architectural design and consulting firms are also situated in either the St. Louis or Kansas City metropolitan areas. One of the largest of such firms in the world, Sverdrup Corporation (also an engineering and construction firm), has offices in both St. Louis and Kansas City. Sverdrup was the lead engineering company for the Alaskan Pipeline Project, which was directed by the U.S. Army Corps of Engineers, and also designed Busch Stadium in St. Louis as well as the New Orleans Superdome, the Chesapeake Bay Bridge Tunnel, and the Stennis Space Center rocket test facilities. Another nationally known architectural firm, Kansas City–based Gould Evans Goodman Associates, is one of the fastest-growing architectural firms in the country and is the principal architect for the Kansas City Jazz and Negro Leagues Baseball Museums project.

In the Columbia metropolitan area, an innovative architectural firm is Chinn & Associates, which was established in 1960 and is responsible for such highly

GEORGE GRAHAM VEST (1830–1904) SERVED IN THE CONFEDERATE LEGISLATURE AS REPRESENTATIVE OF MISSOURI'S QUASI-LEGAL "SECESSIONIST" GOVERNMENT DURING THE CIVIL WAR. HE LATER WORKED IN THE FIRM OF A UNION OPPONENT, COL. JOHN PHILLIPS, IN SEDALIA, AND ARGUED A CASE INVOLVING THE KILLING OF A HOUND DOG THAT EVENTUALLY REACHED THE MISSOURI SUPREME COURT. DURING LITIGATION VEST DELIVERED THE "EULOGY TO A DOG," WHICH GAINED HIM NATIONAL ATTENTION. HE LATER SERVED IN THE UNITED STATES SENATE AND WAS A CHIEF PROPONENT FOR ESTABLISHING YELLOWSTONE NATIONAL PARK (SHOWN).

FACING PAGE: *This walkway at the Missouri Botanical Garden is an attractive example of architectural form and function working hand in hand. © Lewis Portnoy/Spectra-Action, Inc.*

A St. Louis chapter of IMC was also established about this same time.

Many Missouri consulting firms specialize in areas such as information technology, health care, nonprofit organizations, cost management, human resources, and marketing. One of Kansas City's largest and most successful consulting firms, the Corridor Group, Inc., focuses much of its attention on both small home health care organizations and large health maintenance organizations. In 1998 the company had revenues approaching $6 million and was ranked 412th on *Inc.* magazine's list of the five hundred fastest-growing privately held small companies in the country.

When a large number of middle managers were laid off during the corporate downsizing of the 1980s and 1990s, many of them turned to consulting to make a living. In St. Louis, Data Management Consultants, founded in 1985 and specializing in data and systems management software, grew by more than 520 percent between 1992 and 1996. Another major St. Louis–area consulting firm, Magnum Technologies, founded in 1990 as an engineering consulting firm with a special emphasis on industrial automation and computer-assisted design services, was cited in 1995 by *Inc.* magazine as one of the nation's fastest-growing companies. In 1997, it became a wholly owned subsidiary of General Electric.

ine and certify the growing number of unregulated consultants. In Missouri, Tom Lawrence (president of Lawrence-Leiter & Company, one of the old-line area consultant businesses formed in 1950) and Hal Wood (president of Advisory Management Services of Kansas City) established a Kansas City chapter of IMC in 1968.

According to all economic indicators, Missouri's service industries should continue to increase in importance during the first decades of the twenty-first century. Experts predict that professional services, in particular, will occupy the top spot among the many services in this sector.

LEFT: *Planning for retirement is an important service offered by the state's many accounting firms. © Michael Goldman/FPG International LLC*

The St. Louis skyline is seen here from the Morton D. May Memorial Amphitheater. © James Blank

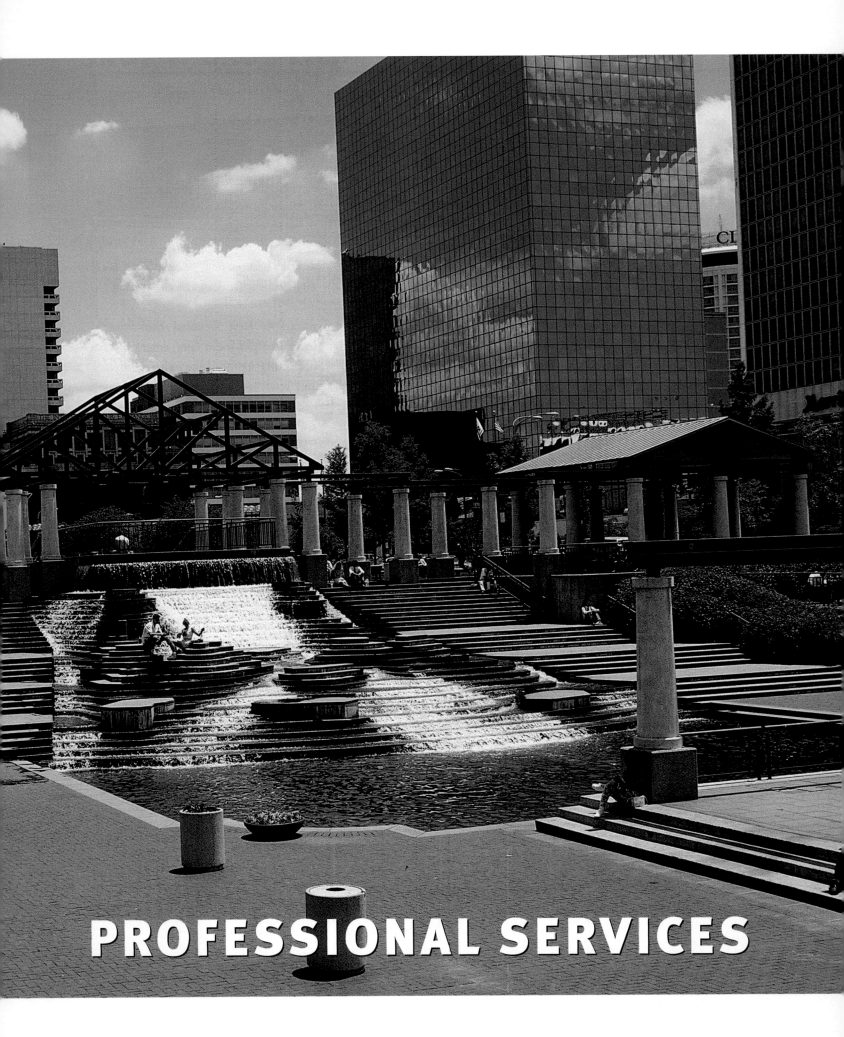

PROFESSIONAL SERVICES

OCCU-TEC, INC.

OCCU-TEC, INC., OFFERS PROACTIVE TRAINING AND ASSISTANCE TO BUSINESSES HANDLING EVER-INCREASING RESPONSIBILITIES IN THE AREAS OF WORKPLACE SAFETY AND ENVIRONMENTAL REGULATIONS

Based in Kansas City, OCCU-TEC, Inc., was formed in 1983 by Duncan Heydon and Skuli Gudmundsson. It is a full-service consulting firm that gives special assistance and training in occupational safety, industrial hygiene, and environmental issues. Its mission is to proactively provide cost-effective, timely solutions to environmental and safety concerns that affect industry and government.

OCCU-TEC provides consulting and training in the areas of safety, asbestos and lead management, environmental services, industrial hygiene, and indoor air quality.

In today's competitive market, businesses have elected to reevaluate their workplace and operational processes in order to eliminate loss associated with waste and preventable injuries. OCCU-TEC's safety consulting experts address these safety and loss concerns and provide cost-effective solutions that can substantially increase its customers' productivity and bottom line.

As a full-service training provider, OCCU-TEC offers courses that are ready to be custom-designed for each customer's needs. Its goal is to help companies become proactive in safety and environmental management—and meet compliance requirements—while integrating safety and health into a firm's overall management plan.

An effective health and safety program is essential for businesses in today's regulatory environment. OCCU-TEC takes a proactive approach to managing safety and environmental issues by providing leading companies with powerful, high-quality safety and environmental assistance and support.

Field project managers from OCCU-TEC visit a client's workplace to survey the physical site and the business's operational processes. After evaluating the existing levels of safety and environmental protection, OCCU-TEC provides practical solutions for meeting compliance regulations, which also can lead to financial benefits.

The asbestos management and lead management services that OCCU-TEC provides to industry and government effectively minimize workers' health risks and client liability. OCCU-TEC focuses on giving practical solutions to the environmental and safety concerns that affect each business.

Businesses must comply with an ever-increasing number of complex local, state, and federal environmental laws and regulations. Violations of these environmental requirements carry serious civil and/or criminal penalties. Additionally, in view of the public's demand for a clean and healthy environment, companies realize they can ill afford to ignore their environmental responsibilities. Property owners, lenders, and buyers also are recognizing that environmental management must be part of sound business practice.

"OCCU-TEC's staff of safety and environmental professionals understands the challenges faced by businesses today, and we offer innovative and cost-effective solutions for handling these issues," says Skuli Gudmundsson, OCCU-TEC president. "When top management treats company safety as a business function, their companies reap financial benefits."

Members of the management team at OCCU-TEC work closely with clients to create safety and environmental programs, which are custom-designed for each company.

WORLD-CLASS DEVELOPMENT

CHAPTER TWENTY

In Missouri if a newcomer asks a real estate agent, "Show me," he'll find himself faced with an amazingly wide range of choices, and all available for the right price. For, whether suburban, urban, rural, or small-town, Missouri properties (both old and new) are selling at prices well below the national average. The median single-family home price for Missouri's two largest

metropolitan areas, for example, was about $96,500 in 1997, whereas the U.S. median price was $123,200. The 1997 median single-family home price in the Springfield, Missouri, area was $80,900 in 1997. Real estate buyers from the East and West Coasts, especially, will be pleasantly surprised at how far their dollars will go in the Show Me State.

The wealth of styles available in Missouri's properties mirrors the widely varying rural and urban settings themselves. The suburbs of Kansas City and St. Louis, for example, offer restored nineteenth- and early twentieth-century classics as well as contemporary custom-built homes. The older neighborhoods of these two great cities are filled with the architectural personalities of Victorian town houses, trendy rehabilitated warehouse lofts, swank condos, and upscale apartments. A few hours' drive

beyond city limits, rustic cabins set harmoniously among thickly wooded acreage allows homeowners and vacationers to step into the rugged Ozark Mountain countryside. The construction of timber-frame lakeside getaways at the Lake of the Ozarks and other recreational lakes is skyrocketing at the end of the 1990s, reflecting a desire among people to escape the frenetic trappings of the city for more serene settings.

In the friendly middle ground of the heartland, small and midsize towns offer a down-home comfort missing elsewhere. Missouri native Walt Disney knew this when he immortalized his hometown of Marceline by reconstructing its early twentieth-century atmosphere in Disneyland's Main Street, U.S.A. As for farmland, two-thirds of the state is blanketed by it, from small "hobby" farms to large livestock and crop farms.

FACING PAGE: *The sky's the limit for Kansas City as it heads into the new millennium. A revival of several downtown neighborhoods, including 18th & Vine and River Market, and the continued popularity of others, such as Country Club Plaza, make Kansas City one of the most exciting cities in the nation. © Dan Wolf/Midwestock.* THIS PAGE: *Those seeking the quiet life head for the country, where timber-framed homes, such as this one built of cedar, blend in with the lovely surroundings. © Gay Bumgarner/Tony Stone Images*

© Dave G. Houser

Rural acreage accounts for 82.4 percent of Missouri's total area, yet 65 percent of Missouri's population lives and works on the 17.6 percent of land in the state's six large metropolitan areas: St. Louis, Kansas City, Springfield, Columbia, Joplin, and St. Joseph, in descending order. While the most active real estate and new construction markets are understandably in and around the two largest cities, the Lake of the Ozarks region and the Columbia and Springfield metropolitan areas have also grown steadily in the 1990s. As a whole, the real estate market in Missouri may be measured by the presence of more than four thousand real estate companies and their twenty thousand employees, who produce annual personal earnings of just over $3.5 billion.

DREAM HOMES IN ST. LOUIS

In 1996, *Fortune* named Greater St. Louis the nation's sixth best place to live and work; Greater St. Louis has the second-lowest cost of living and most affordable housing rates among major metropolitan areas. It is not surprising, then, that the largest real estate firm in the state, Colliers Turley Martin, is based there. This company, with three major offices and seventeen satellite offices, more than doubled its revenue between 1993 and 1998. The largest residential sales real estate company in the St. Louis area,

In this image circa 1960, stately Victorian and early twentieth-century homes stand out among wintry trees in St. Louis's Portland Place north of Forest Park. © Robert Srenco/FPG International LLC

A new home goes up in Kansas City, where in 1994 the median price of a single-family home was $88,600, well below the average for homes in other major U.S. cities. © Bruce Mathews/Midwestock

accounting for more than one-third of all transactions, is Gundaker Realtors/Better Homes and Gardens.

The commercial real estate market in the St. Louis area has been gradually moving to the outer fringes of the metropolitan area, mainly west and south of the city proper, though efforts are being made to revive interest in commercial properties in both the central business district and other parts of the city. Despite high vacancy rates in the older Class B and Class C

With its stunning scenery and wealth of recreational opportunities, Lake of the Ozarks is one of the top retirement and vacation-home communities in the nation. © James Blank

BY 1996, ST. LOUIS WAS THE FIFTH MOST SPRAWLING URBAN AREA IN THE NATION. IN 1997 ST. LOUIS PROPER RECORDED A POPULATION OF ABOUT 351,000. IN THE COUNTIES SUR-ROUNDING ST. LOUIS, ST. CHARLES COUNTY HAS GROWN FASTER THAN ANY OTHER PART OF THE REGION.

downtown commercial buildings, the modern Class A office buildings have a relatively low vacancy rate. The Metropolitan Square and MCI buildings, for example, reported occupancy rates above 90 percent in 1996. Efforts to revive the downtown business district focus on the St. Louis riverfront, with its Gateway Arch, Laclede's Landing, Busch Stadium, and the newly expanded America's Center/Trans World Dome convention complex. These attractions, along with the refurbished Union Station, once the railway hub of St. Louis but now a huge enclosed shopping mall and hotel, assure that the downtown will continue to be a vital part of the city's economy.

In 1998, the older premier industrial site in St. Louis County, Earth City, was being challenged by new commercial developments in Elm Point Business Park just off Route 370 in St. Charles and the Gateway Commerce Center between Granite City and Edwardsville on the Illinois side of the Mississippi River. At the same time, a marketing and development firm called the Discovery Group was promoting the Riverport industrial section,

area is Cohen-Esrey Real Estate Services, Inc., though Foster 7 Associates is also a major player in Kansas City's commercial real estate market.

CONSTRUCTING A BUILDING BOOM

Considerable construction activity in both St. Louis and Kansas City is focused on warehouse space, since warehouses are one of the most stable and cost-effective of all forms of commercial real estate. In fact, the largest segment of building activity in the state over the last ten years has been the construction of industrial buildings and warehouses, followed by office buildings and single-family residences. There has also been increased activity in hotel and convention center construction in both downtown St. Louis and Kansas City. Despite a construction slowdown in the late 1980s and early 1990s, the construction trades have experienced a comeback in

TOP: *Kansas City's H. R. Bartle Exposition Hall undergoes expansion.* © *Jim Hays/Midwestock.* BELOW: *Commercial construction is booming in Kansas City.* © *Steve Drews Photo*

the latter half of the century's final decade. In 1997, personal earnings by the construction industry were just over $5.2 billion, accounting for about 6 percent of all personal earnings in the state.

Commercial construction in the Kansas City metropolitan area is dominated by two firms, Dunn Construction Group and Black & Veatch, both of which got their starts locally but have since expanded to national prominence. Dunn Construction Group is one of Kansas City's largest and most respected commercial construction companies, employing more than one thousand people locally and generating gross revenues of $632 million in 1996. The company is rated in the top ten nationwide for hospital construction and forty-fifth nationwide among all contractors.

Kansas City–based Black & Veatch, founded in 1915, began as a small engineering firm handling projects like street paving, small water systems, electric plant appraisals, sewer systems, and street lighting. Today, the company is one of the largest and most diversified engineering and construction firms in the world, specializing in energy and environmental engineering as well as construction. In 1997, Black & Veatch generated nearly $2 billion in gross revenues and employed about eight thousand professionals in more than ninety offices worldwide. More than three thousand of the employees work in the Kansas City area.

Kansas City and St. Louis are not the only areas of major real estate development in Missouri. Garnering national attention in recent years has been the remarkable growth of a formerly sleepy town named Branson nestled in the Ozark hills. From 1959 when the "Baldknobbers Hillbilly Jamboree" opened the first music and comedy show downtown until today when more than thirty-five music theaters have made Branson America's "Live Music Show Capital," the growth in the area has been dramatic. In 1970 Branson had a population of about 2,000, and by 1996 it had grown to more than 5,000. But the increase in Branson's population is only the tip of the iceberg. Taney County, where Branson is located, has grown from about 20,500 in 1980 to nearly 34,000 in 1997. Nearby Springfield has grown from just over 133,000 in 1980 to about 143,500 in 1996. How long this southwestern Missouri boomtown atmosphere will last is anybody's guess, but at present it shows no apparent sign of slowing down.

Surrounded by lakes, Branson has become one of the Midwest's most popular tourist attractions. Its fame has sparked tremendous growth in the region. © James Blank

A construction crew pours a floor slab in Kansas City. © Eric R. Berndt/Photo Network

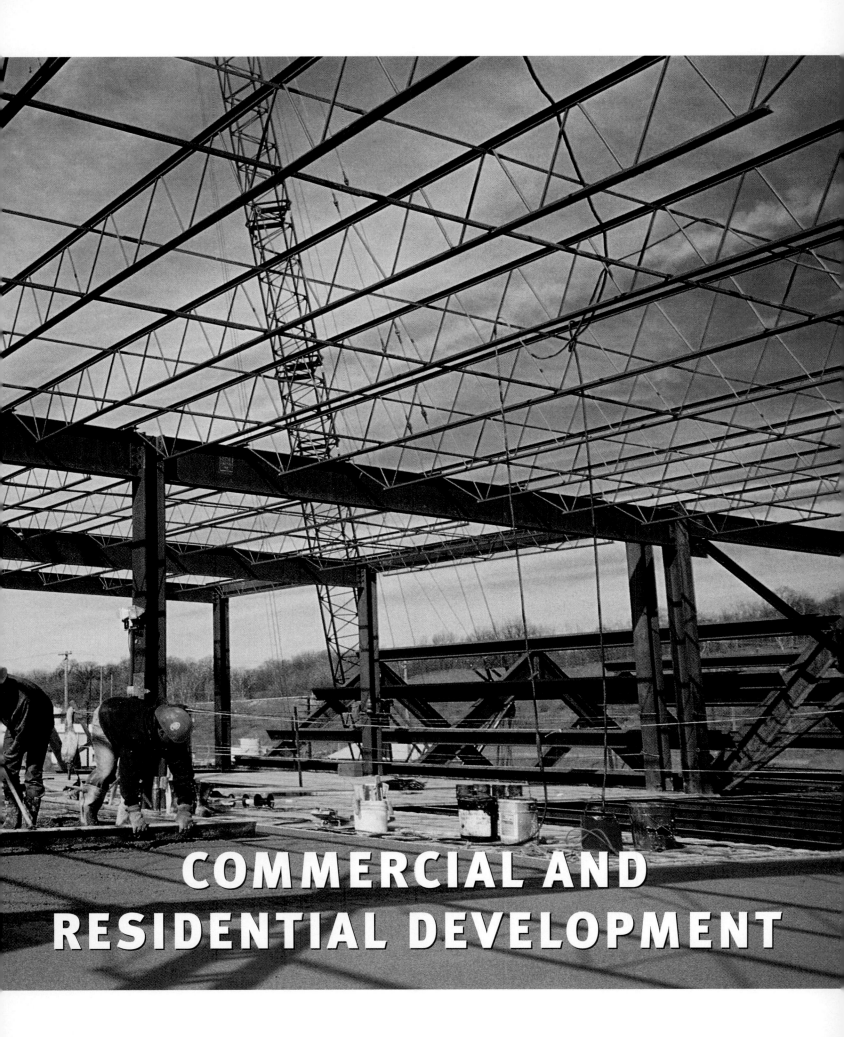

COMMERCIAL AND RESIDENTIAL DEVELOPMENT

THE MANY SUPPORT PROGRAMS OF THE MISSOURI DEPARTMENT OF ECONOMIC DEVELOPMENT ARE DESIGNED TO FACILITATE EMPLOYMENT AND ECONOMIC GROWTH FOR THE BUSINESSES AND THE PEOPLE OF MISSOURI

The Missouri Department of Economic Development (DED) is committed to fostering and supporting economic security, opportunity, growth, and a high quality of life in Missouri. The department offers direct assistance to businesses and industries, communities and regions, and individuals and organizations to promote economic development throughout the state. To meet its goals, DED created four groups to oversee the department's efforts.

The Community Development group encourages and fosters community growth. It administers the Missouri Community Betterment Program, the Neighborhood Assistance Program to encourage business participation in neighborhood development, the Main Street Program to revitalize the downtown areas of smaller cities, and the Office of Rural Development. Its Community Development Block Grants Program administers grants from the federal Department of Housing and Urban Development. Its Youth Opportunities and Violence Prevention Program creates positive opportunities for youth to discourage violent behavior. A Community Development Corporation (CDC) Program serves as a clearinghouse for information about local CDCs and awards grants, financing, and loans for developments in the community.

The DED Business Expansion and Attraction group works directly with Missouri businesses and communities to retain and expand job opportunities and investment. Its field staff markets the state by providing a comprehensive array of services, programs, and assistance to meet businesses' needs. This staff also works with community leaders to develop vital communication links with local industry through business retention programs.

The DED Business Development group includes the Office of Productivity; the Office of International Marketing; and

This brilliant display of holiday lights adorns Country Club Plaza from late November through late December, dazzling spectators who visit Kansas City during the holiday season.

the Office of Business Information, which encompasses the Missouri Economic Development Information System (MEDIS), the Missouri Product Finder, and the Missouri Business Assistance Center. The Business Development group's Office of Minority Business assists businesses owned by women and minorities in obtaining technical and financial assistance through federal, state, and local sources. The Office of Business Finance administers programs designed to increase private investment in Missouri companies, new business incubators, and research activities.

The DED Job Development and Training division, called the Workforce Development group, administers federal and state funds for training and employment opportunities in Missouri. The Missouri Customized Training Program, through agreements between state education agencies and local private industry councils, prepares eligible individuals for jobs with new and expanding businesses.

In a cooperative effort, the DED division of Job Development and Training, the Department of Economic Development, and the Missouri Community College system administer a Community College New Jobs Training Program. This program offers a new or expanding industry the resources necessary to train workers in new jobs at a reduced cost. Participant-based training helps ensure that comprehensive training is available not only at the state level but also at the local level.

The St. Louis Arch is one of the most well-known pieces of architecture in the United States. It is a magnificent symbol of the city's nickname, "Gateway to the West."

THE IBEW–NECA LABOR MANAGEMENT COOPERATION COMMITTEE

WITH SUPERB TRAINING

PROGRAMS AND GOOD

LABOR RELATIONS,

THE IBEW AND NECA

IN KANSAS CITY,

THROUGH THEIR

LABOR MANAGEMENT

COOPERATION

COMMITTEE, PROMOTE

HIGH-QUALITY

ELECTRICAL

CONTRACTING SERVICES

FOR BUSINESSES

The IBEW–NECA Labor Management Cooperation Committee is noted for its non-traditional approach to labor-management relations. Its approach is considered nontraditional because its emphasis is on labor and management working together. As a result of this close working relationship, everyone wins—the employees (electricians), the employers (contractors), and, most importantly, the businesses who are the customers.

The International Brotherhood of Electrical Workers (IBEW), Local Union No. 124, founded in 1892, and Kansas City Chapter, National Electrical Contractors Association (NECA), founded in 1929, have been building a relationship that is uncommon and unparalleled throughout the United States. A group known as the Labor Management Cooperation Committee (LMCC), comprised jointly by the IBEW and NECA, is forging this positive working relationship. Under the authority of federal law, this committee is empowered to create opportunities for both labor and management to further expand its "win-win" relationship.

NECA was formed to promote the electrical contracting industry, represent its contractor members, promote sound labor relations on the basis of labor management cooperation in the public interest, and jointly operate a practical and ongoing program of training for apprentices and journeymen. The IBEW was formed to organize electrical workers, promote reasonable methods of work, improve standards of living, cultivate feelings of friendship among those in the industry, and elevate the standards of citizenship of its members.

In Kansas City the IBEW and NECA are noted for their excellent training programs. Their electricians receive more training, both in the classroom and on the job, than

IBEW–NECA electricians and contractors are uniquely qualified to perform even the most sophisticated electrical projects, such as this data closet installation work.

virtually all other electricians. To complete the IBEW–NECA program, 8,000 hours of on-the-job experience, in addition to 900 hours of classroom instruction, is needed.

As part of a coordinated, nationally recognized five-year apprenticeship program, IBEW–NECA apprentices receive individual hands-on training from experienced journeyman electricians. In addition, classroom training offers theoretical and practical applications for motor-control systems, transformers, fiber-optic cabling, wiring methods, and electrical safety, to name just a few. The training program is recognized by the American Council on Education (ACE), and graduates of the program are entitled to receive up to fifty hours of college credit.

"We train electricians better than just about anyone," says Lindell Lee, business manager of the local union. "We require that a rigorous apprenticeship program be completed before electricians are allowed to work in the field on their own. This kind of training wouldn't be possible without cooperation between labor and management. The ultimate winners resulting from our excellent labor relations and comprehensive training are the businesses that use the services of IBEW electricians and NECA contractors."

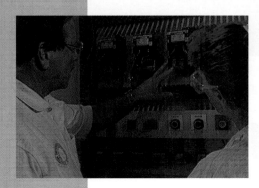

One-on-one hands-on training is the foundation upon which IBEW–NECA develops the most skilled electricians.

largest banking institution in the United States.) Two other prominent Missouri banking organizations are the Kansas City–based Commerce Bancshares and UMB Financial Corporation, with Missouri deposits of $6.5 billion and $3.9 billion, respectively. Mercantile Bancorporation recently acquired another of the Missouri-based banks, Mark Twain Bank. Mercantile is one of the oldest banking houses in the state, with a history that extends back to 1855. UMB Financial Corporation was established as a storefront bank in 1913 by the well-known Kemper banking family of Kansas City and is now a $10.4 billion multi–bank holding company with branches located throughout Missouri, Illinois, Kansas, Colorado, Oklahoma, and Nebraska.

Four of the state's 399 commercial banks are located in the Columbia metropolitan area, eight are located in the Joplin metropolitan area, five are in the St. Joseph metropolitan area, and fourteen are in the Springfield metropolitan area. Banks account for 13 percent of the total number of establishments, 30 percent of the employment, and nearly 39 percent of the payroll within

BANKING ON WHEELS

IN 1928 THE CITY CENTER BANK IN KANSAS CITY, ESTABLISHED BY R. CROSBY KEMPER SR. AND NOW KNOWN AS THE UNITED MISSOURI BANK, ADDED A "DRIVE-UP" WINDOW TO ITS BANKING SERVICES. IT IS BELIEVED TO HAVE BEEN THE FIRST OF ITS KIND IN THE COUNTRY.

the larger sector of the state's economy that includes finance, insurance, and real estate. In addition to commercial banks, Missouri has about forty-one savings and loan associations and more than two hundred credit unions.

GROWTH THROUGH VENTURE CAPITAL

Nine venture capital companies operate in Missouri. Five of these companies are in Kansas City, including Kansas City Equity Partners, Kansas Venture Capital, Invest America Investment Advisers, Capital for Business, and

For projects as large as Science City at Union Station in Kansas City, many people and institutions invest financial resources to make a city's vision come true. © Bob Barrett

LET THE GAMES BEGIN

Shelter Insurance in Columbia, Missouri, is a principal corporate sponsor of the Missouri Show Me State Games, an amateur athletic festival that draws more than thirty-four thousand participants statewide. It is the largest of the state games in the nation.

FACING PAGE: *The Arrow Rock Bank building is part of the Arrow Rock State Historic Site, which preserves a town founded in 1829 along the Santa Fe Trail. © Kevin Sink/Midwestock*

Enterprise Fund. The other four companies are in St. Louis, and include Gateway Venture Partners, Capital for Business (affiliated with Commerce Bank), Advantage Capital Partners, and Civic Ventures Investment Fund (the only company providing venture capital specifically for African-American enterprises). In 1996 these venture capitalists injected nearly $70 million into twenty-two Missouri companies. Although this figure represented a decline from the $133 million invested in Missouri companies by venture capitalists in 1995, the number of companies receiving venture capital grew by more than

50 percent from that year. Topping the list of Kansas City companies receiving venture capital funding in 1997 (though all of this funding came from outside Missouri) was Golden Sky Systems, a direct TV distributor, which received $91 million. Heading the list of St. Louis companies receiving venture capital funding in 1997 was Savvis Corporation, an Internet access provider.

Susan Catts, president of the Silicon Prairie Technology Association, in a March 1998 interview with the *Kansas City Business Journal,* said that the relative lack of activity in venture capital investments in Missouri resulted from the inherent conservative nature of the Midwest. "Missouri has the Show Me State as its slogan," Catts said, "and I think that's probably a reflection of how the investors are. They're not as freewheeling as they are in California [for example]."

INSURING THE FUTURE

Since 1869, state government has regulated the insurance industry in Missouri. The Division of Insurance formerly

Courteous bank tellers make a visit to the bank a pleasant experience. © Steve Smith/FPG International LLC

Closed

operated under the old Department of Business Administration, now called the Department of Economic Development, but in 1990 Missouri voters passed a constitutional amendment to elevate the Division of Insurance to the status of a department unto itself. The department, based in Jefferson City, with branches in Kansas City and St. Louis, oversees the more than six hundred insurance companies that sell policies in the state, more than one-third of which are Missouri-based. In fiscal 1990, the department spent nearly $2 million on its programs, processed about eight thousand complaints, issued more than ten thousand agent licenses, examined about seventy-five companies, and recovered almost $6 million for insurance customers relating to product liability and medical malpractice claims.

Among the top twenty-five insurance carriers in Missouri, three of the top five are based out of state: State Farm Mutual, the largest U.S. insurer of autos, homes, and pleasure boats (Illinois); American Family Mutual (Wisconsin); and Prudential Insurance (New Jersey). The two Missouri-based companies in the top five are Healthy Alliance (HALIC) and Blue Cross and Blue Shield of Missouri (the state's largest health insurance company). Three other Missouri-based companies are also in the top twenty-five: General American Life (among the top one percent of life insurance carriers in the United States), Missouri Employers Mutual, and Shelter Insurance, one of the few major Missouri-based insurance companies based outside of Kansas City and St. Louis.

General American Life, which made the Fortune 500 list in 1996 for the first time, with $2.74 billion in revenues and more than $82 million in profits, was established in 1933 and now has about 4,500 employees as well as some 6,000 sales agents. Individual life and group life and health insurance are the company's mainstays, but it has also become involved in asset management and research as well as reinsurance. The company also worked with Missouri legislators in 1997 to become one of the few mutual insurance firms with the power to convert to a stock company. Beyond its business dealings, General American Life has been actively engaged in civic activities in the St. Louis area. Dick Liddy, the company's chief executive officer, for instance, has been deeply involved in the planned expansion of the St. Louis Art Museum and chaired the local United Way fund drive in 1995, raising more than $49 million.

Shelter Insurance, established in 1946 to provide affordable car insurance to Missourians, is based in the university town of Columbia. Over the years, Shelter has grown from a

Financial advisors who come to the home make planning for medical and household needs—or a vacation—less intimidating and more convenient. © Gary Buss/FPG International LLC

number of surrounding states and do business not only nationwide but worldwide. This widening scope of operations is testimony to the up-to-date expertise of Missouri's professionals in all economic sectors and their ability to keep abreast of state-of-the-art technologies and apply them in day-to-day business.

single-line, single-state insurer into a multiple-line company with 1,300 agents in thirteen midwestern states. Shelter is one of the most successful and financially sound regional insurance groups in the country and employs more than 1,600 people in its Columbia headquarters.

As Missouri enters the twenty-first century, the challenges facing financial institutions and insurance providers will be related to how these institutions cope with the demands of an expanding economy and the vicissitudes of world markets. Banks and insurance companies have been growing larger through corporate mergers in the final decades of the twentieth century, and the increasing globalization of business and the economy poses its own challenges. No longer do banks and insurance companies in Missouri serve only Missourians. Many banks and companies in the Show Me State have branches in a

MISSISSIPPI VALLEY TRUST COMPANY, WHICH BECAME PART OF MERCANTILE BANK OF ST. LOUIS IN 1929, PLANNED THE FINANCING OF THE ST. LOUIS WORLD'S FAIR OF 1904, WHICH TOOK PLACE 101 YEARS AFTER THE LOUISIANA PURCHASE.

© Archive Photos

THE PILLARS OF FINANCE

A young couple applies for a home loan. © Michael Krasowitz/FPG International LLC

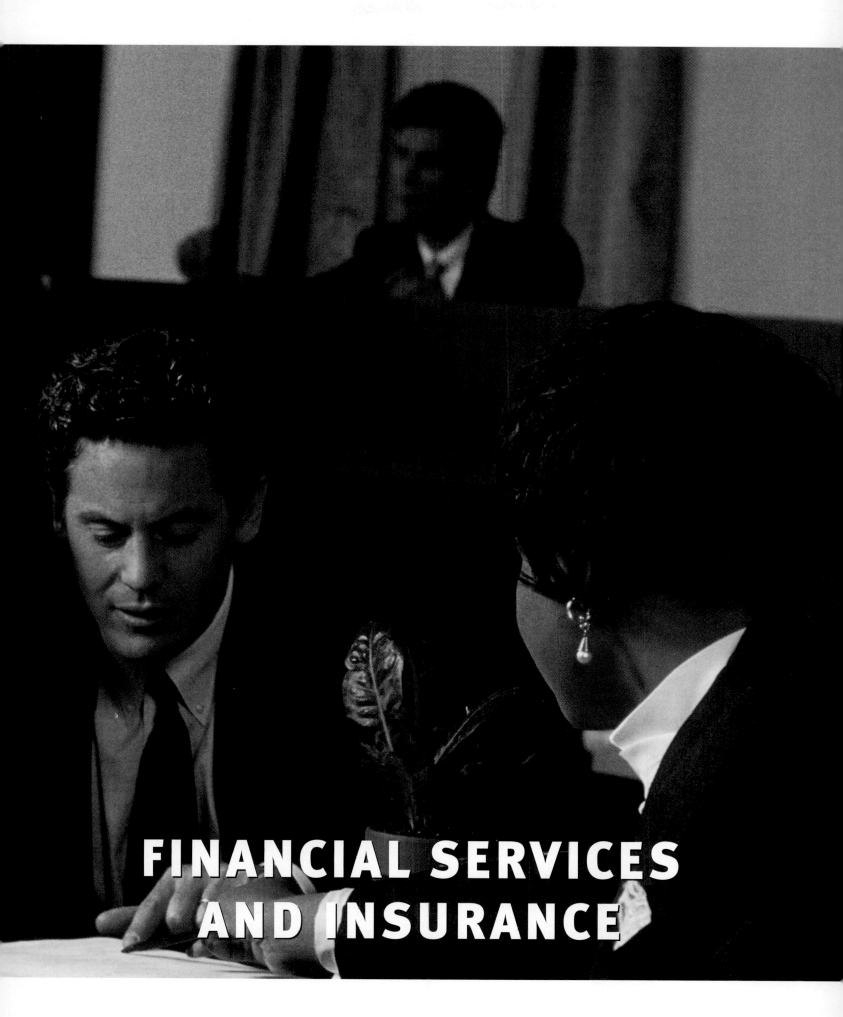

FINANCIAL SERVICES AND INSURANCE

DEUTSCHE FINANCIAL SERVICES

The headquarters of Deutsche Financial Services is located in modern offices at Maryville Centre, in west St. Louis County.

Chances are, every day you see or use a product financed at one time by Deutsche Financial Services—whether it is the computer on your desk, the school bus your child rides, or the recreational vehicle (RV) your neighbors just purchased. Deutsche Financial Services (DFS) provides specialized financing and servicing programs that promote manufacturing, distribution, and sale of technology products, consumer durables, and industrial equipment.

DFS has long-standing relationships with many of the world's leading manufacturers and distributors of consumer and commercial durable goods. These strong ties enable DFS to develop specialized programs, often sponsored by manufacturers, designed to help distributors, dealers, and resellers reach their sales and profit objectives. DFS programs and services include:
- Inventory finance
- Accounts receivable finance
- Purchase order funding
- Retail finance
- Equipment finance
- Leveraged acquisition finance
- Franchise finance
- Private-label finance programs
- Credit and collection services

Robert M. Martin, president and CEO of DFS, has led the company through expansion, acquisitions, and impressive growth since 1994.

- Collateral management services
- Extended warranty and service agreement programs

Often, DFS adds value and efficiency to the financing process by providing several types of financing options to one business—in effect, offering the business one-stop shopping. For example, an RV dealer benefits from DFS inventory financing programs, retail financing options, collateral management services, and service agreement programs. In this way, many DFS customers gain added value from their financing relationship with DFS.

"DFS has assembled a full range of high-value financing products and services to support the manufacture, distribution, and sale of goods on a global basis," explains Robert M. Martin, president and CEO of DFS. "We now have highly specialized business units that can provide fully integrated, end-to-end distribution financing solutions for our customers." DFS headquarters is located in St. Louis, Missouri. Its operations may be traced back to 1971 when the company began providing inventory financing to manufacturers and dealers of consumer electronics and appliances. The company has grown steadily since then, increasing managed receivables from under $50 million in 1975 to billions today. DFS, as it is known today, is a combination of two companies with related businesses and strategies. In May 1995 Deutsche Bank Group acquired ITT Commercial Finance, a subsidiary of ITT Corporation, and merged its activities with Deutsche Credit Corporation (DCC), a leader in equipment finance.

The parent company of DFS, Frankfurt, Germany–based Deutsche Bank Group, is one of the world's largest financial institutions. With assets in excess of $600 billion and significant capital strength, Deutsche Bank Group has earned a reputation as a well-managed and highly respected organization. The bank has more than 2,400 branches in more than fifty countries throughout Europe, Asia/Pacific, and the Americas.

The acquisition by Deutsche Bank brought dividends to both the bank and DFS, as synergies developed in international markets. Today DFS, still headquartered in St. Louis, reaches out to customers worldwide.

The years since the acquisition have seen rapid growth for DFS. In 1997 the company announced the formation of the Consumer Finance Group, which offers retail finance programs to dealers in the manufactured housing, recreational vehicle, marine, and lawn and garden equipment markets. This important addition was enhanced by the DFS acquisition in 1997 of Ganis Credit Corporation, a California-based company specializing in marine and RV loan originations and servicing.

Additionally, DFS formed the new Leveraged Finance Group to provide senior secured revolving and term credit facilities for middle-market manufacturers and distributors—those with revenues between $25 million and $1 billion. The group primarily focuses on revolving lines secured by inventory and accounts receivable but also offers machinery, equipment, and real estate term loans.

DFS supports a variety of charitable, cultural, health care, and educational organizations in the St. Louis area, as well as in other communities where DFS operates. DFS employees are encouraged to request support for the organizations of their choice. Additionally, the DFS Matching Gift Program matches contributions made by employees to educational institutions.

DFS has long defined itself by its entrepreneurial team of employees, who strive to improve the way the company does business and search for new opportunities for growth. It is this spirit that led DFS to be the first independent lender to work with computer manufacturers in the late 1970s, as the technology industry began its rapid expansion. A popular company anecdote recalls that, in 1979, DFS first began negotiations to finance the inventory of a young upstart company. DFS looked beyond

Consumer and commercial products seen every day—from PCs to powerboats—move through the distribution process aided by DFS financing programs and services.

Steven Jobs's sandals and youth to his business plan and product and agreed to design and provide an exclusive financing program to this innovator and his new company, Apple Computer.

Since then DFS has grown to become a top provider of financing to the information technology (IT) market. In 1997 DFS generated more than $20 billion in IT financing volume through relationships with nearly 400 manufacturers and distributors and more than 3,000 resellers. The successful expansion of DFS into the European IT market was demonstrated by announcements from Hewlett-Packard, Ingram Micro, Digital Equipment Corporation, and Apple Computer that DFS had been chosen to provide their customers with distribution financing programs to help build sales through Europe.

As DFS faces the new millennium, the company plans to continue its expansion into new markets and industries, while continually adapting and refining its financing options to customer needs. It is this continuing process of improvement and growth that has led DFS to the leadership position it now enjoys and that promises to underline its success in the years ahead.

Deutsche Financial Services
Deutsche Bank Group

MISSOURI EMPLOYERS MUTUAL INSURANCE

WITH ITS CREATIVE

WORKSAFE^{SM}

PROGRAM AND

ITS DEDICATION

TO PROVIDING

RESPONSIVE

SERVICES, MISSOURI

EMPLOYERS MUTUAL

INSURANCE

PROMOTES A HEALTHY

AND ACCIDENT-FREE

WORKPLACE FOR

MISSOURI

EMPLOYERS

Workplace accidents leave many employees' lives hanging in the balance. In Missouri alone there is an average of 513 workplace accidents every workday. Each of these disabling injuries costs an average of $26,000 in medical costs, lost time, and lost income.

Missouri Employers Mutual Insurance (MEM), headquartered in Columbia, Missouri, believes it doesn't have to be that way—accidents don't have to happen. MEM believes so strongly in this philosophy that it has built its company around one vision: a healthy and accident-free workplace for Missouri employers.

In the early 1990s insurance costs were escalating and the residual market was growing within Missouri's workers' compensation system. The enactment of the 1993 Workers' Compensation Reform Act created MEM as a mutual insurance company that would act as a catalyst for change in Missouri's workers' compensation market. MEM was presented with an opportunity to do what no company had done before: create a unique new paradigm for workers' compensation insurance that would break through traditional barriers to develop innovative ways of providing services.

The act worked. The change MEM generated in the workers' compensation market has been embraced by Missouri insurance agents and employers alike. Shortly after MEM was founded, increased competition produced an average decrease of

The corporate headquarters of Missouri Employers Mutual Insurance is centrally located in Columbia, Missouri. The company operates field offices in St. Louis, Kansas City, and Springfield and has employees in locations all across the state.

M
Missouri Employers
Mutual Insurance
Insuring a Working Missouri

more than 5 percent in workers' compensation premiums, making policyholder firms more competitive in their markets.

"MEM set out to become Missouri's premier workers' compensation provider," says Dennis Smith, MEM president and CEO. "Early on we knew we'd accomplish this goal by doing two things. One, compete based on our customer-focused services, such as safety and facing fraud. Two, partner with our policyholders and producers to create a relationship based on trust. Today many of the policyholders who leave MEM due to price inevitably return because of our value-added services."

Through its loss prevention services, MEM has changed the concept of workplace safety and created a revolutionary program: WorkSAFE^{SM} (Work Smart in an Accident-Free Environment). WorkSAFE is a comprehensive training program designed to give policyholders the safety resources they need to promote safe workplace behaviors. WorkSAFE takes the issue of workplace safety to a new level. It creates an awareness of accident prevention methods that is long overdue and emphasizes a commitment to workplace safety that benefits every Missourian.

MEM concentrates on building relationships with Missouri's insurance agents. It maintains an open-door policy and invites agents to share their concerns and offer suggestions. Many of its services and products were developed in response to agent requests.

For example, one policyholder, Cerebral Palsy of Tri-County Missouri, found bottom-line benefits from MEM's WorkSAFE program. The policyholder's staff transformed WorkSAFE into a custom-designed safety tool. Employees designated a safety coordinator, formed a safety committee, and completed a written safety program for the center.

"We all worked together, and one by one, we fixed the problems—everyone's safety awareness increased," says Pauline Newton, the center's safety coordinator. "WorkSAFE worked because our employees made it work. It's their WorkSAFE attitude that keeps the company healthy and accident free." As a result of the company's safety commitment, its premium dropped 74 percent.

MEM's claims and loss prevention departments work closely together, based on the philosophy that preventing accidents is the best form of claims management. However, in the unlikely event that an accident occurs, MEM's claims team is set up to respond quickly and to ensure high-quality medical care in order to facilitate an employee's early return to work. MEM's managed care approach focuses on two things: effective case management and cost containment through high-quality health care.

MEM's adjuster-to-caseload ratios are dramatically lower than the industry norm. This ensures that injured employees are well cared for and communication lines are open. As a

MEM's employees are its sharpest competitive edge in the workers' compensation market. The company depends on their energy, knowledge, and creativity. MEM taps into employees' combined talents by grouping them into strategic teams. These cross-departmental teams explore ways to make MEM's services better and develop action items designed to achieve corporate objectives.

result, injured employees feel they are being treated fairly, and the company's litigation rates remain low.

One claims success story involves a Missouri police officer who was tragically injured in a traffic collision. His condition was critical: severe multiple head injuries and extensive internal injuries. As soon as MEM was notified of the accident, the company pulled together an experienced claims team to work with the officer's doctors and help coordinate his care. MEM arranged for salary disability coverage and assurance that his employer would have a place for him when he was ready. All the officer had to do was fight his way back to health. And fight back he did. Seven months after his accident, the man was back on the job in a part-time clerical position. Fourteen months later he was working as a full-time dispatcher. Today, three years after his ordeal began, he is working as a detective.

Another important factor that contributes to MEM's excellence is its team of highly skilled workers' compensation insurance professionals. MEM's employees are its sharpest competitive edge. They have the talent and know-how to better serve agents and policyholders. Employees know that each and every policyholder has unique circumstances, so they take special care in delivering individualized products and service.

MEM encourages employees to become involved in the community. As a company created to benefit Missouri, MEM believes it is important to invest in the communities in which employees live and work. It is so important to the company, in fact, that being a good corporate citizen is designated as one of its ten corporate values. Employees regularly participate in the Adopt-a-Highway program, United Way, food pantry drives, public school programs, and Red Cross blood drives. MEM is also the sole sponsor of the Show-Me State Games basketball tournament.

"Our promise to our more than 15,000 policyholders is to lead, never follow; innovate, never imitate; set a new pace and never fall behind," says Smith. "Our determination to be the best continually forces us to create—and re-create—MEM to meet the needs of Missouri."

Policyholder Rosemary Wiedeman, director of Cerebral Palsy of Tri-County Missouri, embraces WorkSAFE^SM. She and her staff transformed the program into a custom-designed safety tool for their center and the effort has paid off: their commitment to safety was a key factor in a 74 percent decrease in their insurance premium.

RIGHTCHOICE MANAGED CARE, INC.

RightCHOICE
Managed Care, Inc.,
uses technology
to streamline
operations,
provide excellent
customer service,
and prepare for
future growth

In the face of constant change occurring in health care financing for the past decade, RightCHOICE Managed Care, Inc., headquartered in St. Louis, has evolved to remain in the forefront of this highly competitive industry.

RightCHOICE, which does business as Alliance Blue Cross Blue Shield, has succeeded because it has been able to reinvent itself while the very definition of health insurance changed because of social, economic, and political demands. Regardless of the changes needed, however, taking care of its members and providing value always have remained at the heart of the RightCHOICE corporate philosophy.

"Our focus is to differentiate ourselves from other health insurers through service excellence, high-quality products, and a benefit design that meets the needs of the marketplace," says RightCHOICE CEO John A. O'Rourke. "Of course we also have our emphasis on wellness, prevention, and disease management."

RightCHOICE Managed Care, Inc., was founded in 1994 as a vehicle to facilitate the continued growth and success of Blue Cross and Blue Shield of Missouri. Today RightCHOICE is one of the largest managed care companies in the

RightCHOICE headquarters is located at 1831 Chestnut Street in downtown St. Louis, across from Union Station.

Midwest. RightCHOICE and its subsidiaries have a total enrollment of approximately two million members. Its provider networks cover a seven-state region and include 10,000 physicians and about 250 hospitals.

RightCHOICE offers a full complement of both fully underwritten and self-funded programs, including managed indemnity, preferred provider organization (PPO), point-of-service (POS), and health maintenance organization (HMO). It also offers drug, dental, and mental health programs, and third-party administrator, network rental, and life insurance programs.

In 1995 RightCHOICE acquired HealthLink, Inc., in order to enter new managed care business arenas, including network rental, stand-alone utilization review and large-case management, and workers' compensation. In 1997 RightCHOICE began offering fully insured products outside its Missouri service area using the HealthLink network. HealthLink is a crucial component of RightCHOICE's future expansion and growth strategy.

"We're targeting the full spectrum of the marketplace, from individuals and small groups to medium-size and very large groups," says O'Rourke. "Traditionally we have focused on the smaller end of

John A. O'Rourke is the chairman, president, and chief executive officer of RightCHOICE.

the marketplace. But as we grow and look at the future, we also think that the large-group market is very fertile ground for us."

Moving to better serve both ends of the market, RightCHOICE participates in the national BlueCard PPO program, which expands benefits for large, multistate employers, and offers an Options for Small Business program that it launched, which gives expanded choices in affordable employee health insurance to small businesses.

Under BlueCard PPO, RightCHOICE PPO members have access to a national health care network that encompasses 95 percent of the U.S. population. This means that multistate employers can offer all their employees the same, hassle-free benefits no matter where they are located.

The Options for Small Business program offers individual coverage for the sole proprietor or freelancer just starting out; billing options for small employers who do not pay for employee health insurance but want to make it available with simple, paperwork-free administration; and an array of PPO, POS, and HMO options for the small business that pays for employee health care insurance. Short-term medical insurance also is available to fill the gap when a small business has a probationary or waiting period before new employees are eligible for coverage.

Continuing to best serve the market in the future requires that RightCHOICE maintain its ongoing investment in the new generations of managed care, including investments in technology.

Information technology is a key to effective managed care, and RightCHOICE has been described as a technology leader in its industry by *Insurance & Technology* and *PC Week* magazines. To remain a leader in the health benefits management market, RightCHOICE is dedicated to remaining a leader in health care information. "To maintain our technology edge, we launched our Information and Operations Strategy (IOS)—a five- to six-year, $70 million to $80 million program designed to move RightCHOICE from a transaction-based system to an information management system," O'Rourke says. "IOS provides better information that lets us make more knowledgeable business decisions. It prepares us for growth, year 2000 issues, changes in our product portfolio, and benefit design issues. IOS replaces manual processes with technology, and that streamlines our operations."

Another technology tool, the company's Strategic Data Initiative provides aggregate information about claims to help employees make

The latest managed care technology helps experienced RightCHOICE nurses and case managers ensure that members receive the appropriate health care in the right setting.

strategic decisions. RightCHOICE also integrates voice and data networks to connect company headquarters with RightCHOICE's lower-cost satellite offices statewide.

"Keeping costs down through the use of technology helps our company and our customers," says O'Rourke. "Providing cost-effective service excellence to our members, our brokers, and the physicians in our networks is our goal today and for the future."

The philosophy at RightCHOICE is to manage provider networks rather than to manage members. "Members want physicians to manage their individual care, and they want us to provide access to that care through efficient hospitals, physicians, and disease management programs," O'Rourke says. RightCHOICE works with physicians through the Physician Group Partners Program and the Physician Consultative Committee.

"Our mission is to provide value to our clients through superior service and coordinated access to effective managed health programs at an affordable cost," O'Rourke says. "With a single-minded dedication to doing the best for our customers the first time, every time, and an infrastructure that supports that dedication, we're fulfilling that mission. The future looks very good for RightCHOICE."

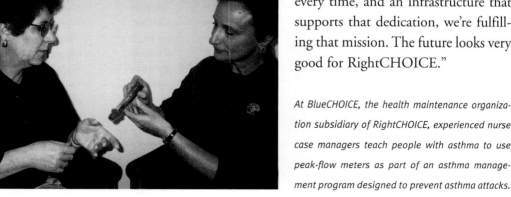

At BlueCHOICE, the health maintenance organization subsidiary of RightCHOICE, experienced nurse case managers teach people with asthma to use peak-flow meters as part of an asthma management program designed to prevent asthma attacks.

GEORGE K. BAUM & COMPANY

The municipal bond trading desk and the equity trading desks in George K. Baum & Company's Kansas City, Missouri, headquarters are always alive with activity.

Since its founding in 1928, George K. Baum & Company has been committed to helping clients meet or exceed their expectations for prosperity. The firm's scope includes six distinct but related businesses: Investor Services/Retail Sales, Public Finance/Municipal Bonds, Investment Banking, Equity Capital Markets (Research, Institutional Sales and Trading), Professional Investment Advisors Division, and Merchant Banking.

The firm's equity analysts cover more than eighty companies, focusing on small and mid-cap firms in industries driving the economy. Industries covered include agriculture and food; building and building components; capital and industrial products; consumer goods and services; energy, oil, and gas companies; restaurants; telecommunications; temporary staffing; rent-to-own; trucking and transportation services; and utilities.

George K. Baum & Company, with offices in thirteen cities, is a member of the New York Stock Exchange, Inc., and the National Association of Securities Dealers (NASD). Client accounts are protected by the Securities Investor Protection Corporation (SIPC). The firm is noted for its expertise in structuring, underwriting, and marketing tax-exempt and taxable municipal bond issues. Its Denver-

Jonathan E. Baum is the chairman and CEO of George K. Baum & Company.

based municipal finance headquarters has helped establish the company as a leading underwriter of municipal bonds nationwide.

The firm's equity strategy remains focused on the continuing development of expertise in advising and raising capital for small and mid-cap companies, all the while creating superior proprietary investments for clients. The Investor Services division, serving the complete investment needs of thousands of individuals, currently has nearly $3 billion in assets under management. The firm's sister company, George K. Baum Trust Company, offers a full range of trust, investment management, and custodial services for individuals, families, individual trustees, and employee benefit plans of all types.

In 1994 G. Kenneth Baum, son of the founder, passed his forty-two-year stewardship of the firm to his son, Jonathan E. Baum, who now serves as chairman and chief executive officer. Jon Baum continues his family's history of dedication to clients, employees, and the community.

"We now are in our third generation of family ownership and management, and the company has never been better positioned to provide strategic and valuable solutions to the financial needs of our clients," says Jon Baum. "In fact, George K. Baum & Company's value system is based on the belief that the firm will succeed only if clients succeed."

KANSAS CITY LIFE

The promise of financial security is only as good as the company that makes it. When Kansas City Life makes a promise, it stands behind the pledge. Since 1895 Kansas City Life has seen its policyholders through world wars, the Great Depression, and various periods of recession and inflation. Today the company maintains its long-standing, steadfast commitment to its customers.

"Kansas City Life's reputation is built on integrity, sound investment strategies, and honest business practices," says R. Philip Bixby, president and chief executive officer of Kansas City Life. "To us, integrity is not an outdated notion in today's fast-paced world. It is the guiding force behind every decision we make. Every policy we sell is backed by a century of quality service and financial security."

Kansas City Life today has nearly $20 billion of life insurance in force and serves more than half a million policyholders from coast to coast. An agency force of more than one thousand sells variable, individual life, annuity, and group products through approximately 110 career general agencies in forty-eight states.

Deeply rooted values, a strong commitment to policyholders, and more than a century of experience make Kansas City Life a steady force in an

Located between downtown and the Country Club Plaza, the Kansas City Life Insurance Company home office complex at 3520 Broadway has served as an area landmark for many years.

ever-changing industry. Built on a solid foundation, the company continues to reach into the future by offering new and improved products and developing new relationships with individuals, families, and businesses that are in need of financial security.

Founded on 1 May 1895, in Kansas City, Missouri, the company today is a well-known and respected leader among the more than 1,200 life insurance companies in the United States. Its corporate group includes Kansas City Life and two major subsidiaries: Sunset Life Insurance Company of America, purchased in 1974, and Old American Insurance Company, purchased in 1991. The consolidated group's assets total nearly $3.5 billion with more than $26 billion of life insurance in force.

Now well into its second century, Kansas City Life Insurance Company can look back proudly on a history that began long ago in a three-person office. Through years of astute planning and management, Kansas City Life has grown into a highly respected family of companies. While many businesses have come and gone, Kansas City Life has remained a strong force in the marketplace.

Kansas City Life's 100th Anniversary Commemorative Plaza features a Kugel floating ball as its focal point. The 2,155-pound granite ball perpetually rotates on a film of water thinner than a business card.

EDWARD JONES

Edward Jones, headquartered in St. Louis, is one of the nation's most convenient suppliers of reliable financial products for individual investors. In 1989 the company became one of the six firms in the industry that serve one million investors or more. Today ten firms serve two million investors. Among the ten, Jones is one of the only firms to serve individual investors exclusively. With nearly 4,000 offices across the country, including all fifty states, Jones has more branch offices than any other brokerage firm in the United States.

"Our philosophy is that service to the individual is of utmost importance," says CEO John W. Bachmann. The more than 4,000 Edward Jones investment representatives provide this personal brand of service by discussing their clients' individual investment needs on a one-on-one basis. Having cultivated a previously untapped market of individual investors, Jones representatives offer predictable, long-term investment opportunities including a broad mix of municipal, government, and corporate bonds; mutual funds; common stocks; and tax-advantaged securities.

The firm was founded more than a century ago in 1871. It began as the bond house of Whitaker & Company. In 1922 Edward D. Jones Sr. founded the St. Louis brokerage house of Edward Jones, which then merged with Whitaker in 1943.

After working a rural territory in Missouri and Illinois, Ted Jones, the founder's son, decided to position the company in the increasingly competitive marketplace as a specialist in providing investment advice to rural Americans.

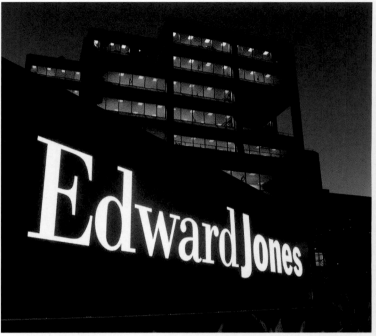

Based in St. Louis, Edward Jones has more than 4,000 investment representatives, serving two million individual investors from nearly 4,000 offices nationwide. Edward Jones also serves investors in Canada and in the United Kingdom through affiliate organizations.

John W. Bachmann, who now manages the firm on a day-to-day basis, has continued this tradition but also has replicated the success of his predecessor by expanding the one-person office concept into a select number of metropolitan areas. Bachmann also has led the firm to the forefront of its industry in terms of technology. In fact, Jones maintains the largest satellite network in the financial-services industry. The firm was ranked number one in *Money* magazine's 1995 survey of twenty-one leading full-service brokerage firms.

Jones brokers complete an intensive three-month training before opening an office. Although many of the firm's offices are in rural communities, Jones is developing a strong presence in urban areas, including Chicago, St. Louis, Atlanta, Oklahoma City, Kansas City, and Seattle. Currently 65 percent of Jones's offices are in metropolitan areas.

"Our brokers live where they work, and come from all walks of life—they are former engineers, attorneys, teachers, bank presidents, and military officers," says John Bachmann. "We go where there is a sense of community."

Managing principal John W. Bachmann brought Edward Jones to the forefront of the financial services industry during the 1980s and 1990s. He is now leading the firm into the twenty-first century by focusing on customer needs, healthy growth, and visionary technology.

MADE IN MISSOURI

CHAPTER TWENTY-TWO

IN THE PRESENT ECONOMIC ATMOSPHERE OF MULTIMILLION-DOLLAR MERG-

ERS AND CORPORATE TAKEOVERS ENGINEERED BY TEAMS OF LAWYERS, IT IS

HARD TO IMAGINE SEALING A CORPORATE DEAL WITH LITTLE MORE THAN A

HANDSHAKE. YET THAT IS HOW E. M. STAFFORD, PRESIDENT OF THE FAMILY-

OWNED WORK-CLOTHING BUSINESS J. A. LAMY MANUFACTURING COMPANY

IN SEDALIA, BECAME A MANUFACTURER OF LEVI JEANS IN 1946.

For fifty-two years, a dedicated force of some 375 workers turned out nearly two million pairs of Red Tab Levi Strauss jeans a year. Before its relationship with Levi's began, J. A. Lamy Manufacturing had been making men's apparel in Sedalia since 1866. The pride in craftsmanship, focus on production efficiency, and personal integrity of management that were represented in J. A. Lamy Manufacturing are typical qualities of Missouri's manufacturers, both small and large. Although Stafford's handshake arrangement with the Levi Strauss Company ended at the beginning of 1999 after Levi's announced a restructuring that would result in the plant's closing, Lamy executives said they were looking for ways to reopen the plant that has been such a fixture in Sedalia life for generations.

Clothing is just one of the wide array of items that have been created by Missouri hands for more than one hundred years. With each passing decade, the number of manufacturers has continued to

grow. In the past ten years the state has averaged nearly two hundred new and expanded manufacturing facilities annually. By 1996 the number of manufacturing establishments stood at just over eight thousand, with a total value added to the economy of about $17 billion.

In the first decades after statehood, Missouri manufacturing efforts were focused on milling, distilling of grains into alcohol, meat packing, production of smoking and chewing tobacco, rope making, and a variety of craft industries such as the manufacture of guns, soap, candles, clothing, furniture, pottery, leather goods, carriages, and wagons. By 1850 Missouri manufacturers were employing more than fifteen thousand workers and the primary market was New Orleans. With the development of railroads in the mid-1800s, and with the decimation of the agricultural economy of the South as a result of the Civil War, Missouri manufacturers shifted the marketing of their products

FACING PAGE: *With its central location and government incentive programs, Missouri is attracting increasing numbers of manufacturers, with production of transportation equipment accounting for 25 percent of the state's manufacturing revenue.* © Bruce Mathews/Midwestock. THIS PAGE: *From its humble beginnings in 1865, the Stetson Hat Company has grown into a multimillion-dollar concern. The company's St. Joseph factory is one of the largest in the nation.* © Phil Schermeister/Tony Stone Images

© Courtesy, Purina Mills, Inc.

Western Auto in
Kansas City is the
official parts store of
NASCAR and NHRA.
© Chuck Pefley/Tony
Stone Images

lishments in the
state, most of
which were situ-
ated in Kansas
City and St. Louis.
The number of
manufacturers and
workers fluctuated
over the next fifty
years in response

from the South and New Orleans to the North and East.
Chicago, New York, Philadelphia, Pittsburgh, and
Cincinnati then became the prime trading centers for
products from Missouri.

After the Civil War the number of manufacturing
establishments in Missouri increased and a shift in population from rural areas to urban areas began. These ten-
dencies became even more pronounced after 1900. By
the 1920s there were more than two hundred thousand
wage earners employed in 8,500 manufacturing estab-

to the Great Depression and World War II but reached a
point of relative stability by the 1970s. After a period of
downsizing in the 1980s, the numbers of new manufacturing businesses as well as firms expanding existing
plants began to noticeably increase in the 1990s.

For the last seventy-five years Missouri has been
known as a leading producer of transportation equip-

*A new Ford awaits engine inspection at the company's manufac-
turing plant in Claycomo. © Bruce Mathews/Midwestock*

which employs thousands of people. St. Louis also has seven of the other top ten manufacturing firms in the state, including the Chrysler, Ford, and General Motors auto assembly plants (Kansas City also has a Ford assembly plant); along with several companies that originated in St. Louis, such as the Brown Group (formerly Brown Shoe, established in 1878), Emerson Electric, Monsanto (established in 1901), and Anheuser-Busch (founded in 1852).

Production of transportation equipment is one of Missouri's principal manufacturing activities, accounting for more than 25 percent of the total manufacturing revenue in the state. Among the top twenty-five manufacturing firms in Missouri by employment in 1991 were Buick Oldsmobile Cadillac in Wentzville; Ford Motor Company in Claycomo and Hazelwood; and Chrysler Motors in Fenton. Statewide, automobile manufacturing accounts for more than one-half of the state's seventy thousand workers in the transportation

ment as well as defense and aerospace technology. The manufacturing of shoes and other leather goods, furniture and wood products, metal and clay products, beer and other beverages, and garments also have a long tradition in Missouri. In the last part of the twentieth century, food processing has become the state's fastest-growing industry.

The Kansas City and St. Louis metropolitan areas account for about 70 percent of Missouri's manufacturing businesses and about 75 percent of such workers. St. Louis, the state's top manufacturing city in terms of number of firms and employees, is the location of Boeing's Military Aircraft and Missile Systems unit,

industry. Four companies in the Springfield area make more than 25 percent of all the stretch luxury limousines in the country. Also in Springfield is Aaron's Automotive Products, which employs about 1,600 workers in the rebuilding of auto engines and transmissions. The company has a satellite operation in Joplin.

Missouri has also long been known as a source for aircraft and aerospace transportation equipment, mainly because of the long-time presence of McDonnell Douglas, now The Boeing Company. And aircraft-parts manufacturer AVMATS in St. Louis provides parts for Sabreliner, Hawker, Falcon, Gulfstream, Jetstar, Learjet,

ABOVE: *Purina products feed millions of farm and domestic animals worldwide. Courtesy, Purina Mills, Inc.* LOWER LEFT: *Hard at work, Missouri's manufacturing employees on the average give 16 cents more per payroll dollar in value than their counterparts in the rest of the country. © Chris Salvo/FPG International LLC*

Westwind, and Citation aircraft. AVMATS has grown substantially since 1982 and has expanded from parts sales to include maintenance, accessory and engine repair and overhaul, instrument repair, avionics repairs and installations, major airframe repair, and other services.

In Kansas City two top-ten manufacturers, New Jersey–based AlliedSignal (an advanced technology and manufacturing company) and Hallmark Cards (established in Kansas City in 1910) employ five thousand and 5,500 people, respectively. Kansas City is also home to the North-American headquarters of Hoechst Marion Roussel USA, one of the nation's leading pharmaceutical producers, and a major manufacturing facility for Harley-Davidson motorcycles.

BEYOND THE BIG CITIES

Manufacturing is not limited to the state's eastern and western borders, however. Springfield, the third-largest city in the state, is

At a ground-breaking cere-
mony for Harley-Davidson's
320,000-square-foot assembly plant in Kansas City, Harley
riders attend in typical fashion. © Jim Hays/Midwestock

home to major manufac-
turing facilities, including
divisions of the food-processing giants Kraft and
Tyson Foods, General
Electric, the Sweetheart
Cup Company, and Mid-
America Dairymen. The
latter employs about 550
people and produces vari-
ous milk, cheese, butter,
and dehydrated dairy
products. Nearby Joplin boasts several important
regional employers: an Eagle-Picher Industries plant,
which employs more than 1,600 people in the manufacture of aerospace and military batteries; significant manufacturing facilities for ICI Explosives; a plant for St.
Louis–based LaBarge Electronics; and a plant for King
Press Corporation, a subsidiary of Publishers Equipment
Corporation of Dallas, Texas.

St. Joseph is home to divisions of such national
firms as stationery manufacturer Mead Products; the
Quaker Oats Company; Johnson Controls, a maker of
wet and dry auto storage batteries; and one of the largest
Stetson hat factories in the country. Until 1995 St.
Joseph was also the national headquarters of the Wire
Rope Corporation of America (WRCA), a maker of electrical cables and wire rope primarily used in aircraft, as
well as cable for truck, automotive, and construction
uses and specialty-wire products for appliances. In 1995
WRCA moved its headquarters to Chillicothe, Missouri,
while retaining a manufacturing facility in St. Joseph.
WRCA is the largest producer of wire rope in North
America and employs about six hundred people in its
two Missouri facilities.

The Columbia metropolitan area is home to a large
3M manufacturing facility; the Textron Automotive
Interior plant, which specializes in automobile instrument panels; and the Square D Company, which specializes in the production of circuit breakers. Several other
central-Missouri towns also have large manufacturing
facilities, like Jefferson City's Chesebrough-Ponds USA
plant, which makes a variety of personal care products;
Centralia's A. B. Chance Company, which manufactures
electrical products for utilities; and Mexico's A. P. Green
Industries, which manufactures various refractory items.

IRRESISTIBLE INCENTIVES

Much of this strong and highly diversified manufacturing
base can be attributed to an attractive business climate
stimulated by regional commerce and growth commis-
sions as well as state programs and incentives. The
Missouri Department of Economic Development
(DED) groups, such as the Business Expansion and
Attraction Group, the Business Development Group, the
Office of International Business, the Office of

SELLING FOR A SONG

BEFORE RADIO AND TELEVISION, THE ANHEUSER-BUSCH
COMPANY IN ST. LOUIS USED SHEET MUSIC TO ADVERTISE ITS
BRANDS. THE COMPANY COMMISSIONED SONGS THAT CON-
TAINED REFERENCES TO THE COMPANY OR THE NAME
BUDWEISER IN THE TITLE OR LYRICS. THE SONG
"BUDWEISER'S A FRIEND OF MINE" WAS INTRODUCED IN THE
ZIEGFELD FOLLIES OF 1907.

When completed after the year 2000, Crown Center's new 85-acre complex will house shops, exhibits, restaurants, theaters, and hotels. © Hallmark Cards, Inc.

Productivity, and the Workforce Development Group, help existing businesses in the state expand and become more competitive in both national and international markets and provide financial and service incentives to attract new businesses to the state.

One example of how the DED assists businesses is the case of Orscheln Industries of Moberly. The DED helped Orscheln develop a highly lucrative joint venture with a Japanese company that resulted in company

exports of more than $30 million a year. The DED also awarded the town of Moberly an Industrial Infrastructure Grant to provide new and needed services for a plant expansion of the New York–based boxing-gear manufacturer Everlast Fitness. The Moberly plant, a community fixture since 1954, employs about one hundred people. The DED also worked closely with the Kansas City Chamber of Commerce and Kansas City–area colleges to provide an attractive package of services and incentives to the South Dakota–based personal-computer company Gateway, which opened a 1,600-worker technical support and customer service facility in Kansas City in 1994. Among the programs and incentives offered by the DED are industrial development and tax-exempt bonds, linked timed deposits in Missouri lending institutions, an Action Loan Fund, and various tax credit programs, including a Seed Capital Tax Credit program that provides capital to small, innovative businesses and that offers tax credits to contributors.

Small and midsize manufacturers in Missouri can take advantage of low-cost, hands-on consulting services provided by the nonprofit Mid-America Manufacturing Technology Center (MAMTC), which has twenty-seven

The Hallmark commitment to excellence requires attention to detail throughout each step of the printing process. These cards are being printed at Hallmark's headquarters in Kansas City. © Hallmark Cards, Inc.

offices in a four-state area that includes Kansas, Missouri, Colorado, and Wyoming. This organization, established in 1991 as a subsidiary of the Kansas Technology Enterprise Corporation, has formed state partnerships with the Missouri Department of Economic Development, the state of Colorado, and the Wyoming Science, Technology and Energy Authority to help manufacturers improve quality, productivity, and sales.

STORING AND DISTRIBUTING GOODS

The robust climate for manufacturing in Missouri has also made the state an active center for warehousing and distribution. Key factors here are Missouri's central location, diversified transportation network, and low cost per square foot for warehouse construction and leasing, along with the availability of well-developed industrial parks and warehousing areas in the major urban areas of the state.

Some of the prime St. Louis industrial parks and warehousing developments are Earth City, Corporate

Woods, and Riverport, along with newer developments such as Elm Point Business Park in St. Charles, the Highway 40 high-tech corridor, and Lambert Corporate Center II at Missouri Bottom and Fee Fee Road. Many of Kansas City's newest industrial parks and warehousing areas are located in the Kansas suburban areas of Lenexa, Overland Park, Riverside, and Olathe. But Kansas City also has a number of older warehousing districts near the

Silgan Holdings, Inc., produces steel and aluminum containers, as well as plastic containers and packing items. © Steve Drews Photo

EMERSON ELECTRIC, FOUNDED IN 1890, IS NOW A GLOBAL MANUFACTURER OF A BROAD RANGE OF ELECTRONIC, ELECTRICAL, AND RELATED PRODUCTS. IT HAS MORE THAN SIXTY DIVISIONS AND 100,000 EMPLOYEES WORLDWIDE, INCLUDING SOME 2,500 EMPLOYEES IN THE ST. LOUIS AREA. ITS FISCAL 1997 SALES EXCEEDED $12 BILLION.

urban center, some of which are in the process of being revived. The U.S. Post Office has, for example, acquired the old Sears Warehouse near I-70 and Truman Road for use as a distribution center.

Kansas City has the unique distinction of leading the country in underground storage capacity, a residue of abandoned limestone mining activities. Four of the area's five largest industrial parks are underground and contain

Manufacturing, warehousing, and distribution firms all benefit from Missouri's abundant storage space, both above and below ground. © Telegraph Colour Library/FPG International LLC

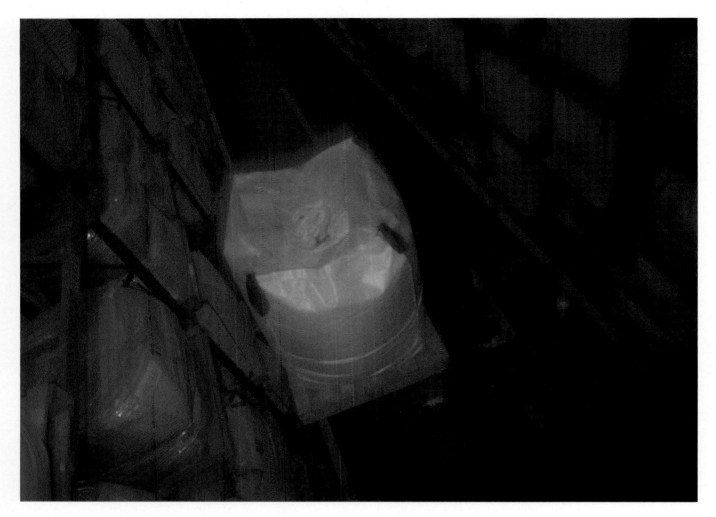

a combined total of 16.5 million square feet of space. American Meat Company, one of the top five food distributors in the Kansas City area, uses an underground storage facility in east Kansas City. And the National Archives and Record Administration has 170,000 square feet of storage space at Space Center Summit, an underground industrial park in Lee's Summit.

Missouri Governor Mel Carnahan has often referred to Missouri's bright economic future, pointing out that unemployment is at its lowest level in twenty years (4.2 percent in 1998), and that exports to foreign countries are at an all-time high. He credits Missouri's central geographic location as one of the key factors that make it a popular site for warehousing and distribution. Carnahan has also outlined a development strategy for the future that consists of eight key areas necessary for Missouri to grow and prosper economically. Those areas—technology, access to capital, job training, promotion, marketing, community development, infrastructure development, and the elimination of bureaucratic barriers—are the focus of Missouri's economic development efforts as the state enters the twenty-first century.

Missouri is within 500 miles of 43 percent of the U.S. population and 45 percent of U.S. manufacturing plants, making it an ideal distribution center. © Telegraph Colour Library/FPG International LLC

WASHINGTON, MISSOURI, IS KNOWN AS THE "CORNCOB PIPE CAPITAL OF THE WORLD." THE MISSOURI MEERSCHAUM COMPANY WAS STARTED IN 1869 IN WASHINGTON AND HAS BEEN MAKING CORNCOB PIPES THERE EVER SINCE. THE COMPANY MADE ALL OF GENERAL DOUGLAS MACARTHUR'S CORNCOB PIPES. ALSO LIGHTING UP MEERSCHAUM PIPES WERE GENERAL JOHN J. PERSHING, PRESIDENTS GERALD FORD AND DWIGHT D. EISENHOWER, AND CARL SANDBURG. ABOUT SEVEN THOUSAND PIPES ARE PRODUCED, PACKED, AND SHIPPED EVERY DAY, IN EIGHTEEN DIFFERENT STYLES, TO NEARLY EVERY STATE AND SEVERAL FOREIGN COUNTRIES.

© Randall Hyman

Shipments are prepared at the House of Lloyd distribution center in Kansas City. © Nick Vedros, Vedros & Associates/Tony Stone Images

MANUFACTURING, DISTRIBUTION, AND WAREHOUSING

QUAKER WINDOWS AND DOORS

BACKED BY

FAMILY HISTORY

AND DEDICATION,

QUAKER WINDOWS

AND DOORS

OFFERS DIVERSIFIED

PRODUCT LINES OF

EXCELLENT QUALITY

IN A RANGE OF

PRICE LEVELS,

WITH RESPONSIVE

CUSTOMER SERVICE

Whether a customer needs a high-performance window for a mountaintop getaway or a stylized door for a home in a quaint historic neighborhood, there is a Quaker window or door engineered specifically to meet the need.

Founded in St. Louis in 1949 by Marge and Harold "Bud" Knoll, Quaker Windows and Doors will celebrate its fiftieth anniversary in 1999. The Knolls' three sons—Ken, Tom, and Mike—represent the second generation to own and operate the business, now based in Freeburg, Missouri. In keeping with the business philosophy established by the founders, today the company's motto is A Tradition of Quality. The philosophy includes dedication to detailed workmanship. Quaker combines a history of artistry with a passion for continual improvement.

The company's roots as a family-owned business are reflected throughout its operation. There are 450 employees, and many of the people who were hired in the early days of the company are still employed there today. Other members of the Knoll family, including cousins, aunts, and uncles, work in the business. Many of the products are named after the founders' children and grandchildren. The company is the biggest employer in the county, employing more people than there are residents in the town of Freeburg. With such strong local roots, Quaker actively participates in many charities, belongs to professional associations, and is involved in community organizations.

From motels and apartment complexes to nursing homes, government buildings, and schools, Quaker's aluminum-frame windows and doors are installed in commercial projects nationwide. William Woods College, above, in Fulton, Missouri, has found Quaker's windows to be perfect in keeping with its efforts to preserve the original look of its campus.

"As a family business, we have a hands-on relationship with our customers," says Tom Knoll, executive vice president and general manager. "All three brothers are involved in every aspect of the business, and we each take a personal interest in keeping customers satisfied. Our employees are part of our extended family. As the backbone of the company, they share our dedication to customer service."

The company began as Quaker Shade Company in St. Louis, selling venetian blinds. Shortly thereafter, it moved to Freeburg, the birthplace of Marge Knoll, who currently serves as president of the company. Quaker began diversifying its business by producing awnings.

In the 1950s the company diversified further, producing aluminum storm windows and doors. Aluminum replacement windows and patio doors were added in the early 1960s. In 1985 the company started making vinyl windows and patio

(From left) Ken Knoll, Tom Knoll, and Mike Knoll are the owners of Quaker Window and Doors.

doors, and in the late 1980s, wood-clad windows and patio doors. The most recent additions to the Quaker product lines are heavy commercial aluminum windows and wood-clad windows with prefinished white interiors. Today the company offers more than sixty different lines of windows and doors, a selection created to fit any residential or commercial project according to the customer's budget and taste.

Quaker's well-constructed products offer many unique features to ensure weather protection. Glass is cut with an Optimizer, which minimizes waste and ensures the highest quality cuts with perfect edges. For an airtight seal, Quaker insulated glass uses Swiggle Seal® with warm-edge technology. On wood windows, solid wood frames of ponderosa pine are specially treated to eliminate deterioration and provide long-term durability.

Quaker's extruded aluminum window and door exteriors have a factory baked-on finish that is maintenance free, sturdy, and can be painted any color. The company offers these at various price levels. Each product line is diversified, so that there are numerous shapes and construction options within a particular style. Quaker also is unique in having the manufacturing capability and flexibility to offer custom-made versions of its products.

Quaker manufactures windows using in-house equipment that includes the most up-to-date computer technology and on-site testing facilities that enable tight control over the production

The offices and manufacturing facilities for Quaker Windows and Doors are located in Freeburg, Missouri. The complex has more than seven-and-one-half acres of production space under roof.

process. With its passion for continual improvement, Quaker tests products on site by simulating extreme weather conditions, including rain, wind, and sun. The company's seven-and-one-half-acre manufacturing facility has recently been refurbished, with two new buildings that increased its floor space by 80,000 square feet. It also added an upgraded year 2000–compliant state-of-the-art computer system and automated manufacturing equipment and increased the number of trucks in its in-house shipping department.

The Quaker dealer network is concentrated throughout a thirteen-state region in the Midwest, in Missouri, Illinois, Indiana, Arkansas, Kentucky, Tennessee, Wisconsin, Minnesota, Iowa, Kansas, Nebraska, Oklahoma, and Colorado. However, Quaker dealers also are found throughout the continental United States. The company works closely with its more than 1,700 dealers, providing product, sales, and installation training. Quaker customers range from authorized dealers to commercial users of heavy-duty windows to national hotel chains and military bases. The company is equipped to serve the needs of individual homeowners as well as such large projects as the installation of 20,000 windows for the Los Angeles Housing Authority.

"We offer customers excellent quality, responsive service, and pricing to match any budget," says Tom Knoll. "Building on the foundation established by our parents, we expect to continue growing as a business for many generations to come."

Wood-clad windows and patio doors were added to Quaker's product line in the late 1980s. Along with their striking appearance, test ratings show these products to be among the best manufactured.

FAULTLESS STARCH/BON AMI COMPANY

The Faultless Starch/ Bon Ami Company is a privately owned business whose principal activity is the manufacturing and sales of laundry and household cleaning products for consumer and commercial use. In addition, it sells unique home and garden tools and gift products for the consumer market.

With seventy-five products in its Laundry Products Group alone, and now having added a Home and Garden Tool line, including the Garden-Weasel® and the Garden-Claw®, the company is selling products in thirty countries. Its spray starch is one of its best-selling products in the United States.

Faultless Starch/Bon Ami products are distributed through supermarkets, discount department stores, hardware stores, drugstores, home centers, and mail-order catalogues. The products are distributed nationwide.

One of the company's best-known product lines is Faultless® Spray Starch. It is so popular that it is sold in grocery stores in thirty countries and continues to mold the ironing habits of people around the world. The company's Bon Ami® product line is known worldwide for the yellow chick on its label and the slogan that heralds it as a nonabrasive cleanser: Hasn't Scratched Yet!®

The Faultless Starch/Bon Ami Company headquarters, the company's laboratory, and its distribution center are located on three sites in Kansas City, Missouri. The manufacturing plants are in Kansas City and Humansville, Missouri.

The company's original product was dry laundry starch. Later, it developed the spray-on version, which now is sold in thirty countries worldwide.

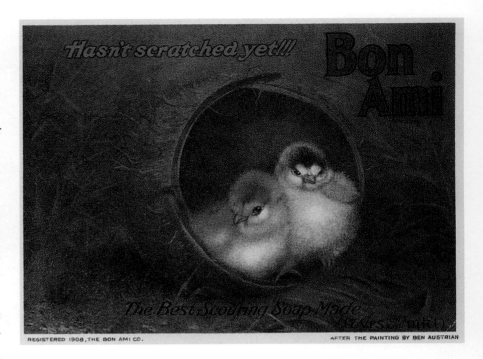

REGISTERED 1908, THE BON AMI CO.   AFTER THE PAINTING BY BEN AUSTRIAN

The yellow chick on the Bon Ami label with its companion slogan "Hasn't Scratched Yet!®" has become a textbook example of early American trademarks.

The company was founded in 1887 by Major Thomas G. Beaham and has been owned by the Beaham family ever since. It began with just a few workers and has grown through four family generations. Major Beaham's great-grandson, Gordon T. Beaham III, is the current president and chairman of the board. The fifth generation, Robert and David Beaham, are preparing to eventually lead the business.

THE HISTORY OF FAULTLESS STARCH

In 1886 Major Beaham came to Kansas City from Zanesville, Ohio, and bought into Smith & Moffit, a company that sold coffee, tea, and spices. This company became Beaham & Moffit. Later, Beaham & Moffit bought the formula for Faultless Starch from Bosworth Manufacturing Company, and in 1891 the name Faultless Starch Company was adopted. The company was incorporated in 1902. It was in 1974, after adding Bon Ami products to its line, that the firm became known as the Faultless Starch/Bon Ami Company.

Major Beaham's first product, dry white starch, earned immediate acceptance in the late 1880s. Faultless soon became a household word in

Bon Ami was first made in 1886 as a polishing soap and, over the next fifty years, developed into the familiar cleaning powder. After a hiatus in the 1960s, Bon Ami re-emerged and, in a major consumer magazine, topped the ratings.

the Midwest and Southwest, as many uses were discovered for the product beyond starching clothes—such as adding an elegant finish to embroidery and lace, treating skin irritations, and serving as a bath powder.

Further enhancing its popularity, Faultless published some charming books, many of which became the *Faultless Starch Library* (see photo, below). A company salesman named John Nesbitt took wagonloads of these books to Texas in the 1890s and attached the books to Faultless Starch boxes with rubber bands. The books supplemented or substituted for school texts and primers, and people actually practiced reading by studying the thirty-six books that the company published from the 1890s to the 1930s. "Many people in Texas and Indian country learned how to read with them," says president Gordon Beaham.

During the 1940s Faultless also sponsored half-hour segments on the *Grand Ole Opry* radio show, which was widely listened to before the days of television. "Our jingle became so popular," says Beaham, "that they played it during half-time at football games.

"From 1887 to 1954, we were a single-product company," he says.

In fact, packing and selling dry laundry starch was the company's only business until 1960 when, working with Arthur D. Little, the company developed a unique, high-quality liquid starch suited for use in aerosol cans. High-speed equipment for

Today, the Faultless Starch/Bon Ami Company boasts a wide array of laundry and household cleaning products.

processing aerosol cans was purchased, and the new aerosol starch, called Faultless Spray-on Starch, was an instant marketing success. It was followed by Faultless Fabric Finish, added to the product line in 1964; Faultless Hot Iron Cleaner in 1965; and Faultless Spray Pre-Wash in 1968.

The total aerosol starch category was among the top-ten fastest growing categories in the nation's supermarkets for three years in the 1960s. This success was partly due to the new twenty-two-ounce size for aerosol cans, pioneered by Faultless. It also was spurred by an improvement to the starch that Faultless made in 1964. The new version didn't clog the aerosol can's spout, and the starch sprayed evenly. When the company began selling this new version, the convenience of spray-on starch in a can made it popular all over the world.

Since 1964 the company has actively marketed starches and other chemicals to the commercial laundry market. The Faultless Laundry Products Group now offers more than seventy-five starches, chemicals, and specialty products to laundries and dry cleaners. Faultless continues to be active in

In the 1890s the company's popularity was enhanced by the Faultless Starch books attached with rubber bands to the boxes of starch. The books were designed to supplement or substitute for school texts and primers, and people actually learned to read by studying them.

creating new fabric care products. During the late 1980s it launched Faultless Lemon Starch, Lite Starch, Heavy Starch, and Wrinkle Remover.

"Today we probably have about 10 percent of the world's market and a third of the U.S. market for spray starch. I would estimate that nearly a half-billion cans of this product have been sold in world markets," says Beaham.

THE HISTORY OF BON AMI

Bon Ami polishing soap was first manufactured by the J. T. Robertson Soap Company of Manchester, Connecticut, in about 1886. Robertson formed his venture and began operations in an unused gristmill located on property owned by Gurdon Hicks Childs. Feldspar was ground to a fine powder, mixed with liquid soap in wooden troughs, cured and cut into cakes, imprinted with the Bon Ami name, and wrapped and packed in quarter-gross boxes for market.

William H. Childs, son of Gurdon Hicks Childs, and his cousin, William Henry Harrison Childs, formed the firm of Childs and Childs in 1890; and the firm became the exclusive sales agent for Bon Ami.

By 1896 Bon Ami had become quite successful, and the bar with the yellow chick on its label was evident in households throughout the Northeast. The yellow chick had the slogan "Hasn't Scratched Yet!" because neither chicks nor Bon Ami scratch. This has become a textbook example of early American trademarks. During Bon Ami's 110th anniversary, its new motto became "The 110-year-old chick that hasn't scratched yet."

Above: Expanding into the gift market, the company now offers its Trapp® Private Gardens® product line of candles and room sprays with natural fragrances made of the finest oils, spices, and essences. The line was created by Midwesterner Robert Trapp, acclaimed as a botanical, floral, fragrance, and interior decorating specialist.

Left: Major Thomas G. Beaham founded the company in Kansas City in 1886 with just a few workers; it now has grown through four generations.

After fifty years of growth, Bon Ami sales began to decline. Several changes of ownership and management occurred, and the product almost had disappeared from the market by the late 1960s. The Faultless Starch Company's major acquisition came in 1971 with the purchase of the Bon Ami Company. The Bon Ami products included the original-formula Cleaning Cake, the original-formula Bon Ami Cleaning Powder, and new Bon Ami Deluxe Polishing Cleanser, which was a formula updated from the original, containing detergent and bleach.

To emphasize the return of Bon Ami to the market, the name of the company was changed in 1974 to Faultless Starch/Bon Ami Company. It launched a new ad campaign that led to a 12 percent sales increase. Today, Bon Ami maintains a 6 percent share of the cleanser business, ranking as the third best-selling powdered cleanser in the United States. In the September 1986 issue of a leading consumer magazine, Bon Ami topped the ratings as the most effective scouring cleanser, ahead of such competitors as Comet®, Ajax®, Soft Scrub®, and Old Dutch®.

In the 1970s, Faultless Starch/Bon Ami began bringing garden tools and other household products to the retail market. Shown above, from the top, are: the WeedPopper®, the Mini-Claw®, the Garden-Weasel®, and the Garden-Claw®.

AN EXPANDED PRODUCT LINE

In 1968 the company acquired the Kleen King Company, one of the leading makers of consumer metal-cleaning products.

The International Division of Faultless Starch/Bon Ami Company has exported many of the company's specialty cleaning and laundry care products to overseas markets for years. Since 1962, the company's products have been sold worldwide through United States military commissaries and exchanges.

drugstores. In the early 1990s the company continued to expand its lines with extensions of its older brand names. It also added a number of imported and domestically produced products. Today it has a Web site (www.gardenweasel.com) to encourage the development of similar products for the mass retail market.

"The new products we look for are not necessarily garden tools, because our methods work across many retail categories," explains Gordon Beaham. "We also market household cleaners, ironing aids, folding dollies, a natural drain cleaner, and many other products. We offer companies and individuals a method of getting products to retail, if a product meets our criteria. Ethical treatment of manufacturers and inventors is of utmost concern to us. We want to find the next Garden-Weasel. Our business is the marketing of products." Since the Garden-Weasel, the company's other successful new products include the Garden-Claw, the WeedPopper®, the Gold-Digger™, and the HoeDown®.

"We appreciate the efforts of all of the people who help us manufacture, sell, and distribute our products to homes around the world," he continues. "We are proud to be carrying on the family tradition and the formulas that have made Faultless Starch and Bon Ami two of the best-selling brands in the United States."

During the late 1980s and early 1990s company sales of powdered cleansers were strengthened by the addition of Steel Glo® metal cleaner.

In 1976 the company acquired the exclusive sales rights in the United States to the Garden-Weasel, a German garden tool. In the years 1979, 1980, and 1981, the Garden-Weasel was one of the best-selling spring items of all such products sold through chain

BELOW: Gordon T. Beaham III, chairman and president of Faultless Starch/Bon Ami Company, and Nancy Beaham, director of consumer affairs, continue the long-standing family tradition of bringing fine household products to market. CENTER: David G. Beaham, vice president/planning, has served the company since 1987. FAR RIGHT: Robert B. Beaham, vice president and treasurer, has served the company since 1989.

U.S. PAINT CORPORATION

USING ADVANCED

RESEARCH AND

TECHNOLOGY,

U.S. PAINT

CORPORATION

DEVELOPS

HIGH-PERFORMANCE

COATINGS TO

MEET THE DEMANDS

OF HARSH

ENVIRONMENTAL

CONDITIONS

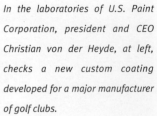

In the laboratories of U.S. Paint Corporation, president and CEO Christian von der Heyde, at left, checks a new custom coating developed for a major manufacturer of golf clubs.

A proud leader in the technology of cutting-edge coatings, St. Louis–based U.S. Paint Corporation specializes in the development and manufacturing of highly advanced coatings for the marine, aerospace, and automotive industries, as well as for industries offering a wide variety of specialized products. Essentially, if a product needs to look beautiful and at the same time must withstand the harsh environment, U.S. Paint has the ideal line of products.

An inspirational combination of dedication, pride, and leadership is evident throughout the

Timeless, a 1972 Burger Yacht owned by David Ross, president of Burger Boat Company, was refinished with U.S. Paint's AWLGRIP®2. A custom color, Timeless Green, was specially formulated for this project.

entire group of 150 men and women at U.S. Paint. The company's commitment to providing the highest-quality products available is evident at its plant in St. Louis. U.S. Paint employs more chemists and technicians than most companies many times their size, indicating the importance the company places on being on the leading edge of the coatings industry.

Staying far ahead in technology is a tradition at U.S. Paint. For more than twenty-five years the company's well-known AWLGRIP® brand of linear polyurethane topcoat has been synonymous with high-quality long-lasting finishes seen on the world's finest yachts. When applied to new yachts under construction or to older yachts during refinishing, AWLGRIP produces an incomparable level of high gloss and durability. AWLGRIP allows yachts to look new and beautiful for years with minimal maintenance. Thanks to the color specialists at U.S. Paint, many finer yachts are now being finished in beautiful, rich colors such as Jade Mist Green or Flag Blue, in addition to the more traditional Matterhorn White. One yachtsman in Florida even had his multimillion-dollar sport fishing boat refinished to match the flamingo-pink hotel across the waterway from his estate.

AWLGRIP's sister product, ALUMIGRIP®, is equally respected in the aerospace industry. In fact, U.S. Paint's dominance in high-performance aviation coatings dates back to the specification of ALUMIGRIP by McDonnell Douglas for its first DC-9 aircraft and by NASA for the space

program. Today U.S. Paint's products are preferred by owners and operators of leading commercial, corporate, and general aviation enterprises throughout the world. Among aircraft, Northwest, U.S. Airways, and JAS planes show the high gloss and rich colors of U.S. Paint products.

Beyond the marine and aerospace industries, U.S. Paint products have been found to have a surprisingly wide number of other uses. Motorcycles, snowmobiles, golf clubs, automobile parts, sports stadiums, and even amusement park rides have all benefited from the durable qualities of U.S. Paint coatings.

However, U.S. Paint has not depended on its past successes. Today an all-new, high-solids-formulation topcoat is available under the AWLGRIP®2 name. This highly advanced product took ten years to develop, and it is quickly becoming known as a "miracle in a can." This environmentally friendly topcoat offers higher gloss and greater durability than AWLGRIP or ALUMIGRIP and is equally applicable to both the marine and aerospace industries. Although it once seemed there would never be a better product than AWLGRIP, AWLGRIP2 is now considered to be the new leader for years to come.

Recently, in a move to provide an even greater range of highly advanced products in the aerospace and automotive markets, Christian von der Heyde, president and CEO of U.S. Paint, announced the formation of a strategic alliance with Germany's Mankiewicz Gebr. & Company. This alliance includes the rights to comanufacture and codistribute Mankiewicz's ALEXIT® interior coatings in the United States and U.S. Paint's AWLGRIP2 throughout Europe.

"This alliance provides new opportunities for both companies in the aviation and automotive markets, promotes exchange of technical information, and ensures a greater focus on the globalization of our collective coating products," comments von der Heyde.

Part of U.S. Paint's worldwide success is due to its excellent corporate culture, which is exemplified in its ISO-9001 certification, the most prestigious level of certification for quality assurance. From customer service to vendor relationships, from product development to providing a safe working environment, everyone at U.S. Paint is unified in a commitment to excellence and quality. Armed with the world's most advanced technology and focused on a common goal of uncompromising quality, U.S. Paint is positioned within its industry to lead the way into the twenty-first century.

J. F. DALEY INTERNATIONAL, LTD.

J. F. DALEY INTERNATIONAL, LTD., WITH SUBSIDIARIES ACROSS THE CONTINENT AND INTERESTS AROUND THE WORLD, IS WELL KNOWN FOR ITS HIGH-QUALITY BRAND-NAME AND PRIVATE-LABEL INSTITUTIONAL CLEANING CHEMICALS

A nationwide firm with a major presence in St. Louis, Missouri, J. F. Daley International, Ltd., is one of the largest manufacturers of private-label and brand-name institutional and industrial cleaning products in the United States. The corporation is headquartered in Chicago and spans the continent with nine manufacturing plants (three of which are in Missouri), thirteen warehouses, and twenty-four sales offices; operations in Canada and Mexico; and ties to international manufacturing and distribution facilities.

In 1980 J. F. Daley International acquired two cleaning-chemical manufacturing companies: Candy & Company, and Peck's Products Company, founded respectively in Chicago in 1891 and St. Louis in 1918. Thus the corporation's roots can be traced more than 100 years to the genesis of Candy & Company, whose original product line consisted of waxes and shellacs for the confection and paper trades, wire-coating compounds, and battery seal. Today Candy & Company manufactures base emulsions for sale to the secondary manufacturing market, as well as an extensive line of institutional cleaning and building maintenance chemicals. Candy is one of the largest producers of floor finishes, waxes, and ancillary floor care products.

J. F. Daley International broadened its lines with subsidiaries such as the St. Louis family business of James Varley & Sons, acquired in the late 1980s. Shown above is a portrait of its founder, entrepreneur James Varley, in the company's reception area.

The J. F. Daley Bulk Warehouse in St. Louis inventories raw materials and packaging for distribution via company-owned trucks to its nine manufacturing plants.

The early manufacturing of Peck's Products Company was simple soap bases and other janitorial-type cleaners. Today Peck's has national distribution of institutional warewash, laundry, and housekeeping products and also supplies cleaners, sanitizers, and conveyor lubricants to industries that process and package food and beverages.

Through vigorous acquisition of companies that strengthen and complement J. F. Daley's original lines, the corporation now produces brand-name and private-label products. For example, James Varley & Sons, Inc., a family business founded in St. Louis in 1921, became a subsidiary of the Daley organization in the late 1980s. Varley institutional cleaners and floor care products are sold internationally through distributors. Cynamic Chemical Company, of Chicago, produces Cynamic-brand commercial and industrial products. HiTech, headquartered in San Antonio, Texas, provides services, products, and programs to retail chains and supermarkets.

Pecci, Inc., in Naples, Florida, packages personal care products for salons and department stores.

The Daley corporation's auspicious customer base includes Anheuser-Busch, Seven-Up Bottling, Sears, Walmart of Mexico, Kmart, A & P Supermarkets, Shoprite, General Motors, Hilton Hotels, Mirage Casinos & Resorts, AT&T Company, Prairie Farms Dairy, Inc., Kohl's, Cole's Australia, Shaw's Markets, HEB Supermarkets, and many other well-known retailers.

Much of the corporation's strength and continued growth can be attributed to dedicated employees as well as to sound management and a philosophy of "independent/interdependency," in which plants operate autonomously but share resources. Manufacturing sites are strategically located throughout the United States (in New York, Florida, Illinois, Texas, Missouri, and Colorado) to speed shipment, reduce freight, and provide personal service to distributors within geographic regions. Ample raw materials are stocked at these sites to meet anticipated production schedules. To ensure uninterrupted production, each plant has access to additional raw materials from

Each J. F. Daley manufacturing site has a fully equipped laboratory and an experienced technical staff for quality control management.

the corporate bulk-storage facility in St. Louis, via company-owned and operated trucks.

Internal resource centers support the manufacturing effort. A central purchasing and bulk warehousing group in St. Louis negotiates prices and stocks bulk raw materials that meet stringent quality specifications. J. F. Daley Trucking's bulk tanker-and-van fleet, based in Chicago, guarantees on-time deliveries of raw materials and packaging supplies to the manufacturing plants and finished goods to large-volume buyers.

Great Impressions, Ltd., Daley's in-house graphic arts firm, located in Chicago, produces labels, silk screens, literature, forms, and sales-support materials. J. F. Daley Marketing in St. Louis handles advertising, public relations, and video production; develops sales aids and presentation materials; coordinates conventions and exhibits attendance; and acts as the intermediary for national and international trade associations.

Daley's research and development group is headquartered in Chicago, as is the corporation's engineering and technical staff. In addition to product development, this group assists customers and provides liaison with various federal and state regulatory agents.

As the twenty-first century approaches, J. F. Daley International deepens its commitment to manufacture effective, environmentally compatible, user-safe products; to build relationships with its employees, distributors, suppliers, and customers; and to contribute to the economies of its national and international communities.

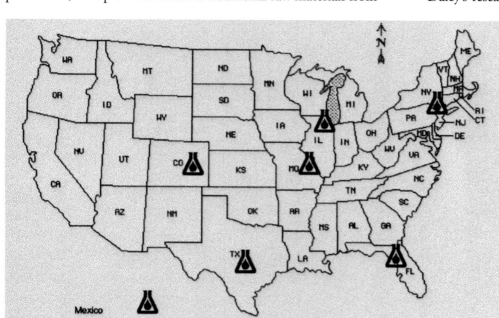

The corporate logo pinpoints the sites of Daley manufacturing plants. Three of its nine plants are in St. Louis.

A NATIONAL LEADER

IN THE DOOR

AND HARDWARE

INDUSTRY,

H & G SALES, INC.,

HAS PROVIDED

HIGH-QUALITY

PRODUCTS FOR

THREE DECADES

BY USING

STATE-OF-THE-ART

TECHNOLOGY

AND CREATIVE

PROBLEM SOLVING

One of the nation's most successful door and hardware distributors and fabricators, H & G Sales, Inc., started out with a simple idea: to develop better methods of getting materials to customers on time. Its owners, Irv Hill and Don Guenther, achieved this goal, and now, thirty-two years later, they have set into motion a vision to lead their company into the future.

Hill and Guenther started H & G Sales in St. Louis in 1967 as fabricators and distributors of hollow metal doors and frames. With a small warehouse in Westport Industrial Park and two employees, the partners sought customers for their doors and hardware products. Although their company was small, they felt that there was plenty of room for growth by selling what they had in stock, standard profile door frames.

At that time many architects specified custom-made frames that required long lead times and had to be shipped long distances by truck, often incurring damage in the process. Project delays were commonplace. If the architect made modifications after materials had been ordered, even more delays could be expected.

Guenther says, "We realized that shifting from custom-manufactured products to customized standard products was the direction to go, since such a shift would address many of the problems inherent in made-to-order products." Having a fabrication shop right in St. Louis would enable H & G Sales to provide customers with a local source for doors, frames, and hardware

Project management teams work together using the latest computer technology to coordinate doors, frames, and hardware, providing single-source responsibility for the complete door or window opening and the total project.

H & G Sales, Inc.

and eliminate problems related to distance, such as shipping delays and damage.

Getting off the ground was another story. Customized standard products were a slow sell. Jobs were small at first. The nature of the business dictated keeping a large inventory, which meant capital was needed. But the company delivered on its promises, and after adding a leading lock maker to its list of suppliers, H & G Sales took off.

Among the early clients that boosted the company's sales and reputation were Shell Oil Company, which used H & G products in its service stations nationwide; and Red Lobster restaurant chain, which eventually ordered products for more than 500 restaurants. It was on these early challenges that Hill and Guenther cut their teeth. Turning out

Steel entry systems such as this are fabricated in the H & G Sales shop in St. Louis.

quality products in large quantities on a weekly basis was no easy task, but once they developed their system, Hill recalls, "It was just a matter of finding out whether a particular building was a right-hand or left-hand structure and then supplying the product."

Eventually H & G took on significant projects for commercial giants such as Anheuser-Busch, McDonnell Douglas, Monsanto, Mallinckrodt, and the Salk Institute. By 1982 the company had moved from its warehouse of eleven years on Fee Fee Road to its present 43,000-square-foot facility on Lackland Road. In 1996 H & G opened a branch in Columbia, Missouri, to accommodate its growing number of customers in outlying parts of the state.

Today H & G is a nationally recognized leader in the door and hardware industry, marketing products by the world's leading manufacturers: the Essex Group, Ingersoll-Rand, Weyerhaeuser Company, Best Lock, and others. Its once-cutting-edge approach has become the standard of the market. While many of the custom manufacturers Hill and Guenther competed with are no longer in business, the partners' foresight and wisdom enabled them to prevail, serving the construction industry for more than three decades.

Good judgment, good ideas, and vision still power the company, starting with its embrace of new technology. With the industry becoming more heavily involved in electronic security, the challenges ahead are clear. "I see secured doors that will recognize you, unlock and open for you, and then close and lock behind you without your ever having to touch them," predicts Hill. At H & G the latest technology is a sophisticated Microsoft® Windows™–based computer system released to the market in mid-1998 that will enable orders to be entered directly into a cooperating vendor's production system, bypassing that company's screening program and further cutting lead times.

H & G's 43,000-square-foot facility in St. Louis houses all the necessary components to create doors and windows for projects of all sizes.

Wisdom and vision also come to the fore when Hill and Guenther talk about the principles by which they've guided the company. Their threefold philosophy centers on craftsmanship, creative problem solving, and respect. For its emphasis on craftsmanship, H & G was selected to reproduce in steel several sets of ornate wood doors for the University City School District, which wanted to maintain its schools' historic character but add durability. Demonstrating creativity in problem solving, H & G devised a six-story hollow metal framework system for an atrium in a downtown St. Louis office building instead of the heavy steel curtain wall framing called for in the original plans. H & G's framework was easier to handle and install and cost the client significantly less. Respect, the company's third maxim, is shown on every H & G project and extends to everyone involved—beginning with the company's own employees.

In the ultimate show of respect, Guenther and Hill have turned 80 percent of the company ownership over to their staff as the two prepare for eventual retirement. "They helped build the company," Guenther says, "they should share in its ownership." The company and its employee/owners are committed to meeting the challenges of the future and to searching continually for ways to add value to their products and services.

Everything from a single frame to an interior or exterior multistory wall system is fabricated in-house.

D & K HEALTHCARE RESOURCES, INC.

A FULL-SERVICE

REGIONAL

WHOLESALE DRUG

DISTRIBUTOR,

D & K HEALTHCARE

RESOURCES, INC.,

OFFERS ADVANCED

INFORMATION

SYSTEMS, SERVICE,

AND SOLUTIONS

FOR CUSTOMERS

Success for D & K Healthcare Resources has been attained by rapidly adapting to the changing health care marketplace and keeping customers' needs as the primary focus. Dedication and commitment to customer service are the core of D & K's achievement.

A full-service wholesale drug distributor serving customers in twenty-one states throughout the midwestern and southern United States, D & K is among the top-ten pharmaceutical distributors nationally. The company supplies pharmaceuticals, over-the-counter products, and health and beauty care and related items to customers such as retail drug chains, independent pharmacies, and health care institutions.

D & K customers are serviced from distribution centers in Cape Girardeau, Missouri; Lexington, Kentucky; and Minneapolis, Minnesota. Company headquarters are located in St. Louis, Missouri.

In today's fast-changing health care market, D & K is large enough to have effective distribution and sophisticated information system solutions for its customers, yet small enough to ensure that customers still receive personal attention.

Founded in 1987 as D & K Wholesale Drug, the company has exhibited rapid internal growth augmented by a series of acquisitions and mergers. After acquiring Delta Wholesale Drug, Inc., W. Kelly Company, Northern Drug, and Krelitz Industries, the company changed its name to D & K Healthcare Resources. Since then it has acquired Viking Computer Systems, Tykon, Inc., and a 50 percent equity interest in Pharmaceutical Buyers, Inc. (PBI).

"With its regional focus, D & K is a more flexible organization compared to large national wholesalers," says J. Hord Armstrong III, chairman and chief executive officer. "We can respond to change quickly and can custom-fit systems to our customers' requirements.

At D & K Healthcare Resources, Inc., a customer order is scanned using radio frequency technology to ensure that the order is complete and accurate.

As our customers are under pressure to drive system costs down, D & K finds ways to help them reduce costs, provide value-added services, and improve the quality of care."

Computerized information services form a critical link to the pharmaceutical supply chain. D & K has virtually 100 percent electronic communication with customers and suppliers. Its user-friendly information systems help D & K customers manage their businesses better, reduce costs, and increase productivity. Customers are able to exchange information electronically with suppliers, managed care partners, and third-party payers.

"We changed our name in 1997 from D & K Wholesale Drug to D & K Healthcare Resources, Inc., to have a name that more clearly defines the scope of our services," Armstrong says. "We believe that health care distributors need to offer their customers more than just distribution services. They need to offer solutions. Our new logo has our customer as the center of our business focus. In this changing universe of health care, it is important to know that our company is designed to revolve around the customer."

A D & K distribution center employee fills a customer order for pharmaceuticals and over-the-counter products for next day delivery.

D & K HEALTHCARE RESOURCES, INC.

UNITED INTERNATIONAL INDUSTRIES

United International Industries supplies ingredients across the nation and around the world to companies that make high-quality food products, premium pet foods, and on-farm stock feeds. The company's food ingredients go into the hands of bakers, into grocery store dairy cases, and into the commercially prepared dinners and snack foods that have become a mainstay in today's busy households.

Founded in 1993, United International Industries has offices in Wentzville, Missouri, and Newport News, Virginia. Its geographic trading area is worldwide, and its products are exported to, among other countries, Mexico, Japan, and Canada. To give the company stability, diversification, and steady growth, United has adopted a three-pronged business approach. Its divisions include the Agriculture Division, the Food Division, and the Nutritional/Pharmaceutical Division.

United's Agriculture Division handles grains, grain by-products, and specialty feed ingredients that are used in making pet food and livestock feed. For instance, the shrimp meal it supplies may be used as an additive in flamingo feeds to help the birds maintain their bright pink color.

The vast majority of feed ingredients in the United States are actually by-products of milling and processing rice, soybeans, wheat, and other grains. These by-products are used either for their protein value or for fiber value, and prices can vary depending on factors such as weather, international markets, the size and condition of the nation's field crops, and even the activity of futures contracts. United's ingredients salesmen often use the Chicago Board of Trade for benchmark prices when buying and selling feed ingredients. To successfully compete in the nation's feed industry, United's traders maintain close relationships with numerous manufacturers and factories. This enables them to competitively supply a wide range of ingredients as well as to keep pace with developing market

United International Industries supplies grains and specialty feed ingredients to "feed the farms that feed the world." © Corbis

trends. United's broad base of diversified customers includes multifacility manufacturers of internationally recognized name brands, single-factory manufacturers, and manufacturers of all types of pet foods and livestock feed.

United's Food Division supplies the basic ingredients for making food products, ranging from snack foods to frozen entrees. The responsibilities of the Food Division include buying and selling cheese, dairy proteins, miscellaneous ingredients, and packaged finished goods.

United supplies ingredients called "nutraceuticals" for use in products targeted for weight control, bodybuilding, infant formulas, and geriatric nutrition supplements. Special protein ingredients are supplied for making specific kinds of IV-administered nutrition and for trauma-patient nutrition sources.

"We expect to maintain United's strong and steady growth pattern," says United CEO James Dolson. "We expect not only to maintain our position within the industry as a supplier of premier ingredients but also to continue to grow in the industries in which we specialize. I believe our success is due to our consistency in supplying a high-quality product, to our flexibility during market changes, and, most important, to United International's dedication to The Adventure of Business and the Customer's Profitable Bottom Line."

Supplying ingredients to serve nutritional needs, United is dedicated to The Adventure of Business and the Customer's Profitable Bottom Line. © Corbis

DT INDUSTRIES, INC.

DT INDUSTRIES, INC.,

MAKES AUTOMATED

ASSEMBLY AND

PACKAGING SYSTEMS

AND PLASTICS

PROCESSING

EQUIPMENT TO

HELP CUSTOMERS

WORLDWIDE

INCREASE

PRODUCTIVITY

DT Industries, Inc., of Springfield, Missouri, creates integrated systems, such as the automated welding system, above, for manufacturing office partitions.

Headquartered in Springfield, Missouri, DT Industries, Inc., is an engineering-based designer, manufacturer, and integrator of automated production equipment and systems used to assemble, test, or package a variety of industrial and consumer products. DT Industries is the leading company in North America—and one of the largest worldwide—providing integrated systems for the assembly, testing, packaging, and handling of discrete products. DT Industries also has established itself as a leading global manufacturer of systems for the processing, counting, and liquid-filling of tablets.

By operating a family of complementary technologies and capabilities under the DT Industries banner, the company creates solutions to meet customer needs such as increased demands for productivity, quality, and flexibility within manufacturing. Through the development, integration, and cross-selling of various technologies and capabilities, DT Industries helps its customers bring their product innovations to market faster—resulting in increased profits.

The company is structured into three groups: Automation, Packaging, and Plastics. The Automation Group designs, engineers, and manufactures integrated systems for precision assembly and testing, heavy assembly, material processing, and handling of consumer and industrial products. The Packaging Group offers a range of branded technologies, which allows it to serve as a single source for a complete line of integrated systems that perform processing and packaging tasks. The company's newly structured Plastics Group has a strong presence in the production of processing equipment such as thermoforming, blister packaging, heat sealing, and foam extrusion.

Markets served by DT Industries include electronics, automotive, pharmaceutical/nutritional, recreational products, agricultural equipment, heavy truck, tire, electrical components, appliance, plastics, food and beverage, medical devices, and cosmetics. The company employs approximately 3,200 people at twenty-three facilities in the United States, Canada, the United Kingdom, and Germany.

DT Industries has sustained its consistent growth by meeting industry challenges for improved competitive cost advantages, shorter lead times, flexibility, and modularity in equipment. Strategic acquisitions also have enabled the company to expand its marketing reach and production capabilities.

"The key element to our success is our people," says Stephen J. Gore, president and chief executive officer. "We are taking aggressive steps to acquire new business and improve the efficiency of our service to existing customers. Many exciting new opportunities for business growth exist on the horizon."

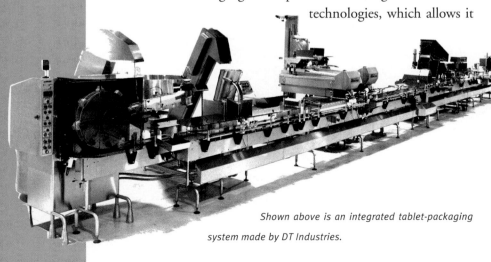

Shown above is an integrated tablet-packaging system made by DT Industries.

Systems for Success
DT INDUSTRIES

COPELAND CORPORATION

Since its founding more than seventy-five years ago, Copeland Corporation has been a pioneer in the world's air-conditioning and refrigeration industries and has earned a reputation for creating leading innovations.

It started in 1918, when founder Edmund Copeland introduced the nation's first successful household refrigerator. Copeland was the first manufacturer to develop a thermostatic cooling control. The first true heat pump compressor also came from Copeland. In 1977 Copeland unveiled its "CR" hermetic reciprocating design, a compressor line that today has grown to more than thirty million installations.

But perhaps the company's greatest contribution to the global HVAC/R (heating, ventilation, air-conditioning/refrigeration) marketplace was the development of its patented Compliant Scroll® design, a revolutionary technology that raised the standards in compressor efficiency, reliability, and sound ratings. This technology is based on the concept of compliance—the method in which two scroll members move in an orbiting fashion to compress refrigerant gas and simultaneously achieve high efficiency and durability. Copeland's scroll compressors have brought new meaning to the term *performance* since the product's launch in 1987.

Copeland is a world leader in its industry, with more than twenty locations around the globe. A subsidiary of St. Louis–based Emerson Electric since 1986, the company is a supplier to almost every well-known manufacturer of refrigeration, air-conditioning, and heat pump systems worldwide.

Copeland's state-of-the-art manufacturing facility in Lebanon, Missouri, lives up to the company's reputation for leadership. Copeland Lebanon is the industry's first dedicated, high-volume scroll manufacturing facility, designed and

Copeland's manufacturing facility in Lebanon, Missouri, is the world's first dedicated, high-volume scroll manufacturing plant.

Copeland's Lebanon plant, capable of producing more than two million scroll compressors annually, strives to build high-quality, reliable compressors for use in residential air-conditioning systems worldwide.

built in 1992 for the sole purpose of producing scroll compressors. This 400,000-square-foot facility has the capacity to produce more than two million pieces per year. Its 1,000 employees share a common mission: to build the highest-quality, most reliable compressors available anywhere, and to provide Copeland customers with precision delivery. The plant received ISO-9002 certification in 1998 for achieving international quality standards.

Copeland Lebanon strives to be the world's premier high-volume compressor factory. It has already manufactured more than four million compressors for the residential air-conditioning market, and it works hard at continuously improving performance in manufacturing and delivery. Copeland Lebanon has been particularly successful at involving all its employees in its facilitywide effort to extract the maximum output from its capacity and to produce scroll products at the best cost levels in the world.

At the start of the twenty-first century, more than fifteen million scroll installations will be in place worldwide. Copeland Lebanon will continue to play a vital role in heating and cooling homes around the globe throughout the new millennium.

INTEGRAM–ST. LOUIS SEATING

INTEGRAM–ST. LOUIS SEATING DESIGNS AND MANUFACTURES AUTOMOTIVE SEATING SYSTEMS, APPLYING INNOVATION, ADVANCED TECHNOLOGY, AND HIGH STANDARDS TO ACHIEVE GROWTH AND INDUSTRY RECOGNITION

Built on a commitment to clients and employees alike, Integram–St. Louis Seating is known for innovation and the ability to exceed expectations. When ingenuity is combined with a corporate philosophy of continuous improvement, the results can be impressive. That is how Integram–St. Louis Seating, established in 1989 by Magna International, quickly became an industry leader in automotive minivan seating systems.

The St. Louis company opened as a tier-two automotive foam manufacturing plant with a 120,000-square-foot facility and 400 employees. Within a year it became the tier-one seating-systems manufacturer for all Chrysler minivan AS models. It built a second on-site facility and expanded to 800 employees.

This success quickly led to more Chrysler business. Today, through cutting-edge design and innovative technology, the St. Louis plant has become the supplier of 100 percent of Chrysler's minivan seating. For the new millennium, Integram is designing and manufacturing the seating for Chrysler's new RS-series minivans, scheduled for launch in 2001.

As an industry leader, Integram continues to evolve into a full-system supplier with new and more sophisticated systems that are focused on the complete seating package. Advanced technology and a disciplined product delivery system ensure that products and processes are completed on time and within budget.

J. D. Power and Associates named Integram's 1999 Chrysler minivan seating the best in the industry. As a dedicated Chrysler facility, Integram is a frequent winner of the Chrysler Gold Pentastar for the best in quality and delivery. The St. Louis plant also was one of the first tier-one manufacturers to achieve both QS-9000 and ISO-9001 certification for automotive quality systems.

Integram's proprietary foam-in-place seating technology was developed specifically for the North American automotive industry.

Integram's innovations are many. Its proprietary foam-in-place technology offers freedom in seat styling that is virtually impossible to achieve by other methods. In 1992 Integram became the first in the industry to produce a built-in child-safety seat. This seat, developed in partnership with Chrysler, has set an industry standard.

Integram also excels in the category of workforce quality of life. "Many of our employees say that Integram–St. Louis Seating is the best company they've ever worked for," says Colin Anthony, general manager. As members of the Magna International family, all Integram employees are company stockholders and enjoy guaranteed rights and privileges under Magna International's unique employee charter and corporate constitution.

Magna International is a Canada-based multinational firm specializing in the design and manufacture of automotive systems. Founded in 1957 by Austrian immigrant Frank Stronach in the backyard of his Canadian home, Magna International boasts 35,000 employees at 150 facilities in North America, Europe, and Asia. Annual sales top $7 billion.

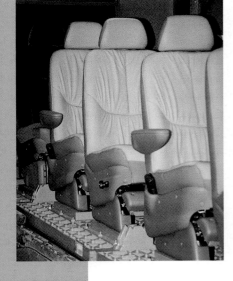

Three different Integram assembly lines produce Chrysler minivan seats on a just-in-time basis at rates up to 1,300 vehicle sets per day.

INTEGRAM-ST. LOUIS SEATING

AT THE TOP OF THE CLASS

CHAPTER TWENTY-THREE

WHEN THE SOLDIERS OF THE SIXTY-SECOND AND SIXTY-FIFTH REGIMENTS OF UNITED STATES "COLORED" TROOPS RETURNED TO MISSOURI AT THE END OF THE CIVIL WAR, THEY REALIZED THAT WITH THE FREEDOM BLACKS HAD ACHIEVED BY WAR THE NEXT NECESSITY WAS TO EDUCATE THEIR YOUTH. SO THEY POOLED THEIR RESOURCES AND RAISED MORE THAN $6,000 TO ESTABLISH LINCOLN INSTITUTE IN THE STATE CAPITAL, JEFFERSON CITY, IN 1866.

The resolution they drafted to set up the school said that "its fundamental idea shall be to combine study with labor, so that the old habits of those who have always labored, but never studied, shall not be thereby changed and that the emancipated slaves, who have neither capital to spend nor time to lose, may obtain an education." This unique institute, now known as Lincoln University, has thrived for more than 130 years to become a fully integrated (it was desegregated in 1954) state-supported university. Its annual enrollment is more than three thousand students.

Missouri's educational system has a long tradition of exceptional public and private schools. The state ranks tenth in the nation in the number of elementary and secondary schools, and ninth in higher education. Annual enrollment in Missouri's eighty public and private colleges and universities averages above 160,000 students. The oldest and largest of Missouri's public universities is the University of Missouri, established in 1839 in Columbia, which has since grown to include three additional campuses—at Rolla, Kansas City, and St. Louis—with a combined enrollment of nearly forty thousand students. The main campus in Columbia has one of the best-rated journalism schools in the country, as well as a major health sciences center.

Other state-supported public universities are located in every region of the state. Southeast Missouri State in Cape Girardeau has nearly eight thousand students. Its newly established Polytechnic Institute aims to encourage industrial development in the region. Southwest Missouri State, based in Springfield, serves over 18,000 students on three campuses and recently insti-

FACING PAGE: This mother shares a jubilant moment with her daughter on graduation day. More than 290,000 people are enrolled in institutions of higher learning in Missouri. The Show Me State ranks nineteenth in the nation in the percentage of people graduated from college (24.3 percent). © Richard Laird/FPG International LLC. THIS PAGE: This 1914 Sanford-Brown College typing class in St. Louis is part of a 133-year-long tradition of providing career education to Missouri's residents. Courtesy, Sanford-Brown College

A NOBEL COUPLE

IN 1947 DRS. CARL FERDINAND CORI AND GERTY THERESA CORI OF THE WASHINGTON UNIVERSITY SCHOOL OF MEDICINE IN ST. LOUIS WERE AWARDED THE NOBEL PRIZE FOR PHYSIOLOGY OR MEDICINE FOR THEIR DISCOVERY OF THE WAY IN WHICH SUGAR IN THE HUMAN SYSTEM IS CONVERTED INTO GLYCOGEN THROUGH AN ENZYME, OR BIOLOGICAL CATALYST, CALLED PHOSPHORYLASE. THEY WERE THE FIRST HUSBAND-WIFE TEAM IN THE UNITED STATES TO RECEIVE A JOINT NOBEL PRIZE.

tuted a public affairs theme to serve as the integrating principle for the entire curriculum. Northwest Missouri State in Maryville has more than five thousand students and a comprehensive computer network among its residence halls. Central Missouri State University in Warrensburg has more than 11,000 students and offers innovative programs in criminal justice and music as well as elementary education. But the jewel of the state college system is Truman State University (formerly Northeast Missouri State) in Kirksville. For the last five years, *Money* magazine has recognized Truman State as one of

TOP: *Southwest Missouri State University is situated on 225 acres in Springfield.* BOTTOM: *Six Ionic columns are all that remain of Academic Hall, the University of Missouri's first administration building, built in Columbia in 1840. Both photos © James Blank*

A SCHOLARLY ACHIEVEMENT

THE UNIVERSITY OF MISSOURI HAS EXPERIENCED A NEARLY 75 PERCENT INCREASE IN NATIONAL MERIT SCHOLARS SINCE 1994 AND RANKS IN THE TOP TWENTY OF THE NATION'S PUBLIC UNIVERSITIES IN THE NUMBER OF NATIONAL MERIT SCHOLARS. IT IS ALSO AMONG THE TOP FIFTEEN UNIVERSITIES IN THE NATION WITH THE MOST FULBRIGHT SCHOLARS.

Central Missouri State University, in Warrensburg, offers 150 areas of study in four principal academic divisions. © James Blank

schools of business, law, engineering, and medicine. Among the six thousand students annually enrolled, two-thirds of the incoming freshmen come from the top ten percent of their high school classes.

A number of top-rated small independent colleges and universities are situated in central Missouri. William Woods College in Fulton was founded in 1870 by the Christian Church (Disciples of Christ) for girls orphaned by the Civil War. Westminster College, also in Fulton,

the nation's ten best educational values. It is also the only public university in Missouri on *Money*'s "Top 100" list. *U.S. News & World Report* recognized Truman State as the number one public university in the Midwest.

KUDOS, TOO, FOR PRIVATE INSTITUTIONS

Among the superior independent colleges and universities in Missouri, several are located in the St. Louis area, including Webster University in Webster Groves, Lindenwood University in St. Charles (affiliated with the Presbyterian Church), St. Louis University (founded as St. Louis Academy by the Jesuits in 1818, making it the oldest institution of higher learning west of the Mississippi), and Washington University. Established in 1853, Washington University is widely regarded as a school of Ivy League caliber and consistently ranks among the top twenty-five universities in the nation in its overall academic program. Especially notable are its

Students at Southeast Missouri State University may select a major from among 150 areas of study in five colleges, two schools, and one institute. Courtesy, Southeast Missouri State University

© PhotoDisc, Inc.

was established in 1851 and was the site of Winston Churchill's famous "Iron Curtain" speech in 1946. This event is commemorated by the Churchill Memorial and Library, a national historic site featuring the reconstructed Church of St. Mary the Virgin, Aldermanbury, designed by Sir Christopher Wren in 1667 and moved to the Westminster campus from London piece by piece after being seriously damaged during World War II.

Just west of Fulton in Columbia is prestigious Stephens College, the only four-year women's institution

TOP: *Drury College in Springfield has over 1,300 students. © Bruce Mathews/Midwestock.* BOTTOM: *Rockhurst University in Kansas City is one of twenty-eight Jesuit colleges and universities in the nation. © Tatjana Alvegard/Courtesy of Rockhurst University*

of higher education in Missouri and the second-oldest women's college in the nation. Stephens has strong programs in fashion merchandising, theater arts, and equestrian sciences. In Columbia, Columbia College (affiliated with the Christian Church) boasts strong programs in fine arts, education, and social sciences. Central Methodist College in nearby Fayette (associated with the United Methodist Church) excels in business and public administration, the health professions, music, biology, and physical education programs. It is also home to the Ashby-Hodge Gallery of American Art, which houses a notable collection of regional art, including the works of at least ten former students of Thomas Hart Benton. The gallery's regular showings receive national acclaim.

The Kansas City area has several fine private colleges and universities, including William Jewell College in Liberty, affiliated with the American Baptist Church and ranked as one of the nation's top liberal arts colleges by the Carnegie Foundation for the Advancement of Teaching. William Jewell was also ranked as one of "America's best colleges" by *U.S. News & World Report* and is listed among the top one hundred dred "best buys" in college education by *Money*. Rockhurst University in Kansas City, established by the Jesuits, has a national reputation for its biological sciences program. A notable independent specialty college in the Kansas City area is the Kansas City Art Institute. Thomas Hart Benton once taught there, and the campus is now home to the noted Kemper Museum of Contemporary Art and Design.

TOP: *William Jewell College in Liberty is one of the nation's top liberal arts colleges. © Bruce Mathews/Midwestock.* BOTTOM: *Sixth-grade students at Thomas Jefferson Middle School in Jefferson City use blocks to figure a math problem. © Randall Hyman*

Springfield has a number of private religious colleges associated with the Baptist and Assembly of God Churches. The most notable of the small independent colleges in Springfield, however, is Drury College, affiliated with the Congregational Church and ranked number fourteen among regional universities in the country by *U.S. News & World Report.*

Although enrollment in Missouri's public universities and four-year colleges has declined slightly over the last two decades, private college and university enrollment has increased by about 20 percent, and enrollment in two-year public community colleges has increased more than 25 percent.

dents continue to high school graduation, above the national rate of 68.6 percent. Of approximately fifty thousand teachers in the state, more than 78 percent have five or more years of teaching experience, and the average ratio of students to teachers is about 15 to 1.

The state's educational system does more than prepare students for the working life. It also gives businesses access to research tools. The University of Missouri at Columbia, for example, is the nation's only state university

BEYOND THE FOUR-YEAR UNIVERSITY

Among Missouri's network of community colleges, two of the largest are in the Kansas City and St. Louis areas. The state also has three military schools. In addition, in recent years, the state has increased its financial commitment to vocational education: more than three hundred thousand students are enrolled in various phases of vocational training. Expenditures for secondary, post-secondary, and adult vocational training exceed $114 million per year, and training facilities are widely available throughout the state at high schools, vocational schools, community and state colleges, and universities.

Missouri's vocational education system offers courses in the major occupational areas and over one hundred subareas. Special programs can also be tailored to meet a company's individual workforce needs.

Courtesy, Washington University, St. Louis

IN 1869, WHEN THE LAW DEPARTMENT AT WASHINGTON UNIVERSITY ADMITTED LEMMA BARKELOO AND PHOEBE COUZINS IT BECAME THE FIRST CHARTERED U.S. LAW SCHOOL TO ADMIT WOMEN. BARKELOO BECAME MISSOURI'S FIRST WOMAN LAWYER AND THE FIRST WOMAN IN THE UNITED STATES TO TRY A CASE IN COURT. COUZINS WAS MISSOURI'S FIRST WOMAN LAW GRADUATE AND THE COUNTRY'S FIRST WOMAN MARSHALL.

BUILDING A STRONG FOUNDATION

More than 880,000 students are enrolled in Missouri's 536 public school districts. Almost 73 percent of secondary school stu-

Professor Carl Safe instructs a student in the School of Architecture at Washington University. Courtesy, Washington University, St. Louis

WILLIAM JEWELL COLLEGE SPONSORS THE MIDWEST'S PREMIER PROGRAM IN THE PERFORMING ARTS. LUCIANO PAVAROTTI MADE HIS AMERICAN RECITAL DEBUT AT WILLIAM JEWELL, AND OTHER PROMINENT ARTISTS, SUCH AS MARILYN HORNE, THE CANADIAN BRASS, ITZHAK PERLMAN, AND THE ROYAL SHAKESPEARE COMPANY, ARE FEATURED ANNUALLY.

LEFT: *The Winston Churchill Memorial on the Westminster College campus in Fulton features the centuries-old Church of St. Mary the Virgin, Aldermanbury, which was relocated to Fulton from London, England, and reconstructed after World War II. © Bob Barrett.* BOTTOM: *Students learn the ins and outs of robotics at the Washington University School of Engineering. Courtesy, Washington University, St. Louis*

to operate a nuclear reactor (completed in 1966) for educational and research purposes. Other links between educational institutions and research are the Missouri Research Park outside St. Louis, developed by the University of Missouri and affiliated with Washington University and the Monsanto Company, and Kansas City's University Park, a business center linked to the research activities in pharmacology, computer science,

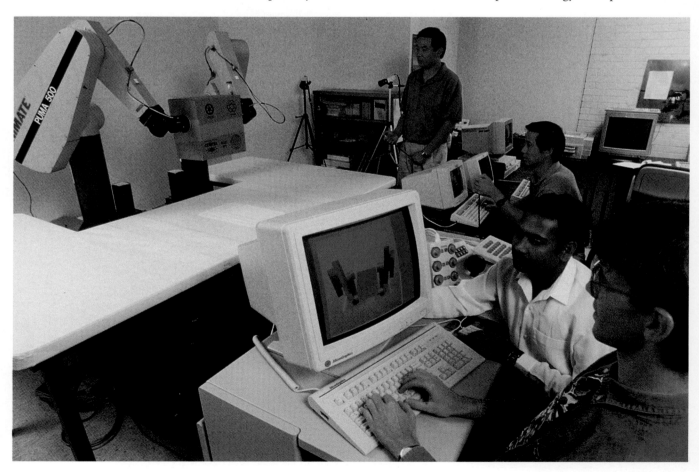

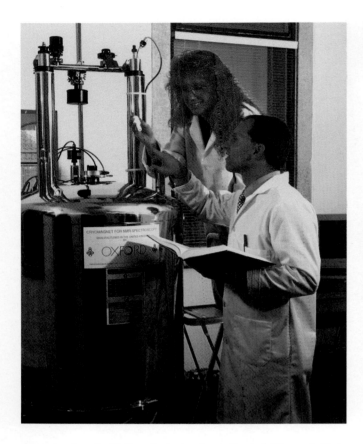

As a leading institution in technology, Central Missouri State University integrates the use of advanced technologies in all of its liberal arts curricula. Courtesy, Central Missouri State University

and telecommunications at nearby University of Missouri–Kansas City.

Businesses can also take advantage of the state-established Innovation Centers in St. Louis, Kansas City, Rolla, and Columbia, which support entrepreneurs and other businesses with low-cost space, shared services, close ties to university research expertise and computing resources. And the Centers for Advanced Technology at the University of Missouri campuses in Rolla and Kansas City and at Washington University in St. Louis encourage commercialization of new technologies.

One unique education story in Missouri is that of College of the Ozarks,

known as "Hard Work U," at Point Lookout near Branson. What makes this independent, privately supported, coeducational four-year liberal arts college different is that most of the 1,500 students pay no tuition. A distinctive work-study program meets the cost of their education. In addition to carrying a minimum of at least twelve academic hours per semester, students work fifteen hours a week, plus one forty-hour week each semester in any one of more than eighty campus work areas. Ranked among the top ten liberal arts colleges in the Midwest by U.S. News & World Report, the College of the Ozarks is dedicated to maintaining high academic standards within a vocational, spiritual, and cultural environment. Nearly every graduate of the college is offered employment before graduation or shortly thereafter. Most important, each graduate leaves not only with indispensable academic and job skills but also with the highly valued character traits of responsibility, cooperativeness, and initiative.

This main entrance sign says it all. © Bob Barrett

Rockhurst University students gather outside Van Ackeren Hall. © Dean Shepard/Courtesy of Rockhurst University

EDUCATION

LINN STATE TECHNICAL COLLEGE

LINN STATE

TECHNICAL COLLEGE

OFFERS TO A DIVERSE

POPULATION

ASSOCIATE LEVEL

ADVANCED TECHNICAL

EDUCATION

IN BOTH EMERGING

AND TRADITIONAL

TECHNOLOGIES,

AND SUPPORTS

ECONOMIC

DEVELOPMENT IN

THE STATE

Responding to the needs of the state's business community for an educated technical workforce, Linn State Technical College helps students develop the knowledge, skills, and attitudes needed to succeed in the workplace," says Dr. Donald Claycomb, president of the college.

As a result of this responsiveness to workplace needs, the college's reputation has continued to grow and become synonymous with quality technical education. Although in existence since 1961, in 1996 Linn State Technical College became the only publicly supported higher education institution in Missouri devoted solely to technical education at the associate degree level. The college has a long-standing reputation for producing graduates with valued technical and interpersonal skills needed for advancement in the workplace.

The Electronics Engineering Technology program qualifies students for employment in industrial electronics, computer technology, biomedical electronics, radio, telephone, television, and satellite communications.

Located on Highway 50 in Linn, Missouri, Linn State Technical College is a two-year public institution that offers Associate of Applied Science and Certificate degrees in emerging and traditional technologies.

The college offers approximately twenty technical programs and is continually enhancing current programs or developing new programs in response to demand. In each program the curriculum includes an integration of theory with hands-on application experience. Such integration ensures the development of functional troubleshooting skills with traditional and innovative techniques, approaches, and equipment. Also emphasized are teamwork, interpersonal skills, and work ethic. To complete a coherent education package, a general education core contributes to the high level of critical thinking and problem-solving ability students have upon graduation. Prior to graduation, many students participate in on-the-job experience in industrial internships.

Linn State Technical College monitors the economic, industrial, and technological needs of the state as new programs are proposed for development. Programs recently developed include Electrical Distribution Systems, Integrated Manufacturing, Medium/Heavy Truck Technology, Heavy Equipment Technology, and Computer Networking Systems. Programs under development include Telecommunications and Civil and Construction Management.

Another factor that supports the institution's responsiveness to the broader community is evidenced by partnerships. As an illustration, Linn State Technical College partnered with the city of Mexico, Missouri, and other higher education institutions to create the Advanced Technology Center. A second example of partnerships involves aviation-related endeavors. Linn State partnered with the Department of Transportation in the development of the new airstrip built on campus. In addition, Trans World Express airline has provided scholarships for Linn State students completing the Aviation program, leading to Federal Aviation Administration licensures for air frame and power plant certification, and the donation of a major teaching aid by The Boeing Company.

The college culture is that of a small (fewer than 1,000 students) Midwestern caring community dedicated to the development of

Graduates of the Electrical Distribution Systems qualify for employment as line workers with one of the state's many electric cooperatives.

the potential of each student. The average class size is fourteen students for each instructor and is purposely kept small to encourage adequate individual attention and faculty-student interaction. The student body consists of traditional students who recently graduated from high school as well as working adults making a career shift or enhancing technical skills. While the majority of the students are from Missouri, increasing numbers are from other states and countries.

Members of the faculty, who are continually involved in updating their skills, have a combination of higher education credentials and real-world experience in their professional areas of expertise. The college is undergoing a construction program that includes an Information Technology Center with state-of-the-art library facilities, distance learning center, a student life center, and new dormitories.

Linn State Technical College evolved from a post-secondary institution governed by the local school district to a state college due to its reputation for excellence and its technological contribution to the state's economy. This special-purpose institution makes available exceptional educational opportunities to individuals interested in technical career training at the two-year level as it fulfills its mission in a responsive manner to a broad constituency throughout the state and beyond.

Students who are enrolled in the college's Medium/Heavy Truck Technology and Heavy Equipment Technology programs prepare for the future with hands-on training.

GUARANTEE

Linn State Technical College guarantees satisfaction with the training it provides. Any graduate . . . who is found by either his or her employer or the graduate to lack entry-level skills (competencies) listed in the graduate's records . . . may return to Linn State for retraining at no cost.*

Certain terms apply. Call the Linn State Academic Affairs office at (800) 743-TECH or visit the college's Web site at www.linnstate.edu for details.

PARK COLLEGE

Mackay Hall, a national historic site situated on the Parkville campus, was built between 1887 and 1892 by student labor; the stone was quarried right on the college grounds. Today the venerable building houses a number of administrative offices and classrooms.

With little more than optimism and one thousand acres of Missouri land, in 1875 Dr. John A. McAfee, an educator, and Colonel George S. Park, a frontier land developer, set forth a goal—to create a college that would be accessible to many who otherwise might not have the opportunity.

Approximately twenty thousand graduates later, "Colonel Park and Dr. McAfee's dream of a quality, affordable education has long since become a reality," says Park College President Donald Breckon. Park College offers more than thirty undergraduate majors and four graduate degrees, including its newly developed master's of business administration program, which began in January 1998. Priced at state university rates, almost unheard of for a private educational institution, Park offers a weekend/evening program for working adults and a work-study program to assist full-time students with tuition.

Park College's diverse student body offers the opportunity to meet and share ideas with people from around the world.

Located in the historic community of Parkville, Park College's home campus sits on 800 acres of wooded hills overlooking the Missouri River. Conveniently situated fifteen minutes from downtown Kansas City, Park is only ten minutes from Kansas City International Airport.

Park College is one of the fastest-growing colleges in the Kansas City area. Approximately seventeen thousand students attend nationwide, including those at its home campus in Parkville, those attending four satellite centers in the Kansas City area, and students attending thirty-three military site facilities around the nation. Boasting a strong diversity, Park College has educated citizens from more than fifty countries and from most states in the nation and has been recognized as a national leader in graduating African Americans.

Striving to stay on the competitive edge, the Parkville campus is a leader in educational technology and telecommunications. Its newly developed electronic classroom allows students to interact in real time with other classes around the nation, providing an even more extensive learning experience.

The school's library is on-line and networked to other Kansas City libraries, allowing students access to two million books. More than two dozen college credit courses are also available over the Internet to students anywhere in the world. On-site degree completion programs are offered in partnership with businesses and industries.

After the college raised more than $3 million, a new science hall wing and renovations to the existing science hall were completed in 1997 and 1998. Also included in the campus facelift was a 1,500-seat soccer stadium, which provides space for concerts, sporting events, and other forms of entertainment for both the college and the community.

Athletics add an extra measure of enjoyment to campus life at Park College. Competing as a member of the National Association of Intercollegiate Athletes (NAIA) and the American Midwest Conference, Park College's athletic teams continue to turn in outstanding performances, often qualifying for postseason tournaments. The men's basketball, women's soccer, and men's volleyball teams have been to the NAIA Tournaments three times in the past four years and consistently finish the season ranked among the top twenty teams.

Park College is also an active participant in the area's economic development. As reported in the September 24, 1997, issue of the *New York Times,* college president Donald Breckon, a member of the Platte County Economic Development Council, promotes the college's role in "growing" this part of Kansas City. As a result, a new commercial underground is taking root beneath the campus with the potential to provide approximately twenty million square feet of warehousing, office space, and light manufacturing. Several tenants are already using the "Parkville Commercial Underground," citing proximity to college amenities

Park College's Council of Vice Presidents comprises (front row, from left) Paul Gault and Virginia Bruch; (middle row, from left) Dr. Clara Brennan, Dr. Donald Breckon, and Clarinda Creighton; (back row, from left) Dr. Tom Peterman, Terry Snapp, and Paul Rounds.

and the cost of the lease—less than half that of surface facilities—as their reasons for locating there. The college is utilizing part of the underground space for classrooms, computer labs, and the library.

Park College has always emphasized the importance of partnerships with the community and has joined forces with numerous organizations, including the American Cancer Society's Relay for Life, Derrick Thomas's Football Camps, and Synergy House/Safe Haven. Community groups that perform at the college include the Bell Road Barn Players, the Kansas City Philharmonia, and two dance troupes. "The Friends of Park," a group of residents of several nearby executive housing developments, especially appreciate these performances.

President Breckon has an additional goal: for Park College to become a university by the year 2000. In the meantime, he says, "Park College continues with its pioneering spirit—advancing education and changing the world, one degree at a time."

Park College's Parkville Commercial Underground leases warehouse and office space to area businesses who appreciate the significant savings it offers.

THE UNIVERSITY OF HEALTH SCIENCES
COLLEGE OF OSTEOPATHIC MEDICINE

THE UNIVERSITY OF

HEALTH SCIENCES

COLLEGE OF

OSTEOPATHIC

MEDICINE IS

RECOGNIZED AS

A MEDICAL SCHOOL

WITH A

RICH TRADITION

OF EXCELLENCE

AND OUTSTANDING

PHYSICIAN

GRADUATES

A "revitalization in facilities, in spirit, and in curriculum"—this is the position that The University of Health Sciences (UHS) has declared for itself in preparing for the coming new millennium.

After more than eighty years of educating some of the finest osteopathic physicians in the nation, UHS is experiencing a whole-hearted renewal. The university is enthusiastically unveiling a new face to its Kansas City community, and continuing to be a major player in the field of medical education. While revamping its curriculum to meet the challenges of the next century, UHS is becoming one of Kansas City's most civic-minded organizations.

Located northeast of downtown on a beautiful ten-acre campus, UHS is the oldest and the only private medical school of the three that call Kansas City home. The school offers a treasury of resources and opportunities to the nearly 800 students enrolled in its four-year academic program. Every year brings an average of twenty-one applicants for each of the 225 first-year seats.

To date UHS has graduated more than 6,400 physicians, who practice in high-tech prestigious medical centers around the country or serve in rural communities as traditional family doctors. A leader among the nineteen osteopathic medical schools in the nation, UHS also is a leader

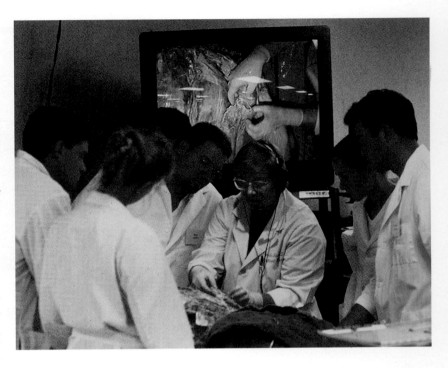

Medical students spend much of their first two years in the new gross anatomy laboratory. An overhead camera follows the instructor's intricate dissections, which are displayed in real time on a monitor at each of the more than a dozen dissection stations throughout the laboratory.

among major allopathic (M.D.) medical schools, offering a rigorous four-year curriculum with preparation for the licensing exams of all fifty states.

UHS students complete two years of on-campus lectures and labs, and then two years of clinical training in hospitals and ambulatory settings, in Kansas City as well as in rural and urban settings throughout the country. After this four-year period, more than half of UHS graduates have chosen to pursue a career in primary care. The area of primary care is experiencing a good deal of growth because of the "gatekeeper" role that primary care physicians play in managed care health care.

In fact, UHS is one of the most sophisticated medical schools in the country with regard to teaching equipment and facilities. It also is one of a handful of medical colleges leading the way in renewing an emphasis on "high-touch" medicine.

"Stressing care with a humane, holistic, and compassionate focus is not simply a philosophy at UHS," says president and chief executive officer,

The university's Roof Terrace, atop the Administration Building, is not only a quiet place to study but also the perfect location for many university-sponsored social functions.

Karen L. Pletz, J.D. "It is the basic premise underlying all that we do here."

In May 1916 the Kansas City College of Osteopathy and Surgery (renamed in 1980 as the University of Health Sciences College of Osteopathic Medicine) was founded. In 1921 the school's permanent address became its present campus, at 1750 Independence Avenue. It is now the largest medical school in the state of Missouri.

The early decades of the century were a time of great growth and prosperity in this area. A prominent Kansas City developer and civic leader, J. C. Nichols, was transforming ten acres of wasteland into the Country Club Plaza district, recognizing Kansas City as the "city of fountains." At the same time, the university's first president, George J. Conley, D.O., was building the city's first medical school, as a virtual fountain of knowledge.

In 1971 the UHS Alumni Association purchased eight and a half acres of land and a building, once the original Children's Mercy Hospital, to serve as a new administration building, a gift that came to greatly enhance the beauty of today's UHS campus. The campus itself is a shining oasis in the Kansas City urban core. The school has made a commitment to continue its work revitalizing this section of the city.

Alumni Hall houses more than sixty individual computer-equipped study rooms with state-of-the-art resources for study, review, faculty-student interaction, and research.

Today the UHS campus sparkles brightly. The stately buildings of yesteryear, with limestone bases and red-brick exteriors, are reminiscent of a rich and proud tradition. Beautifully landscaped grounds are a welcome sight to students, faculty, and visitors. New buildings are architecturally compatible with the historic, picturesque campus, blending artfully and belying the state-of-the-art medical teaching facilities housed within.

The 96,000-square-foot Educational Pavilion, a brand-new $10 million structure, houses a multitude of resources under one roof. Inside, the students and faculty have easy access to a sports-medicine center, a two-story library equipped with every modern electronic resource, and lecture halls and laboratories featuring the most up-to-date technological tools. The contribution of this new pavilion to the local economy garnered a Kansas City Economic Development Council Cornerstone Award for UHS.

Still, the vitality and pride emanating from the school stem from more than bricks and mortar. Students, faculty, and administration alike take a proud and active role in advancing the mission of UHS—a mission that promises the preparation of exceptionally competent physicians who practice with skill and compassion.

As the year 2000 approaches, UHS stands on the leading edge of high-tech medical education, while reaching back to its roots and stressing the kind of traditional, high-touch medicine that places a humane, compassionate emphasis on patient care.

The university has won several awards from Kansas City's Parks and Recreation Department for excellence in the landscape architecture of the campus grounds. Shown at left is the newly opened Educational Pavilion.

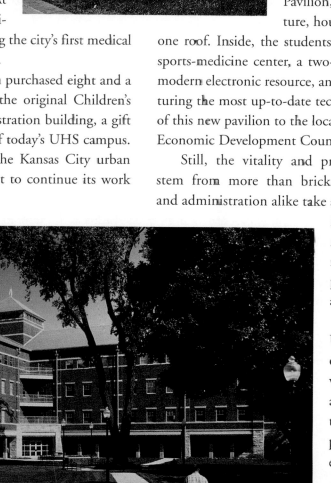

SOUTHWEST MISSOURI STATE UNIVERSITY

WITH THREE

TRADITIONAL

CAMPUSES AND

A FOURTH

"VIRTUAL CAMPUS,"

SOUTHWEST

MISSOURI STATE

UNIVERSITY OFFERS

UNDERGRADUATE,

MASTER'S, AND

SPECIAL PROGRAMS,

AND COURSES

TAILORED TO THE

NEEDS OF LOCAL

EMPLOYERS

Founded in 1905, Southwest Missouri State University (SMSU) is a four-campus metropolitan university with the single purpose of developing educated persons while focusing on five themes: professional education, health care, business and economic development, and performing arts, with a statewide mission in public affairs.

The SMSU system includes a four-year selective admissions campus in Springfield, Missouri; a research campus at Mountain Grove; and a separately accredited two-year open-admissions campus in West Plains. Its 4th Campus is a virtual campus, which uses technology to extend education beyond the reach of the three other campuses. SMSU is the second largest university in the state. Its student body is geographically diverse, with students representing all the counties in Missouri, forty-nine of the United States, and seventy-seven foreign countries.

The university offers baccalaureate degrees in eighty-five disciplines and master's degrees in thirty-two disciplines. These programs are organized into eight colleges: Arts and Letters, Business Administration, Education, Health and Human Services, Humanities and Public Affairs, Natural and Applied Sciences, the University College (for students still deciding on a major), and the Graduate College. In addition, through the College of Continuing Education and the Extended University, SMSU offers evening

The Public Affairs Classroom Building on SMSU's Springfield Campus was dedicated on 13 October 1998. The $20.25 million, 150,000-square-foot building houses the College of Humanities and Public Affairs, a Distance Learning and Instructional Technology Center, KSMU National Public Radio station, and studios for instructional and promotional television. © SMSU Photographic Services

programs, off-campus programs, and distance learning opportunities, as well as a wide range of noncredit courses, seminars, and workshops.

SMSU is distinguished by its statewide mission in public affairs—a university commitment to foster competence and responsibility in the common vocation of citizenship. Integrated throughout the student experience, the public affairs mission seeks to develop citizens of enhanced character who are especially sensitive to the needs of the community, competent and committed in their ability to contribute to society, and civil in their habits of thought, speech, and action.

The campus offers a diversity of activities that are open both to students and to residents of southwest Missouri. These include the athletics

Faurot Hall is the landmark building on the Research Campus at Mountain Grove. The original structure, on the left side of the glass connecting corridor, was built in 1899; it was placed on the National Register of Historic Places in 1979. Faurot Hall was renovated and the addition, on the right, was dedicated on 16 October 1998. © SMSU Photographic Services

program, which competes at the NCAA Division I level (Division I-AA for football); performances offered through the Juanita K. Hammons Hall for the Performing Arts; the popular summer Tent Theatre program; performances by university music ensembles; and more.

Numerous courses tailored to meet the needs of employers in the area are offered as well. SMSU also has the largest cooperative education program in the state, with more than 850 students participating in internships in the public and private sectors.

SMSU's main campus, the Springfield Campus, offers degree programs at the undergraduate, master's, and specialist levels. This campus is located on 225 acres in the heart of the community. It has seventeen classroom buildings, an administration building, a library, residence halls, a multipurpose recreational facility, a sports complex, a health center, a Park & Ride transit facility, and a services support center.

The West Plains Campus is a teaching institution of higher education, offering two-year associate and associate of applied science degrees, certificates, and other courses as needed by employers and citizens of the service area. The college provides a liberal arts transfer curriculum at the freshman and sophomore levels, selected occupational programs, and a variety of continuing education courses.

The 190-acre Research Campus, on the outskirts of Mountain Grove, located sixty-five miles east of Springfield, has a legislative mandate to generate knowledge through research and to disseminate this knowledge for the economic development of the Missouri fruit industry. As an essential component of the Research Campus, the State Fruit Experiment Station, established by a legislative act in 1899, is the oldest identifiable segment of SMSU. The information derived from the research is disseminated through advisory programs to fruit growers and processors throughout Missouri. Located in a

Emory L. Melton Hall, on the West Plains Campus, was dedicated on 19 April 1998; Melton served in the Missouri Senate for twenty-four years. The $2.8 million facility includes six classrooms, faculty offices, a 140-seat auditorium, and computer and science laboratories. © SMSU Photographic Services

natural grape environment, the station has been the site of extensive grape experimentation since 1900, with special emphasis given to research on the hybrid grape varieties and their wines.

SMSU's 4th Campus is a virtual campus, which exists in essence rather than in traditional form. "The virtual campus is, in fact, a logical extension of our growing ability to use emerging communications technologies," says John H. Keiser, university president. "The mission of the 4th Campus is to deliver quality educational services anytime, anyplace, in the most student-sensitive and cost-effective manner possible." The 4th Campus has been under construction for some time. It has an impressive array of distance learning technologies and delivery systems available for use, including audioconferencing, radio, television (interactive video, telecourses, microwave), satellite transmission, audio cassette and video cassette programs, and a variety of computer-based systems, including synchronous computer conferencing.

"Knowledge will be the most valued commodity in the twenty-first century," Keiser says. "Knowledge, unlike coal or iron ore or oil, is never used up. When used, knowledge expands. But it comes only to the prepared mind, and preparing minds is what we as a university are doing well."

SMSU continues to develop its 4th Campus, a virtual campus that uses emerging telecommunications technologies to provide anytime, anyplace learning opportunities. Its distance learning has two major delivery systems: classroom interactive video, in use at left, and Internet-based instruction. © SMSU Photographic Services

SOUTHEAST MISSOURI STATE UNIVERSITY

PREPARING STUDENTS FOR THE FUTURE THROUGH INTEGRATED PROFESSIONAL AND LIBERAL EDUCATION, SOUTHEAST MISSOURI STATE UNIVERSITY PROVIDES PROGRAMS THAT ARE RESPONSIVE TO A CHANGING WORLD

Founded in 1873, the beautiful campus of Southeast Missouri State University, known as Southeast, is situated proudly on the highest hill in Cape Girardeau, overlooking the majestic Mississippi River.

With an enrollment of 8,500 students, Southeast is located in the heart of historic Cape Girardeau, a community of more than 40,000 citizens.

Southeast is a comprehensive state university offering bachelor's and master's as well as post-master's programs. Students can choose a major from among 150 areas of study in five colleges, two schools, and an institute. The university attracts students from all over the world.

Southeast is distinguished for its personalized academic setting and its emphasis on controlled class sizes. It has structured its curriculum around the belief that effective career training involves a broad-based liberal arts education that emphasizes writing and critical thinking. Southeast is the type of teaching and learning institution where students can learn about themselves—they can experiment, have access to faculty, and explore various options. One of the hallmarks of Southeast is its emphasis on internships—about 90 percent of academic programs offer the opportunity for real-life experience.

In 1996 the university completed its strategic plan. The theme of the plan is stated as educating for tomorrow and beyond through integrated professional and liberal education. Through six

For 125 years, Southeast Missouri State University has had a tradition of educating business leaders, renowned scientists, civil and social servants, classroom teachers and mentors, award-winning artists, and other good, decent, honest people who have made the world a better place.

Southeast Missouri State University offers fine science and medical programs. Pre-med majors are accepted into medical school at a rate nearly twice the national average. Nursing, sports medicine, and training as a physical therapist assistant are other examples of programs in demand.

priorities, the university reaffirmed its purpose as an "engaged" university, one that provides students with high-quality, accessible educational programs that are responsive to the needs of the region, the nation, and the world.

In classrooms and at internship sites around the globe, faculty engage students in lively exchanges of knowledge, teamwork, and genuine friendship. Faculty members come from the most prestigious academic institutions in the nation, and they collectively bring to bear hundreds of years of expertise.

"Southeast is committed to providing a well-rounded education to each individual who studies here," says Dale Nitzschke, Southeast Missouri State University president. "Southeast strives continually to be, both literally and figuratively, a student-centered university, for, as we all know, students are the most important resource of all."

Southeast has one of the finest colleges of business in the Midwest, Harrison College of Business, which serves more than one-third of all students with declared majors at the university. The college is accredited by the American Assembly of Collegiate Schools of Business—the International Association for Management Education accreditation—placing it among the top 10 percent of colleges in the nation. The business college is housed in Robert A. Dempster Hall, a state-of-the-art facility featuring eight computer laboratories, two seminar rooms, two business policy classrooms fully equipped for instructional media, and a 400-seat auditorium. Southeast students receive hands-on training, including business internships with major corporations and industries.

The university offers some of the best information resources available. Throughout the Southeast campus, there are more than 1,800 computer workstations, fifteen miles of fiber-optic cable, and 7,000 E-mail accounts. Interactive classrooms and laboratories are networked across campus and have full Internet accessibility. These resources are enhanced by the university's interlibrary research systems.

Southeast's program in teacher education is nationally recognized. The innovative teacher training at Southeast begins during students' first year at the university, with field opportunities that require students to experience a variety of teaching

settings. Senior year culminates with a full semester of student teaching.

Southeast's leadership in its education program has resulted in its acceptance into the prestigious Renaissance Group of institutions with exemplary programs in education and membership in the Coalition of Universities and Businesses for Education (CUBE). Southeast also is the only two-time winner of the Christa McAuliffe Showcase for Excellence Award, which is presented by the American Association of State Colleges and Universities.

Southeast's health and human services programs provide extensive internships and produce graduates who are trained at a competitive level for entering the demanding and ever-growing health care fields.

Study in the Southeast liberal arts program offers an education that prepares students for working and living in a dynamic world. With its new School for the Visual and Performing Arts, Southeast has further committed itself to developing sensitivity to aesthetics and creative talents.

The university's new Polytechnic Institute was established officially in October 1997. It includes a Center of Excellence in Advanced Manufacturing Technology to serve existing industry and encourage industrial development in the region.

"The university has a wonderful opportunity to celebrate," says Nitzschke. "Its roots are deep, and for more than a century it has touched the lives of many people. Throughout its 125-year history, the university has undergone many changes and will continue to experience change. It has been able to withstand the stresses and pressures that come with such change. But all of that has strengthened this university so it can continue to serve people well into the next century and beyond, just as it has served well in the past."

Southeast offers impressive curricula in technology as well as in business. It holds the prestigious accreditation of the American Assembly of Collegiate Schools of Business—the International Association for Management Education accreditation—an honor held by only 10 percent of colleges in the nation.

MISSOURI SOUTHERN STATE COLLEGE

There is a lion in the international arena, and its name is Missouri Southern. Almost ten years ago, Missouri Southern State College, in Joplin, recognized the importance of educating students to function in a global environment and announced its intent to focus on international education.

In 1995 Missouri governor Mel Carnahan signed into law a bill authorizing Missouri Southern "to develop such academic support programs and public service activities it deems necessary and appropriate to establish international or global education as a distinctive theme of its mission." That act allows Missouri Southern to create bold new programs and activities that prepare students well for the challenges of the twenty-first century, and it empowers the college to initiate dynamic programs of outreach to the entire population of the geographical area surrounding Missouri Southern.

Today that distinctive international mission sets Missouri Southern apart and presents new challenges and unparalleled opportunities for

Missouri Southern State College's beautifully landscaped 320-acre campus, one of the showplaces of the region, features twenty-one major buildings, a historic Spanish-style mansion, and a wildlife area visited regularly by Canadian geese.

students and faculty. The philosophy of a strong liberal arts core that supports a variety of areas of career preparation remains central to the education Missouri Southern offers. But the infusion of a global dimension throughout the curriculum gives Missouri Southern students a greater understanding of global interdependence and develops in them a new global empathy.

The Institute of International Studies oversees the myriad activities that make the international mission a reality, including a new major in International Studies. In addition, the institute develops programs that bring the world to the Missouri Southern campus.

Each fall semester is designated for a special focus on a country, a continent, or a culture, such as The China Semester, in 1997, and The Africa Semester, in 1998. The themes derive from the topic chosen for the previous spring's annual Harry and Berniece Gockel International Symposium. The spring symposium features renowned experts on a particular country and global issues, and, throughout the following fall

Underscoring the global mission of the college, international flags are frequently displayed in front of the Billingsly Student Center.

semester, special programs highlight the political, social, and cultural life of the designated country or region.

Enhancing the curriculum, however, is only part of the picture. To develop a global empathy, students must see more of the world firsthand than they've previously known. So travel and study-abroad opportunities abound for students and faculty.

As part of the International Student Exchange Program (ISEP), students study for a semester or a year at universities worldwide for Missouri Southern's modest tuition fees. They may travel and study for a week or a month in programs developed by individual departments, such as art studies in Sweden, language studies in Mexico, biology studies in Belize, or the Oxford and Cambridge programs in England.

The numbers of students coming to Missouri Southern from other countries will undoubtedly increase as the college's reputation continues to spread internationally. They are most welcome and they contribute greatly to the experience the college promotes. However, the college's primary effort is to send its own students abroad.

The students and faculty of Missouri Southern are not the only ones who benefit from this international mission. The college's Institute of International Studies also is developing programs that help the region respond to new multinational needs. The institute's International Language Resource Center is helping

The lanterns that adorn the walls surrounding part of the campus were the inspiration for the college's logo (shown below).

language and geography teachers in nearby public and private schools enhance their skills and materials. The newly established Center for Teaching English to Speakers of Other Languages provides conferences, workshops, and in-service training for teachers in the region.

Local companies receive guidance in developing their business internationally from the International Trade and Quality Center. And the public can enjoy the special music and theater performances, lectures, and symposia that continually enliven the international studies.

One such event, the biennial Missouri Southern International Piano Competition, has gained a worldwide reputation for excellence. Competitors and noted judges from around the globe converge on Joplin, Missouri, for five days of music making in a world-class event. In addition, 88.7 KXMS/Fine Arts Radio International broadcasts classical music twenty-four hours a day, not only over the air but also around the globe on the Internet. Southern Theatre productions for local children bring to life stories and cultures from abroad.

In the late 1930s, when the citizens of Joplin asked the public school district to begin offering college classes, they may not have envisioned the extensive campus and the multidiscipline curriculum that today make up Missouri Southern State College. Throughout the past sixty-plus years, the central goal has remained the same—to provide the best in undergraduate education.

With its added global dimension and its continuing solid academic quality, Missouri Southern State College truly is "a state university for the twenty-first century."

Students can enjoy a class session out-of-doors in many pleasant areas of the spacious campus.

KIRKSVILLE COLLEGE OF OSTEOPATHIC MEDICINE

The Kirksville College of Osteopathic Medicine (KCOM) was founded in 1892 by the developer of osteopathic medicine, Andrew Taylor Still, M.D., D.O., who believed that a consideration of all elements of people's bodies, minds, and spirits should be incorporated into their medical care. His concept embraces a holistic philosophy that considers the body as one unit of interrelated systems that work together to ensure good health.

The main campus of the Kirksville College of Osteopathic Medicine encompasses almost sixty acres and twenty-one buildings.

Today the teaching of osteopathic medicine has grown from one school in Kirksville, Missouri, to nineteen schools nationwide. Together, these schools have produced more than 40,000 osteopathic physicians and are leaders in providing primary care physicians in the United States.

KCOM and the practice of osteopathic medicine constitute a "Missouri original" as the only medical practice actually created in the United States. The college was first named the American School of Osteopathy.

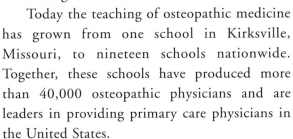

Osteopathic physicians prescribe medication and perform surgery, but they also are trained to use osteopathic manipulative treatments, psychology, and psychiatry to assist in diagnosing and treating patients. In osteopathy, special attention is focused on the neuromusculoskeletal system, which reflects and influences the condition of other body systems.

The osteopathic philosophy recognizes that the neuromusculoskeletal system composes more than 60 percent of the body and that there is a relationship between the structure of the body and the function of organs, giving a broader base for treatment of the patient as a whole.

Training in osteopathic manipulation and structural diagnosis, which is the main difference between allopathic physicians (M.D.s) and osteopathic physicians (D.O.s), focuses on the use of the hands to diagnose and treat patients as a complement to other forms of treatment.

With locations in both Kirksville and Phoenix, Arizona, KCOM is a national advocate for the promotion of integrative health care. The private, nonprofit KCOM offers a four-year doctor of osteopathic medicine degree program to approximately 580 full-time students in Kirksville and master of science degree programs to approximately 340 full-time students at its Phoenix campus, the Arizona School of Health Sciences (ASHS). Admission to KCOM's D.O. program is highly competitive. About 145 out of 4,000 applicants are accepted each year.

The goal of the college's medical curriculum is to prepare osteopathic physicians for primary care and specialty training. The first two years consist of basic sciences with some clinical training. The third and fourth years are composed of clinical training in health care facilities. Students are offered a seamless, vertically integrated, osteopathic curriculum that builds through doctoral and postdoctoral training and then supports continuing education programs and lifelong learning.

The ASHS campus in Phoenix houses the master's degree programs, including medical informatics, physical therapy, physician assistant studies, occupational therapy, and sports health care. In addition, some third- and fourth-year medical students do clinical rotations in the Arizona region.

Medical students may opt for a dual-track degree program in which the doctor's degree is combined with a master's degree in geriatric medicine, health administration, or public health. These dual-track programs give the training and experience to address the health care needs of the nation's population of aging baby boomers and senior citizens, whose life expectancies are longer than ever before.

Although osteopathic physicians constitute only 6 percent of the nation's doctors, they supply more than 10 percent of the nation's medical care.

Osteopathic doctors traditionally practice in small towns and rural areas. The college's curriculum provides for the training of primary care physicians in all communities but with a special emphasis for rural and underserved areas. KCOM ranks second among all medical schools in the United States in producing primary care physicians.

Richard Cenedella, Ph.D., chairperson and professor of biochemistry at KCOM, has received twenty-three years of uninterrupted funding from the National Institutes of Health for his cataract research.

With holistic care at the heart of osteopathic practice, communication skills are of paramount importance. Students are offered training in interpersonal communication skills, which includes videotaping interactive "doctor-patient" role playing.

"We emphasize primary care, prevention, and holistic care," says James J. McGovern, Ph.D., president of KCOM.

The college fosters a lifelong tie to its graduates, even to the extent of helping retiring osteopathic physicians transfer their practices to peers in order to maintain consistent osteopathic care for patients. Faculty members represent a full range of basic and clinical specialty areas. The college is noted for its diversity, actively seeking women and minority students, who are underrepresented among today's physicians.

KCOM'S Still National Osteopathic Museum, located on the Kirksville campus, is the only United States museum dedicated to the history of the profession. KCOM also is producing a 2,000-square-foot interactive exhibition that will tour science centers nationally and around the world. Called "The Healer Within," the exhibition is designed to teach the public, particularly children, the important relationships between structure and function in the body, imparting an appreciation for its self-healing abilities. It includes a history of both allopathic and osteopathic medicine, exploring the patient-centered approach to health care that is now widely accepted.

"The practice of osteopathic medicine requires a special type of individual who is committed to family practice, has excellent communication skills, and wants to empower patients' lives with a preventive rather than a reactive approach to health care," President McGovern says. "We look for individuals who embrace our approach and share our values to enter the field of osteopathic medicine."

Toni R. Smith, D.O., a 1979 graduate of KCOM, associate dean/faculty affairs, and chairperson and associate professor of anesthesiology, supervises a patient's exercise program at the Northeast Regional Health & Fitness Center.

VATTEROTT COLLEGE'S CEDAR CREEK CONFERENCE CENTER

AT ITS

CEDAR CREEK

CONFERENCE CENTER,

A CHARMING

130-ACRE RETREAT

SET IN MISSOURI'S

WINE COUNTRY,

VATTEROTT COLLEGE

OFFERS CUSTOM-

DESIGNED TRAINING

PROGRAMS FOR

LEADING COMPANIES

The Manor House at Cedar Creek Conference Center exemplifies comfort and elegance in the Williamsburg style of design and tradition.

Center in a nutshell—before even mentioning its superb recreational facilities, which are reserved for the private use of its guests. All this is within an hour's drive from St. Louis. Cedar Creek Conference Center is a perfect place for meetings, conferences, and training.

Situated minutes from the village of New

Picture a beautiful 130-acre retreat in Missouri's rolling wine country, one of the most picturesque areas of the Midwest. To this tranquil setting of natural beauty, add spacious, up-to-date facilities for meetings and conferences. And top it off with mouthwatering, imaginative cuisine and quiet, comfortable overnight accommodations. That's Vatterott College's Cedar Creek Conference

Haven in Missouri's quaint wine country, Cedar Creek began as part of an eighteenth-century Spanish land grant. The first structure built on the property, the Rock House, is still used as a guesthouse. In the 1970s owners John and Joan Vatterott converted the historic family farm into a corporate retreat, updating and renovating the original structures. Contemporary Cedar Creek has a magical combination of rustic beauty, comfortable accommodations, exquisite cuisine, spacious conference facilities, abundant recreation options, and a staff of professionals who know what it takes to make a meeting successful.

Leading companies across the nation have used Vatterott College/Cedar Creek Conference Center for Vatterott College's custom-designed training as well as for meetings and conferences, creative brainstorming, or simply rest and relaxation for their staff to develop unity. The specially

Cedar Creek guests gather at the Dining Chalet to enjoy freshly prepared cuisine. The chalet, decorated with antiques, country-style furniture, and quilts from the surrounding region, reflects the warmth of the conference center environment.

designed meeting rooms and adjacent areas can accommodate groups of various sizes. The Cedar Creek staff handles the details necessary to ensure a successful meeting. At Cedar Creek, work and play combine to equal a rewarding professional experience, making it well worth returning to the country.

"We were extremely impressed with the food as well as the accommodations," says Dave Chatmon, Department of the Army, whose unit received voltage regulator maintenance and repair training classes. Such training is necessary to trouble-shoot the generators used in conjunction with the Patriot missile. "It's nice to attend a training class in a relaxing atmosphere like Cedar Creek."

While many businesses use Cedar Creek Conference Center for meetings and training, others bring the skills of Vatterott College instructors directly to their own workplace or have their staff attend classes at one of fifteen Vatterott College campuses. The college specializes in custom-designed employee training, tailoring its programs to each client's needs and offering training twenty-four hours a day, seven days a week, and anywhere in the world.

Among the numerous nationally recognized organizations that have trained with Vatterott College are: the Department of the Army, Chrysler Corporation, Ford Motor Company, Sigma Chemical Company, Bodine Aluminum, and The Boeing Company.

The high rate of repeat business tells Vatterott College administrators that they are on the right track, keeping abreast of new technology and maintaining a strong connection with industry. "The instructor was very knowledgeable and professional," a Boeing employee comments. "I'm looking forward to taking another class in the future."

Formerly a branch of Vatterott Educational Centers, Inc., Vatterott College was established in 1969. In 1985 it opened a spacious new facility in St. Ann and in 1989, when it was issued authority to grant associate degrees, it adopted its present name. The Missouri Association of Private Career Schools named Vatterott College the best private career school in the state. Accreditation has been received from both the Accrediting Commission of Career Schools and Colleges of Technology in Arlington, Virginia, and the Accrediting Council for Continuing Education and Training in Washington, D.C.

Vatterott College has established fifteen locations in seven midwestern states. Five of these are located in Missouri. In

Cedar Creek Conference Center's facilities for training include ten fully equipped meeting rooms of various sizes, which are set up in precise accordance with each company's requests.

1998 the college enrolled more than 4,500 students nationwide. Vatterott College offers hands-on courses ranging from heavy trades to information technology.

The college guarantees the training of its graduates, promising additional course work at no cost if any deficiency stemming from Vatterott College training is found by an employer. Vatterott College's placement rate has proved to be a tremendous success and hundreds of employers attest to their satisfaction.

Honesty and quality education offered both in traditional classroom form and hands-on application settings make up the Vatterott College philosophy. As the new century unfolds, the college will continue integrating its skills as an educator with Cedar Creek Conference Center, eventually using the center exclusively for the Vatterott College Customized Training Division. Visit the college's Web site at www.vatterott-college.com or the Cedar Creek Web site at www.cedarcreekcenter.com for more information.

As it celebrates its thirtieth anniversary, Vatterott College looks to the future with great enthusiasm and the intention of continued growth and success.

Vatterott COLLEGE

Practical, Specialized, No-Nonsense Training Since 1969

CENTRAL MISSOURI STATE UNIVERSITY

Founded in 1871 during the heyday of westward expansion, Central Missouri State University welcomed its first students during a bold new era of economic and technological growth. Then, as now, the future depended on grassroots access to education, a need Central helped fulfill in its early years by preparing teachers. More than a century later, Central's commitment to strengthen Missouri's future by broadening the educational opportunities of its citizens remains undiminished.

Central was among the first institutions in the state to provide students with both a thorough liberal arts foundation and the technical know-how needed to succeed in the world beyond the classroom. Recently this role has expanded into a statewide mission in professional technology, serving as the essential framework for pioneering strategies designed to meet the needs of a new millennium.

Central continues to integrate scores of the latest technologies into more than 150 areas of study, organized into four major academic divisions: Applied Sciences and Technology, Arts and Sciences, Education and Human Services, and Business Administration. The result is a growing corps of Central-educated professionals prepared to move Missouri forward in a global economy and to provide high levels of leadership in industry, government, business, and education.

Central's innovative use of technology dates from the earliest days of the institution.

An integral part of Missouri higher education since its founding in 1871, Central Missouri State University prepares the state's citizens to meet the challenges of the world.

In 1931, for example, the Department of Music broadcast the first radio course ever offered for college credit—sixty years before the phrase "distance learning" became a byword at Central and on campuses nationwide.

The newest milestone in Central's innovative approach to education is the $30 million James C. Kirkpatrick Library. Supporting a full range of on-line research and distance learning, this facility serves as the core information source for Central's diverse academic community. Additional projects include membership in WeMET, Missouri's largest distance learning consortium; continuing education for teachers specializing in technical fields or seeking better ways to use technology in the classroom; customized professional development for business and industry; and a variety of tele-education services via KMOS-TV, the university's 100,000-watt public broadcasting station.

A comprehensive university offering educational opportunities worldwide, Central Missouri State continues to build on more than 125 years of service through fully accredited programs designed to prepare students for the challenges of a new century.

Dr. Ed Elliott has served as Central Missouri State University's president since 1985. Under his leadership, the institution has recommitted itself to quality higher education and put into place extensive assessment and accreditation initiatives.

LOGAN COLLEGE OF CHIROPRACTIC

LOGAN COLLEGE

OF CHIROPRACTIC

IS AN ACCREDITED

INSTITUTION FOR

THE STUDY OF

CHIROPRACTIC CARE,

OFFERING THE

DOCTOR OF

CHIROPRACTIC

DEGREE

An aerial view shows the heart of Logan College's 112-acre campus in Chesterfield, Missouri. Pictured, from left, are the college's campus Health Center; Administration Center; and Science, Research, and Ergonomics building. All buildings feature lecture rooms and classrooms for chiropractic adjusting.

On a spacious, wooded campus in the St. Louis suburb of Chesterfield, Missouri, nearly 1,100 students, representing most U.S. states and several foreign countries, are studying at Logan College of Chiropractic. The college is an accredited, first-professional-degree-granting, nonprofit institution, founded in 1935 by Dr. Hugh B. Logan.

Logan's enrollment has grown from fewer than 700 students in 1992, to today's 1,100 thanks to administrative planning that took advantage of the increasing validation in research literature of the effectiveness of chiropractic care.

Admission to Logan College requires students to complete specific preprofessional course work, creditable toward a baccalaureate degree. Students spend ten trimesters (comparable to five traditional academic years) at Logan, attending classes almost year-round to earn the Doctor of Chiropractic degree. They begin their

The Logan College curriculum includes extensive study of diagnostic imaging. Here, a Logan Radiology Department faculty member reviews X-ray films with clinical interns.

studies with the traditional basic sciences—ranging from gross anatomy (with dissection) to biochemistry. These courses are followed by an extensive curriculum in clinical sciences, focusing on diagnostic methods also used by doctors in other health care disciplines.

In addition, Logan students learn a variety of methods of chiropractic spinal adjusting, in order to provide comfortable treatment for a patient that provides the relief the patient seeks. Logan students complete clinical internships under the supervision of licensed doctors of chiropractic, at facilities operated by the college.

Logan has student/family and outpatient Health Centers on its campus; three outpatient suburban St. Louis Health Centers; and four St. Louis clinics serving the inner city. Three of these are affiliated with St. Louis–area Salvation Army facilities.

Dr. George A. Goodman, Logan's president since 1993, is now leading the college in developing educational partnerships with other institutions. For example, late in 1997 Logan joined the Missouri Gateway Geriatric Education Center (MOGGEC), which is administered by the Division of Geriatric Medicine of the Saint Louis University School of Medicine. At MOGGEC conferences, Logan will have the opportunity to present chiropractic case management methods for geriatric conditions to health care providers representing various disciplines and other professionals serving older patients.

With its strong commitment to educational excellence, Logan College enjoys its Missouri heritage as it plans for the future.

MISSOURI COMMUNITY COLLEGE ASSOCIATION

THE TWELVE MISSOURI COMMUNITY COLLEGES, WITH SEVENTEEN CAMPUSES THROUGHOUT THE STATE, PROVIDE TRAINING GEARED TO THE SKILLS NEEDED FOR THE JOBS OF TODAY AND OF TOMORROW

For most of the twentieth century, Missouri community colleges have educated and trained thousands of Missouri workers, helping to support and stimulate the socioeconomic growth and well-being of the state since 1915. The primary mission of the public community colleges of Missouri is to provide full access to higher-education opportunities to all state residents who are beyond compulsory high school age and can benefit from the colleges' services and programs.

By serving a specific region's needs, ranging from agrarian programs to heavy manufacturing trades, each of the twelve established Missouri community college districts provides its students the right training to do the right job in their own community. Also integral to the mission of the colleges is the availability of remedial assistance, lifelong-learning community programs, and custom-tailored training for business and industry.

All Missouri's community colleges support initiatives such as Tech Prep and School-to-Work programs, designed to prepare today's students for tomorrow's jobs. To ensure that programs stay current, 2,346 citizens from business, industry, and career fields serve on community college advisory boards.

The community colleges work with chambers of commerce, economic development councils, and industry boards to promote economic development, and target job-growth opportunities. More than half of the new jobs created in the near future will require some training beyond high school, predicts the Hudson Institute. Of the ten occupations considered fastest growing by the United States Department of Labor, only four require a bachelor's degree.

With more than 250,000 Missourians enrolled in programs for community college credit, continuing education, and special interests, and another 75,000 trained for new jobs through contract and special trainings, Missouri's community colleges are a key to the state's ability to remain highly productive throughout the twenty-first century.

Missouri's community colleges prepare students for job opportunities in their own communities.

MISSOURI COMMUNITY COLLEGES

- Crowder College, Neosho
- East Central College, Union
- Jefferson College, Hillsboro
- The Metropolitan Community Colleges, Kansas City
  - Blue River Community College
  - Longview Community College
  - Maple Woods Community College
  - Penn Valley Community College
- Mineral Area College, Park Hills
- Moberly Area Community College, Moberly
- North Central Missouri College, Trenton
- Ozarks Technical Community College, Springfield
- St. Charles County Community College, St. Peters
- St. Louis Community College, St. Louis
  - St. Louis Community College at Florissant Valley
  - St. Louis Community College at Forest Park
  - St. Louis Community College at Meramec
- State Fair Community College, Sedalia
- Three Rivers Community College, Poplar Bluff

A TAPESTRY OF CULTURE

CHAPTER TWENTY-FOUR

Missouri has something for every visitor. Man-made wonders like the gleaming, 630-foot, stainless steel Gateway Arch in St. Louis or natural features like the five thousand caves honey-combing the hills and valleys of the Ozark Mountains region are merely two of the reasons that tourism has become one of the leading industries in the state.

The Show Me State offers a wealth of entertainment, recreation, and culture activities—from extravagant stage shows in Branson to the glitzy riverboat casinos in St. Louis, St. Charles, Kansas City, and St. Joseph; from the spectacular natural beauty of fifty-one state parks to the rich historical and cultural heritages preserved at twenty-eight historic sites. Amusement parks, such as Silver Dollar City near Branson, Six Flags Over St. Louis at Eureka, or Worlds of Fun and Oceans of Fun in Kansas City are always crowd pleasers; and the fifty-eight-thousand-acre

Lake of the Ozarks or fourteen other recreational lakes offer both relaxing and adventurous settings, depending on the water sport chosen for the day.

Missouri is also musically rich, and performances of every style abound. Music is everywhere in Missouri—from a weekend of ragtime at the annual Scott Joplin Festival in Sedalia to a few days of traditional folk and acoustic music at the Big Muddy Folk Festival in Boonville; from Kansas City jazz to St. Louis blues; from the "high lonesome" sound of bluegrass to the distinctive mantra of Missouri traditional fiddle music; from Broadway musicals performed at the Starlight Theatre in Kansas City or the Muny Opera in St. Louis to performances by the Kansas City or St. Louis Symphony Orchestras. (The St. Louis Symphony, founded in 1880, is the second oldest in the nation after the New York Philharmonic.) And then, of course, there is Branson, where fans of country and pop music can choose from dozens of shows featuring some of the top entertainers in the United States.

The fine arts are also well represented in Missouri. Kansas City's Nelson-Atkins Museum of Art is noted for

FACING PAGE: *Although formed by the hands of a sculptor, this little girl's form seems full of life. Kansas City is known the world over for its hundreds of beautiful fountains and statues. © Bruce Mathews/Midwestock.* THIS PAGE: *In historic Hannibal, visitors may walk along bluffs overlooking the Mississippi River and muse about the adventures of two mischievous and indefatigable boys named Tom Sawyer and Huckleberry Finn. © Dave G. Houser*

History buffs can keep busy for weeks traveling between sites such as the Pony Express Museum in St. Joseph; the Arabia Steamboat Museum in Kansas City; the National Frontier Trails Center in Independence; reconstructed Fort Osage, which overlooks the Missouri River near Sibley; the lost-in-time river town preserved at Arrow Rock; and the antebellum mansions of Saline, Cooper, and Howard Counties in the Boone's Lick region of central Missouri. Also well worth a visit are the Daniel Boone Home in Defiance; the Lewis and Clark Center and restored riverfront area in St. Charles; the Museum of Westward Expansion beneath the Gateway Arch in St. Louis; the old French town of Ste. Genevieve with its restored French vertical log houses; and numerous sites connected with Civil War battles in Missouri, such as the National Park Service battlefield at Wilson's Creek near Springfield or the state-maintained Fort Davidson battle site in Pilot Knob and Battle of Lexington site in Lexington.

For those interested in the famous and the infamous, there are sites connected with the life of Harry S. Truman in the Independence area, including the Truman Library and the Truman home, and a number of places devoted to notorious outlaw Jesse James, like the James Farm and Museum near Kearney, the house where James met his end in St. Joseph, and the site of his first

A WINNING STRATEGY

IN 1919 BRANCH RICKEY, PRESIDENT OF THE ST. LOUIS CARDINALS, INTRODUCED THE MINOR-LEAGUE "FARM SYSTEM" TO THE SPORT OF BASEBALL AS A MEANS OF DEVELOPING YOUNG PLAYERS AND PREVENTING THE RICHER TEAMS FROM BUYING THEM. HIS INNOVATIONS LED TO THE CARDINALS' WINNING NINE PENNANTS AND SIX WORLD SERIES THROUGH THE 1940S. IN 1947, AS PRESIDENT OF THE BROOKLYN DODGERS, HE ENDED THE COLOR BARRIER IN BASEBALL BY SIGNING JACKIE ROBINSON TO THE TEAM.

A TAPESTRY OF CULTURE

bank robbery (in Liberty). The aura of Mark Twain and his well-loved characters draws thousands of visitors every year to his hometown of Hannibal. And the simple country home of Laura Ingalls Wilder, author of the *Little House on the Prairie* novels, is a popular destination near Mansfield. Other state locations honor ragtime composer Scott Joplin, poet Eugene Field, scientist George Washington Carver, painters Thomas Hart Benton and George Caleb Bingham, film producer Walt Disney, and Generals Omar Bradley, Ulysses S. Grant, Sterling Price, and John J. Pershing.

ON THE PLAYING FIELDS

Missouri boasts the year-round excitement of several professional sports teams, including two major-league base-

From mid-May to early October In Kansas City's Swope Park, the Starlight Theatre produces Broadway musicals, light opera, and big-name concerts of all musical genres in the country's second-largest outdoor amphitheater. © Bruce Mathews/Midwestock

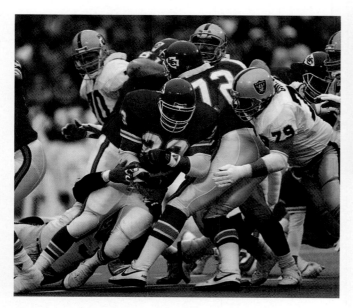

IN 1964 LEGISLATION WAS PASSED CREATING THE OZARK NATIONAL SCENIC RIVERWAYS, TO PRESERVE LONG STRETCHES OF THE CURRENT AND JACKS FORK RIVERS IN THE MISSOURI OZARKS. THIS WAS AMERICA'S FIRST NATIONAL SCENIC RIVER-WAY LEGISLATION. IN 1969 THE ELEVEN POINT RIVER, SOUTH OF THE JACKS FORK RIVER, WAS ADDED TO THE PROGRAM.

Fans rush to Arrowhead Stadium to get caught up in the high-impact drama of Kansas City Chiefs football games. The Chiefs won Super Bowl IV, in 1970. © Ben Weddle/Midwestock

ball teams—the National League St. Louis Cardinals and the American League Kansas City Royals—and two pro football teams—the National Football League's Kansas City Chiefs and the St. Louis Rams. Hockey fans in St. Louis cheer the Blues when they take to the ice at the Kiel Center, and their counterparts in Kansas City root for the Blades in the Kemper Arena.

High school and college sports are also popular in Missouri, especially Missouri Tiger football and basketball at UMC. And recreational sports enthusiasts flock to one of Missouri's biggest tourist attractions, the 270,000-square-foot showrooms and outlet stores that make up Bass Pro Shops Outdoor World in Springfield.

THANKS FOR THE HOSPITALITY

Since 1986 Missouri has had a state lottery, and in 1992 riverboat gambling was legalized. Sixteen casino boats now operate in Missouri, from St. Joseph and Kansas City to St. Charles and St. Louis. In 1997 these casinos added more than $1 billion to the state economy,

accounted for more than $500 million in personal income, generated more than $225 million in new tax revenues for state and local governments, and employed almost eighteen thousand new workers. The casinos are one part of the larger picture of a tourism industry that has shown tremendous growth in the last few years.

Hotels, motels, bed-and-breakfasts, restaurants, convention and visitors bureaus, and a wide assortment of retail and wholesale businesses thrive on the robust tourism and convention business in Missouri. Hotels and restaurants employ more than 160,000 Missourians, with another 50,000 employed in various other tourist-related

These packed stands (and the predominance of the color red) at Busch Stadium in St. Louis might give a little hint of how well loved the home team is. © James Blank

enterprises. Wholesale and retail trades account for another 600,000 workers in the state, and the combined payroll for all of these workers is nearly $8 billion.

The hot spots for much of Missouri's convention business are in the St. Louis and Kansas City metropolitan areas, as well as in the Columbia–Jefferson City–Lake of the Ozarks region. The Marriott, Hyatt Regency, Sheraton, Adams Mark, Holiday Inn, and Doubletree hotel chains dominate the hospitality and convention markets in Kansas City and St. Louis. The new Trans World Dome and America's Center are the largest banquet and meeting centers in St. Louis, and H. R. Bartle Exposition Hall is the largest one in Kansas City. In the Lake of the Ozarks region Marriott's Tan-Tar-A Resort and the Lodge of the Four Seasons tend to be the most popular convention, hospitality, and banquet locales. In central Missouri the Holiday Inns and Ramada Inns in Jefferson City and Columbia are the major convention and hospitality centers.

Tourism is the fastest-growing industry in the state. In 1996 the tourism and travel industry generated $11.1 billion in direct expenditures in Missouri with another $6 billion in businesses and employment that benefit

AT 8:18 P.M. ON 9 SEPTEMBER 1998, MARK McGWIRE OF THE ST. LOUIS CARDINALS HIT HIS SIXTY-SECOND HOME RUN OF THE SEASON, BREAKING THE RECORD SET BY ROGER MARIS IN 1961. THE JUBILANT CELEBRATION THAT FOLLOWED THE 88-MPH LOW BALL TO LEFT FIELD SPARKED AN ELEVEN-MINUTE DELAY. WHILE MARIS ACHIEVED HIS FEAT IN 163 GAMES FOR THE YANKEES, McGWIRE BESTED THAT MARK IN JUST 145 GAMES FOR THE CARDINALS.

© Sporting News/Archive Photos

indirectly from tourism. More than 210,000 people held jobs directly tied to the tourism industry in 1996, while another 80,000 were employed in businesses benefiting indirectly from tourism. Tourism also generated more than $900 million in state tax revenues and nearly $500 million for local governments. The Missouri Division of Tourism predicts that travel and tourism will soon become the largest industry in the state, providing a solid economic anchor in the twenty-first century.

The Union Covered Bridge, five miles west of Paris in Mark Twain country, is the last surviving covered bridge with a Burr arch truss construction. It was built in 1871. © James Blank

Tourism is the fastest-growing industry in Missouri. © Tom McCarthy/Photo Network

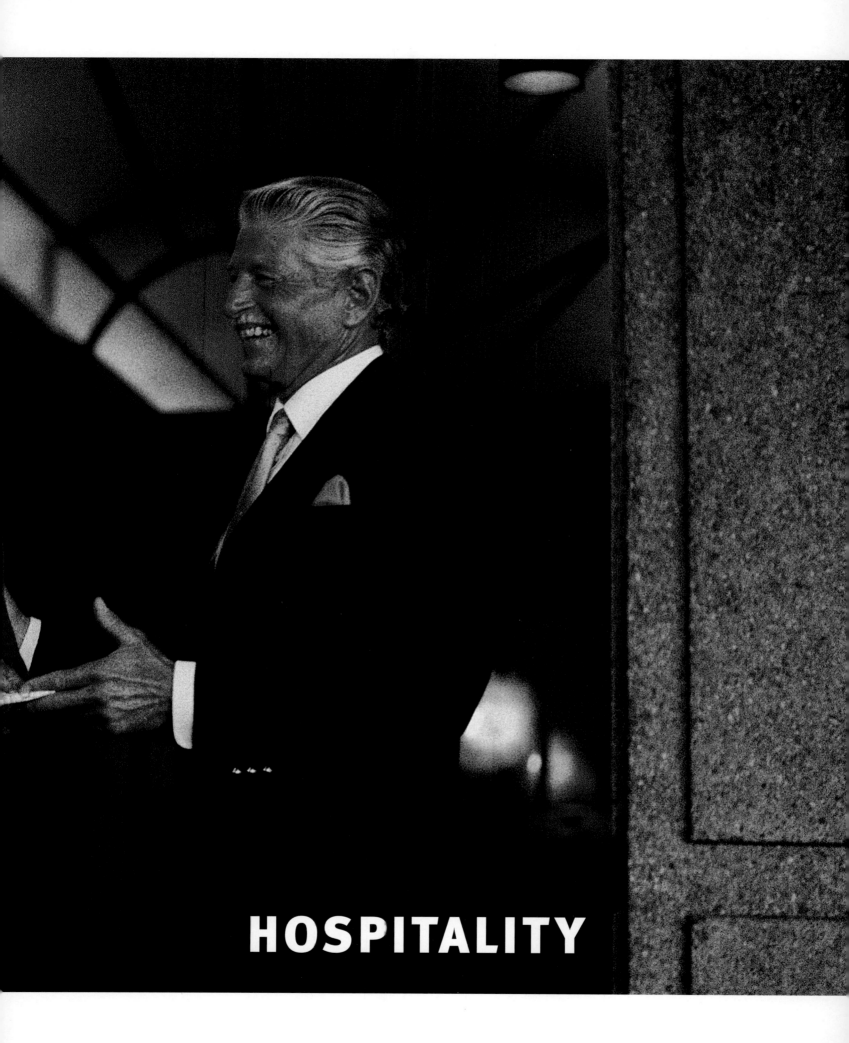

HOSPITALITY

HISTORIC SUITES

Located in the historic Wholesale/Garment District near the River Market in downtown Kansas City, Historic Suites matches historical elegance with contemporary refinement. The hotel began in 1989 with the renovation of three turn-of-the-century structures that helped Kansas City become the urban center it is today: the 1887 Builders and Traders Exchange Building, the 1895 Barton Brothers Shoe Company Building, and the 1892 Burnham-Munger Manufacturing Company Building. These structures all are listed on the National Register of Historic Places.

After detailed restoration and extensive renovation efforts, these three jewels now bring history to life. "You will not find another hotel in Kansas City—or for that matter, the world—that contains the architectural attributes found at Historic Suites," says general manager Carl Galbreath. "We've taken three special buildings and forged a distinctive lodging experience within them."

In addition to its turn-of-the-century architectural charm, Historic Suites offers the latest in hotel and meetings management capabilities and a professional commitment to service. Historic Suites offers a welcome meeting solution, providing the ideal venue for small meetings, strategic planning sessions, and more intimate breakout functions. The hotel is located within blocks of newly expanded Bartle Hall and major corporate headquarters, with access to nearby interstates I-70 and I-35. Corporate clients include such companies as AT&T, Ozark National Life, Nations Bank, and Utilicorp.

Historic Suites can host any meeting, large or small, in a number of settings throughout the property. The hotel's largest meeting

Just one example of Historic Suites's unique and spacious floor plans, this magnificent suite features finely carved wood highlights, twelve-foot-high ceilings, a sweeping spiral staircase, and Palladian windows.

Among the unique architectural highlights of Historic Suites is the soaring atrium rotunda, surrounded in deep mahogany with verdigris ironwork.

space, the 1,750-square-foot conference room, is a wholly dedicated facility with a conference seating capacity of thirty and theater seating for forty-five. The room includes public speaking, audiovisual, and overhead projection capabilities, as well as a built-in kitchenette featuring a refrigerator, an ice maker, and coffee service, with glassware stored within its oak cabinetry.

First-time visitors to Historic Suites of America are always amazed by the sheer size of their accommodations—the total square footage is twice the area of an average hotel room. Beams soar twelve to eighteen feet overhead. Floor-to-ceiling windows flood many suites with light, and each room offers tasteful decor, state-of-the-art amenities, fully equipped gourmet kitchens, and overall convenience. Historic Suites offers an incredible thirty-two different floor plans within its 100 suites, assuring something for every guest.

"As we mark our tenth anniversary in 1999, we will continue our commitment to customer service and quality that has made Historic Suites a very special travel experience," says Beth Krizman, director of sales.

AMERICAN INN

WITH CONVENIENT LOCATIONS THROUGHOUT A FIVE-STATE AREA, AMERICAN INN OFFERS BUSINESS TRAVELERS COMFORTABLE GUEST ACCOMMODATIONS AND A FULL RANGE OF AMENITIES, INCLUDING MEETING FACILITIES

Offering a total of more than 1,500 guest rooms, American Inn provides accommodations at ten locations, covering eight cities in five states.

Each of American Inn's tastefully appointed rooms offers guests comfortable beds, a work area, and plenty of light. Each room has a full bath with a lighted vanity area. Modular telephone jacks allow guests to use their laptop computers or fax services easily. Morning coffee and complimentary local telephone calls are standard amenities at each location, as is cable television, including the Showtime channel.

An American Inn can be found in or near Kansas City, Missouri; Blue Springs, Missouri; Independence, Missouri; Kansas City, Kansas; and Springfield, Missouri; Omaha, Nebraska (served by an American Inn in Council Bluffs, Iowa); Denver, Colorado (Wheat Ridge, Colorado); and Branson, Missouri (Springfield, Missouri).

The location of each American Inn is central to major businesses and entertainment areas. The American Inn in North Kansas City, at Interstates 35 and 29, is near a very active part of Kansas City. North Kansas City is a thriving business, industrial, and residential area. American Inn provides guest room accommodations for many area companies, including Burlington Northern Railroad and Norfolk Southern Railroad. The trucking industry also is a major industry in North Kansas City, and American Inn has many trucking lines as customers.

With theater-style meeting space that accommodates up to 200 people, the American Inn assists many companies that have an array of meeting needs. It rewards with discounts those companies that require guest housing along with meeting space. American Inn

American Inn accommodations are located near business centers and also entertainment areas, such as Missouri's riverboat casinos.

provides the maximum amount of service so that its clients can expend a minimum amount of effort.

North Kansas City also is central to all five operating riverboat casinos. The American Inn has positioned itself as a guest housing option for each of the riverboat casinos to make available for their out-of-town customers.

American Inn has five locations in the Kansas City area and a toll-free reservation center to handle all requests (1-800-90-LODGE). The American Inn has a strong relationship with the Convention and Visitors' Bureau of Greater Kansas City and is a vital partner in handling overflow guest housing during major downtown and citywide conventions and trade shows.

The American Inn in Springfield, Missouri, features the exciting Ozark Style Safari with American Inns and Exotic Animal Paradise, a tour through 400 acres of tamed, exotic wilderness boasting more than 3,000 animals and rare birds from all over the world. This package also includes a visit to one of Missouri's leading attractions, Bass Pro Shops Outdoor World, which features a four-story natural stone waterfall, aquariums, and the Fish and Wildlife Museum.

Both the North Kansas City and Blue Springs American Inn facilities are available for weddings.

Whether visiting for business or pleasure, guests at American Inn are provided with the best available service, comfort, location, and value.

Comfortable guest rooms provide amenities such as well-lighted work areas, telephone jacks for computers, and cable television, including the Showtime channel.

Shuttlecocks *adorns the lawn of the Nelson-Atkins Museum of Art in Kansas City.* © Bruce Mathews/Midwestock

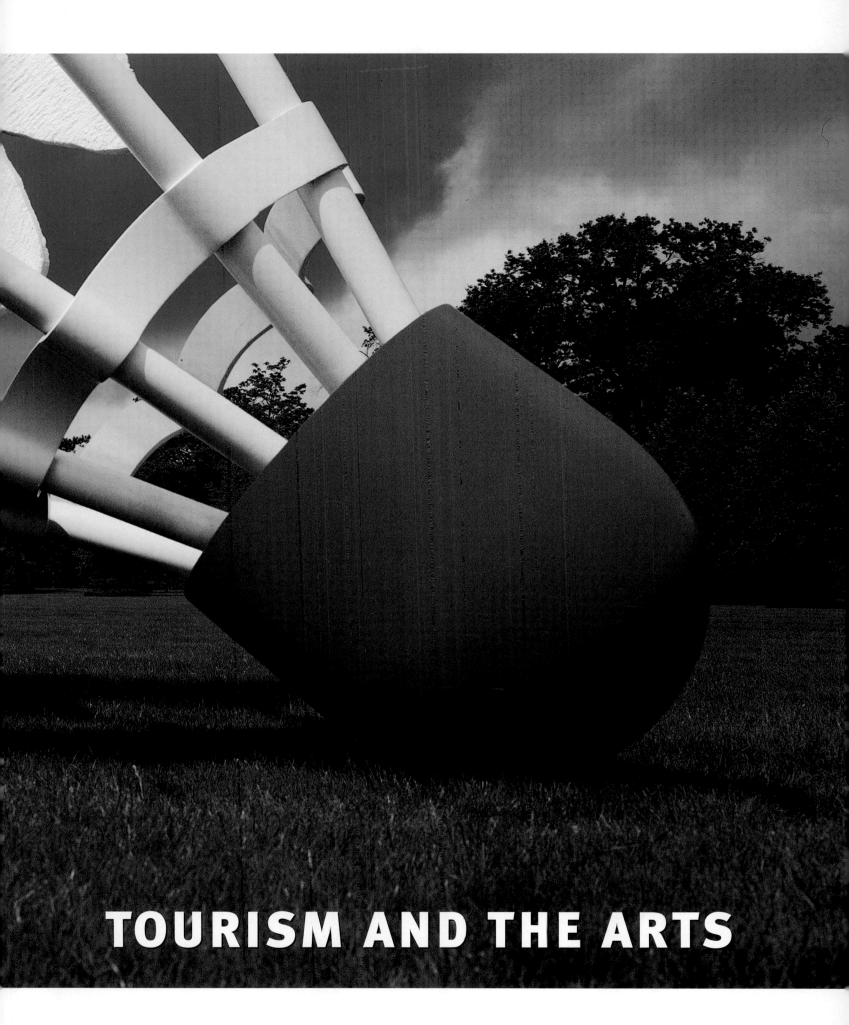

TOURISM AND THE ARTS

PRESIDENT CASINOS, INC.

WITH A HISTORY OF
SUCCESS IN THE
GAMING BUSINESS,
PRESIDENT CASINOS,
INC., DEVELOPS
RIVERBOAT AND
DOCKSIDE CASINO
FACILITIES
THAT BRING
ENTERTAINMENT TO
CUSTOMERS AND
PRACTICAL, VALUABLE
BENEFITS TO LOCAL
COMMUNITIES

The only gaming facility on the St. Louis riverfront, President Casinos, Inc.'s President Casino by the Arch has the perfect ambience for timeless fun and endless hours of entertainment.

The 1907 riverboat that houses the casino has been known since 1940 as the SS *Admiral*. From ferryboat to excursion steamer to dockside entertainment center, today the *Admiral* is a spectacular riverboat casino with soaring atria and glamorous crystal chandeliers. Breathtaking in design, the President Casino by the Arch is more spacious than many land-based casinos. Its extensive gaming facilities include a wide variety of slot and video poker machines. It has a full range of table games and one of the largest poker rooms in the Midwest.

The casino has something for virtually everyone. Guests enjoy the President's Buffet for lunch or dinner and the Champagne Brunch on Sunday. The Four Aces Food Court offers casual dining.

The extensive gaming facilities at the President Casino by the Arch include a great variety of slot and video poker machines.

Docked at the St. Louis Riverfront, the historic SS Admiral *riverboat, which houses the President Casino by the Arch, holds the distinction of being the first riverboat casino in Missouri. It began operations on 27 May 1994.*

The *Admiral* is docked on the Mississippi River at Laclede's Landing, the historic district along the riverfront, next to dining and shopping areas and a few short blocks from the St. Louis TWA Dome and Convention Center. This area continues to be developed as an integrated St. Louis entertainment attraction.

President Casinos has two other gaming facilities, one a riverboat casino, located in Davenport, Iowa, and the other a dockside casino, in Biloxi, Mississippi. The President Casino & Blackhawk Hotel in Davenport, Iowa, is a 35,000-square-foot casino vessel. Formerly a sidewheel riverboat named *The Cincinnati*, the largest overnight passenger steamboat on the Mississippi, this authentic riverboat, now named *The President Casino*, has been certified by the United States Department of the Interior as a national landmark. It features outstanding gambling, restaurants, and accommodations.

The President Casino Broadwater Resort in Biloxi, Mississippi, offers everything from golfing to gaming to world-renowned entertainment. The Broadwater, with more than 500 hotel rooms, overlooks sandy beaches, and has 50,000 square feet of flexible meeting space, three swimming pools in lush tropical settings, a PGA-staffed championship golf course, tennis courts, and one of the South's best covered marinas with charter boat fishing.

John E. Connelly, chairman of the board and chief executive officer of President Casinos, is a pioneer in the gaming business. He is credited with launching the first riverboat casino in 1991, leading the way for today's entire riverboat gaming industry. With a rich history of successful ventures over the years, Mr. Connelly provides the foresight and insight to help President Casinos navigate future opportunities.

"The industry will continue to grow and prosper as riverboat and dockside casino facilities strive to offer their customers more than just gaming," Connelly says. "In other words, a bigger party. It is the philosophy of President Casinos that the real winner in any casino gaming facility that is well conceived, designed, and operated must be the consumer."

Customer service is of paramount importance at President Casinos. Great emphasis is placed on team development and internal training for the staff. All casino personnel approach their jobs not as dealers, cashiers, or waitstaff but as entertainers.

The energy that propels President Casinos also is brought to the community. The company is known for maintaining strong, steady relationships with local businesses and residents. President Casinos offers communities practical, valuable benefits in everything from taxes to tourism. In the states where dockside or riverboat gaming has been approved, more than 75,000 new full-time jobs have been created. Gaming also is an especially powerful and effective way to generate state and local revenues. This eases the tax burden of local businesses and residents, which helps make the region more attractive.

Casino gambling is now one of the most popular forms of entertainment in the nation. In the United States gaming helps attract more than 100 million visitors annually, drawing additional

The President Casino by the Arch offers the President's Buffet for lunch and dinner, and on Sunday there is a Champagne Brunch. Casual dining is available in the Four Aces Food Court.

spending directly into each area where it is offered. Strategic casino development also serves as a catalyst for other related ventures, helping to revitalize downtown urban areas, improve municipal services, and upgrade the infrastructure of the region.

President Casinos has a history of becoming involved in both financial and public support of worthwhile civic and charitable organizations. It has an outstanding record of achievement in providing upward mobility to diverse members of the community. It even helps to energize and develop surrounding public areas, making them more attractive and vital.

"We know this industry," says Connelly. "We understand its history and we are paving the way for its future. Through the years we have earned a reputation for integrity and professionalism and have developed positive, rewarding relationships with the communities in which we have gaming developments."

This group of slot machines characterizes the spectacular design and lighting found in the spacious President Casino by the Arch.

WORLDS OF FUN

Well into their third decade of generating fun for people of all ages, Worlds of Fun and Oceans of Fun make up one of the most popular tourist attractions in the Kansas City, Missouri, area.

Worlds of Fun, an amusement park with international themes, offers a wide variety of rides, shows, and attractions. With five continental-themed areas—Americana, Europa, Africa, Scandinavia, and the Orient—Worlds of Fun covers 175 acres. The park is located on the east loop of route I-435 at exit 54 in Kansas City, Missouri. Right next to Worlds of Fun is the Midwest's largest tropically themed water park, Oceans of Fun, offering more than 60 acres of water-related attractions. These include a million-gallon wave pool; eight water slides; a lazy floating river; special areas for children; sand volleyball courts; a pool for adults only with a swim-up cabana where tropical refreshments are served; and, new in 1999, Hurricane Falls, a high-action superslide the whole family can ride.

Worlds of Fun offers a wide variety of entertainment options. Its rides, shows, and attractions include the gravity-defying Detonator for thrill seekers, Berenstain Bear Country for kids, and a Summer Spectacular Laser Show for everyone.

In 1998 Worlds of Fun debuted its new state-of-the-art steel roller coaster, MAMBA, named for one of the most feared snakes in Africa. One of the tallest, longest, and fastest roller coasters in the world, its first hill takes riders more than 200 feet above the ground and shoots them toward the earth at up to seventy-five miles per hour while pulling 3.5 g's. This is followed by a second hill of 184 feet, plus five camelback bumps and a 580-degree spiral.

Oceans of Fun's Surf City Wave Pool in Kansas City, Missouri, offers a million gallons of water for surfing and swimming. © Cedar Fair, L.P.

"MAMBA is the biggest expansion in Worlds of Fun's history and places the park in an elite class of 'must-visit' roller coaster parks," says Daniel R. Keller, vice president and general manager, Worlds of Fun and Oceans of Fun.

Worlds of Fun is owned and operated by Cedar Fair, L.P., which also owns and operates Cedar Point in Sandusky, Ohio; Valleyfair! in Shakopee, Minnesota; Dorney Park and Wildwater Kingdom in Allentown, Pennsylvania; and Knott's Berry Farm in Buena Park, California. Cedar Fair also manages Knott's Camp Snoopy at the Mall of America in Bloomington, Minnesota.

"With thrilling rides, entertaining shows, and outstanding attractions for the whole family, Worlds of Fun and Oceans of Fun have more fun per square inch than just about anywhere on the planet," Keller says.

At left, Worlds of Fun's mile-long MAMBA, with a 205-foot drop, reaches seventy-five miles per hour, pulling 3.5 g's. At right, the Berenstain Bears add to the excitement at Worlds of Fun. Both photos © Cedar Fair, L.P.

MISSOURI SOUTHERN INTERNATIONAL PIANO COMPETITION

THE MISSOURI SOUTHERN INTERNATIONAL PIANO COMPETITION IS KNOWN FOR ITS WORLD-CLASS STANDARDS AND PERFORMANCES

Every two years, thirty-five outstanding pianists from around the world are selected to participate in the Missouri Southern International Piano Competition at Missouri Southern State College in Joplin. The invited artists compete in the Junior and Senior age-level categories for cash prizes of up to $30,000. In addition, the winner of the Senior competition is awarded a Carnegie Recital Hall debut in New York City.

The competitors dazzle the audience with virtuoso performances, maintaining a standard that is applauded as one that is as high as any of the major international piano competitions in the world.

"I can't think of any competition that is more well-organized or fair in its execution," comments one of the judges. Embraced by the community, the event proceedings

Kriszta Kovács of Hungary, Grand Prize winner of the 1998 Competition, performs before a packed house at the Gala Winners' Concert on the culminating evening of the event. The community opens its homes and hearts to pianists from around the world for the prestigious biennial competition.

are suffused with a warm hospitality that has become a trademark of the competition.

The Missouri Southern International Piano Competition is the only international music competition in the state of Missouri. It has succeeded in acquiring an outstanding reputation on a national and international level. Many musicians consider it to be one of the most outstanding music competitions in the world.

KANSAS CITY ART INSTITUTE

FOUNDED IN 1885, THE NATIONALLY RENOWNED KANSAS CITY ART INSTITUTE PROVIDES A DYNAMIC AND EDUCATIONAL CONTEMPORARY ART EXPERIENCE

One of the oldest and premier colleges of art and design in the nation, Kansas City Art Institute (KCAI) draws some of the most talented students from all over the United States and several foreign countries to its picturesque twelve-acre campus in Kansas City. Situated in the cultural corridor of the city, the fully accredited four-year college offers its 600 students a dynamic art environment.

KCAI awards the bachelor of fine arts degree in art history, ceramics, design and illustration, fiber, painting and printmaking, photography and new media, sculpture, and studio art (creative writing). Intensive classroom time, extensive studio experience, and the benefits of an exceptional faculty combine to provide an ideal milieu for the development of intellect and imagination.

Illustrating its role as an art education leader, KCAI is opening a contemporary art gallery in fall 1999. Officially the H&R Block Artspace at the Kansas City Art Institute, the gallery will organize

Kansas City Art Institute professor Warren Rosser (left), chair of the Painting and Printmaking department, and professor Lester Goldman (right) critique a student's work in her KCAI studio space.

and host temporary exhibitions with a special focus on contemporary art. Through innovative partnerships, local arts-education initiatives, and public programs, the Artspace will serve as "a vital resource for the college, the Greater Kansas City community, and the regional and national arts community," says Kathleen Collins, KCAI president.

Union Station in St. Louis is a shopper's paradise. © Travelpix/FPG International LLC

RETAIL AND WHOLESALE

HELZBERG DIAMONDS

It was 1915 when Helzberg Diamonds began building a business in the heart of America. Since then, the company has focused on providing exceptional jewelry and personalized customer service, to help each and every customer select a true gift from the heart.

Still headquartered in Kansas City, Missouri, Helzberg Diamonds has grown into a national jeweler with sales performance per store averaging more than double that of the industry. The company operates more than 200 stores in twenty-eight states and plans for continued expansion.

Helzberg Diamonds has a reputation for providing style, convenience, and service in power strip centers (example, above) and regional shopping malls (at left) across the nation.

Helzberg Diamonds has two highly successful store formats: that of a jeweler in a traditional mall, with a reputation for quality, style, convenience, and service; and that of a freestanding jewelry store in a power strip center, combining outstanding selection with additional services such as a jeweler on-site and convenient parking just outside the front door.

The company was founded and built by three generations of the Helzberg family, each a leader in the industry and the Kansas City community. This midwestern success story caught the attention of Warren Buffett, and in 1995 the firm was acquired by his holding company, Berkshire Hathaway.

The original 1915 Helzberg Diamonds store was opened by Morris Helzberg at 529 Minnesota Avenue in Kansas City, Kansas. The shop was a small force in its day, but it was established with high

Diamonds and diamond jewelry fashion have always been the merchandising position focal point of Helzberg Diamonds.

principles that would predicate phenomenal growth. After just a few short years in business, Morris Helzberg suffered a stroke and his young son Barnett took over the operation. Barnett Helzberg was determined to build the business and sell diamonds and jewelry in stores across the Midwest. It wasn't long before his dreams began to come true.

By 1929 Barnett had added stores in Topeka and Wichita, Kansas, and downtown Kansas City, Missouri. Helzberg Diamonds was seen as a highly respected business that gave time and money back to the community. The entrepreneur in Barnett was so confident, he denied the miserable economy of the Great Depression. The *Kansas City Star* reported, "When he doubled the size of the store at Eleventh and Walnut in 1932, Barnett Helzberg became a symbol of courage to Kansas City."

Always on the leading edge and concerned about the comfort of customers, Helzberg was one of the first store owners to give customers the luxury of air-conditioned shopping—"cooled by refrigeration," as it was called then. As World War II came to an end, Barnett expanded the Kansas City operation from the single, original store to locations in the growing suburbs, providing jobs for some of the returning servicemen. By 1947 the Helzberg organization operated eight stores in Missouri, Kansas, and Iowa and was billed as the Middle West's largest jeweler. In 1950 Helzberg Diamonds showcased the legendary Hope Diamond at its elegant Country Club Plaza store in Kansas City. All proceeds were donated to the campaign to fight polio.

Barnett Helzberg Jr. became the third-generation leader of the family firm in 1963, taking command of thirty-nine stores. He created a name for himself with his leadership and management abilities, but it was a modest promotional idea of his that made a national name for Helzberg Diamonds.

In 1967 Barnett proposed marriage to a young lady, and, in his euphoria, he developed a small, red lapel button with the words "I AM LOVED®" as a store promotion. He knew firsthand that love was a great feeling. The lapel button was intended to be a two-week marketing campaign, but it evolved into a timeless goodwill gesture delivered across the globe. Since 1967 Helzberg Diamonds has given away millions of such buttons, created in five different languages.

It was in the late 1960s when Helzberg Diamonds opened its first store in a shopping mall, a move that laid the groundwork for today's company structure. Success was immediate, and Barnett decided the best path for the company would be long-term leases in regional shopping malls. An aggressive expansion plan began, with an average of three new stores opening per year.

By 1980 Helzberg adopted a merchandise position that focused on diamonds. Fine quality always had been a requisite for his jewelry designs, and now fashionable style was made an equally important element. By the mid-1980s Helzberg had become one of the most productive jewelers in the country, and rapid growth continued. In 1988 Barnett brought retail leader Jeffrey W. Comment in as president of the family firm. Seven years later, the acquisition of the company by Berkshire Hathaway positioned Helzberg Diamonds for continued growth and strength in the twenty-first century.

As has been the case throughout its history, Helzberg excels at keeping clients happy by offering an exceptional array of fashionable fine jewelry and emphasizing excellent personal service. The company's basic philosophies, backed by its long-standing

Above, a nostalgic photograph of the smiling Helzberg boys (Barnett Jr. and one of his brothers) outside the Country Club Plaza store in Kansas City, Missouri, in the early 1940s.

An advertisement in 1967 announced Helzberg's I AM LOVED® campaign. The slogan survives today as an integral part of the company's corporate identity.

heritage and impeccable reputation, center on ethics, integrity, and courtesy.

"Our mission statement is to serve each and every customer in a very special way, and we really take that to heart. If you're going to work with us, you'll build relationships with the customers; that's a given," says CEO Jeffrey Comment. "We have a reputation of being one of the most service-oriented establishments in the retail industry. When you're selling a product like ours, it's very important that the people who come in have a good experience."

While the company's ongoing mission statement draws its strength from a heritage of service, Helzberg Diamonds' vision statement charts the future for the Kansas City company. Helzberg Diamonds wants to be known for fine jewelry gifts that express the heartfelt emotion of the giver.

As with the "I AM LOVED" promotion, a recent advertising theme, "If it comes from the heart, shouldn't it come from Helzberg Diamonds?" has moved beyond marketing and become part of the company's culture, illustrating Helzberg's commitment to making each customer interaction meaningful. Helzberg Diamonds is in the business of helping people express their love—and it seeks daily to prove that if a gift comes from the heart, it should come from Helzberg Diamonds.

TOWARD THE NEW MILLENNIUM

PART FOUR: ESSAYS

Missouri's top leaders, visionaries in both the public and private sectors, are well positioned to reflect upon the expanding parameters of our world. While looking back at remarkable moments in their sectors' history, representatives from agribusiness, banking, health insurance, education, the media, telecommunications, tourism, and transportation also offer us a glimpse of the future. Of the myriad new challenges coming our way, the greatest, they say, will be embracing nonstop change—the only constant we can count on. The technological leap forward "prepares us for a crossroads with far-reaching implications," says one essayist; in fact, the pace of change may outstrip our ability to imagine all the consequences. Still, the powerful tools at our disposal can create a dimension of life for which even our dreams cannot prepare us. Another essayist reminds us that General Douglas MacArthur once said, "There is no security in life, only opportunity." Thanks to new ways of communicating, businesses throughout the state soon will be defined not just regionally but globally. What kind of leaders can we expect for this new day? Those who think outside the box and have developed that most human of qualities, trustworthiness. "Character counts," says one essayist. So do "hard work, creativity, financial acumen, and a finger on the pulse of the world marketplace," says another. The new millennium actually began yesterday, in terms of preparation—and Missouri is there, our essayists agree, ready to play a major role in the economic, cultural, and social dynamics of the twenty-first century.

Spanning solid ground while reaching for the sky, Kansas City's H. R. Bartle Exposition Hall and its futuristic pylons might be analogous to civilization on the brink of the new millennium, embracing past achievements as a foundation from which to launch new ideas. © Bruce Mathews/Midwestock

FROM MULE TECH TO BIOTECH

H. D. CLEBERG
President and Chief Executive Officer, Farmland Industries, Inc.

H. D. Cleberg is president and chief executive officer of Farmland Industries, Inc., the nation's largest regional agribusiness cooperative. In his position with the farmer-owned system, Cleberg oversees Farmland Industries' highly diversified crop products, livestock feeds, and petroleum business lines and the processing and marketing of pork and beef products and grain. Cleberg, who has worked for Farmland in various capacities since 1968, serves on the boards and committees of a number of Kansas City organizations, including the Greater Kansas City Chamber of Commerce, American Royal Association, Commerce Bank, St. Luke's Northland Hospital, and St. Luke's Hospital of Kansas City.

Outsiders might view Missouri agriculture through the same lens as they do the mule, the state's paradoxically unique but relatively commonplace "mascot." But make no mistake—the Show Me State is no slouch. It ranks second in the nation in both cattle and hay production. It's also the home of leading agricultural families such as Kemper, Busch, Cowden (Farmland's founding family), Danforth, and Litton. Among the Missouri businesses that have accumulated vast renown are Stark Brothers' Nurseries and Orchards in Louisiana, Missouri, the largest family-owned fruit tree nursery in the world; Ralston-Purina, the world's largest producer of dry dog food and dry and soft-moist cat foods; Anheuser-Busch, the world's largest beer maker; and Monsanto, a life sciences company famous for applying advanced bioscience and biotechnology to agriculture, nutrition, and health.

TO FEED HUNGRY MOUTHS AROUND THE GLOBE, U.S. AGRICULTURE MUST DOUBLE ITS PRODUCTION EVERY 20 YEARS

Beyond these singular achievements, Missouri excels in the diversity and scope of its agricultural products. Today agribusiness generates more than $17 billion for Missouri's economy. From woods and hills to flatlands and river bottoms, the state's varied topography produces a wide range of grains, fruits, and vegetables, including soybeans, corn, wheat sorghum, cotton, and rice. Missouri also raises a variety of livestock, including cattle, hogs, chickens, and turkeys, as well as specialty animals such as emus, horses, and ostriches.

PROGRESS ON ALL FRONTS

Perhaps the most important change for Missouri agriculture in the twentieth century has been the shift from mules to machines. Speedier than an ox and hardier than a horse, the mule built many of the state's first roads and bridges and tilled much of the region's soils.

The mule's dominance was challenged with the move to mechanized farming, a feat made possible through the invention of the combustion engine. However, because most farmers were still careening from a series of severe depressions, droughts, and

Agribusiness generates more than $17 billion for Missouri's economy. The state's wide range of crops includes soybeans, shown here during harvest . © James Blank

other crop disasters stretching from the late nineteenth century to the early twentieth, the machine's rise on the farm was fairly slow. Even in 1940 fewer than 20 percent of Missouri farmers owned a tractor.

The tractor advanced nevertheless, becoming a necessary implement to more than 43 percent of Missouri farms by 1950. Mechanical corn and cotton pickers also appeared, enabling more farmers across the state to work faster—picking as many as ten times more bushels than they could by hand—with fewer people.

As important as mechanization was, Missouri farmers' quality of life did not revolve solely around their individual productivity. Agricultural organizations, introduced between 1910 and 1920, were pivotal for giving farmers a louder voice in Washington as well as in the marketplace. The Missouri Farm Bureau Federation, for example, lobbied for farm-favorable legislation and encouraged farmers to organize to leverage their buying and selling power. By 1923 the bureau had helped develop several large consumer and marketing cooperatives for livestock and wheat in East St. Louis and Kansas City.

The Missouri Farmers Association (MFA) was also influential in the cooperative movement. Not only was the MFA instrumental in securing a national alliance to establish stronger representation in government, but it also assisted in the creation of hundreds of co-ops with operations spanning the industry, from packing plants and local livestock shipping associations to grain elevators and producer exchanges.

CHALLENGES AND SOLUTIONS

Today agribusinesses with a presence in Missouri, like Farmland, have a new set of challenges to address. The most pressing is an expanding world population, which is expected to reach 12 billion in twenty-five years. To feed hungry mouths around the globe, U.S. agriculture must double its production every twenty years.

Biotechnology, through the manipulation of plant genes, is emerging as an important means of increasing

Farmers check the progress of piglets in their farrowing pens. In the future, select animals may be sent abroad in an effort to cultivate and strengthen global markets. © Ben Weddle/Midwestock

crop yields and creating specialized grains with particular qualities. Precision farming, which uses satellite technology to maximize production through efficient and precise chemical and fertilizer applications, also appears to be a promising tool for feeding the world.

To make the most of these technologies, agricultural leaders of the future must be prepared to grow and strengthen global markets. They must begin to see the grain and meat that farmers produce not only as everyday necessities but also as incremental ways to improve the quality of health and life of consumers throughout the world.

For Missouri farmers to rise to these challenges, agribusiness leaders must inject more vitality into the state's agriculture. In recent years, Missouri has lost several globally recognized agricultural firms to out-of-state buyers.

My hope is that agribusinesses will not permit this trend to continue. It is up to Farmland and progressive firms like it to prevent Missouri's agricultural leadership from fading, like the mule, into an amusing novelty.

BIOTECHNOLOGY IS EMERGING AS AN IMPORTANT MEANS OF INCREASING CROP YIELDS AND CREATING SPECIALIZED GRAINS WITH PARTICULAR QUALITIES

OPPORTUNITY INHERENT IN CHANGE

ROBERT M. ROBUCK
President, Central Bank

Bob Robuck joined Central Bank in 1968 after working in Kansas City as a certified public accountant with Peat, Marwick & Mitchell (now KPMG). He was elected president of the bank in January 1997 after seventeen years as its executive vice president and eight years as president of the parent holding company, Central Bancompany. Robuck was born and educated in Cairo, Missouri, and received an accounting degree from the Business School of the University of Missouri in Columbia. He fulfills leadership roles in the Jefferson City Chamber of Commerce, United Way, Capitol Region Medical Center, Family Mental Health Center, the Boy Scouts of America, the Council for Drug-Free Youth, and the YMCA.

In the last century we have seen remarkable changes take place, not just in banking but in the way we all do business. Changes are happening more often, more rapidly, and more unpredictably than ever before.

- It took thousands of years to move from the agricultural to the industrial age.
- The industrial age began about 1815 and officially ended only in the last few years.
- We have moved into the information age: from physical power to mind power.

Wealth no longer comprises land, labor, capital, factories, fixtures, and raw materials. A factory can be rendered obsolete overnight with a technological change. Information is doubling every twelve to eighteen months. What is our most valuable asset for cash flow? Our ability to earn by applying learning to our business. General Douglas MacArthur once said, "There is no security in life, only opportunity."

There are a variety of shifts we are experiencing and will continue to experience. The first shift is from one-time learning to lifelong learning. The second shift is realizing that our earning ability, rather than our tangible assets, is the most important resource we have. The third shift is from lifelong employment to lifelong employability. Fourth, reengineering is being forced on companies by the competitive, global marketplace. And the paradigm shift is that our earnings will be in direct proportion to the value of our services.

With the fast-paced, changing environment, we have no time to rest on past or present accomplishments. Financial institutions are changing hands . . . then changing

> **THE PARADIGM SHIFT IS THAT OUR EARNINGS WILL BE IN DIRECT PROPORTION TO THE VALUE OF OUR SERVICES**

Drive-through access to an ATM makes this bank customer's day a little easier. Today convenience is a driving force in choosing with whom to do business.
© Chronis Jons/Tony Stone Images

hands again. As businesses, we will see this as either a threat or an opportunity.

ECONOMIC AND GLOBAL ISSUES

The economic issues facing central Missouri are those facing the nation. The tight labor market is causing costs to rise. Despite the concerns that the Federal Reserve might be forced to raise interest rates to ward off inflation, expectations are that the rates will hold because of the volatility in the Asian financial markets. Growth will continue despite these key economic issues.

There are some indications that events in Asia could be beneficial to the U.S. economy and financial markets. Reduced Asian exports and increased imports on our part will slow the U.S. growth rate just as the economy is pushing the available supply of labor and plant capacity. Less expensive imports will also keep U.S. prices in check. For us, that means a neutral monetary policy from the Federal Reserve, allowing our interest rates to stabilize or even decline.

HIGH TECH—HIGH TOUCH

The greatest competitive challenge we all face today is adjusting to—perhaps embracing—nonstop change. With this new technological revolution, people are meeting themselves coming and going.

Today time is a limited resource; convenience has become the driving force behind how people choose with whom they will do business. Banking customers want to have access to their funds and be able to get a loan where and when *they* want to. The continued growth of two-income families compounds the added

THE GREATEST COMPETITIVE CHALLENGE WE ALL FACE TODAY IS ADJUSTING TO—PERHAPS EMBRACING—NONSTOP CHANGE

pressure to balance home, family, work, and leisure. Brick-and-mortar facilities are giving way to personal computers, the Internet, telephones, and electronics. Because of the changing economic and social environment, business must be committed to making the customer's day easier.

For financial institutions, this all adds up to being a one-stop financial center. Whether the need is for traditional products such as checking and savings accounts, credit cards, and loans or for financial investment alternatives such as brokerage, mutual funds, trust and financial services, insurance, or travel, we must be the ones who make it happen. This need for convenience must, for the same reasons, embrace services for businesses and organizations—services such as employee retirement plans, lock boxes, small business loans, and cash management products.

What do I see in the future? As the use of the Internet, the telephone, and electronic services expands, there must be a commitment to making business services more convenient and easier to use. We need to provide customers with access to their funds wherever they live, work, and play. Our success will be tied to the success of our community. And our community will no longer be defined just regionally but also globally.

Part of a growing trend, this two-income couple consults a counselor who can handle all their financial needs at once. © Arthur Tilley/FPG International LLC

MISSOURI MEDIA AT THE MILLENNIUM

DAVID LIPMAN
Consultant to the Pulitzer Publishing Company

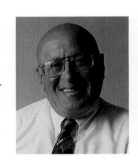

David Lipman capped a thirty-seven-year career with the Pulitzer Publishing Company by being named a consultant to the company on January 1, 1997. He had previously served as chairman of Pulitzer/2000, the new media strategic planning and development arm of the multimedia company, for five years and as managing editor of the *St. Louis Post-Dispatch* for almost fourteen years. He chaired the University of Missouri's 1993 Advisory Committee on the 21st Century, which produced the university's strategic plan for the new millennium. Among many other responsibilities, he was cochair of the 1995 Missouri Commission on Information Technology, whose report laid the groundwork for the current state telecommunication law.

The information revolution is sweeping across the globe, visibly touching government, business, industry, agriculture, science, the media—in fact, all disciplines.

The ability to communicate instantly *around the world,* to distribute massive amounts of information worldwide, demands bold new approaches of not just the media of Missouri but the media worldwide.

The newspaper industry, once virtually alone as the town crier, has moved since 1900 from handset type not hugely different from Gutenberg's to hardcopy scanners, cold type, pagination, and wall-to-wall computer technology.

The dramatic development of radio, television, and cable has shaken the world and reshaped society.

> **COMMUNICATING INSTANTLY AROUND THE WORLD DEMANDS BOLD NEW APPROACHES OF MEDIA WORLDWIDE**

ON THE INFORMATION SUPERHIGHWAY

As the twenty-first century approaches, we are being engulfed by a burgeoning cyberworld of facsimile transmissions, audiotex, cellular telephones, the Internet, and digital interactive technology.

With the magic of wired and wireless, laptops and satellites, we are in touch wherever we are, whenever we desire. *The information superhighway* has become part of our everyday vocabulary.

Some facts:

• The Internet's pace of adoption eclipses that of all other technologies that preceded it. Radio was in existence thirty-eight years before 50 million persons tuned in; TV took thirteen years to reach that benchmark. Once it was opened to the general public, the Internet crossed that line in just four years.

• In 1994 about 3 million people were connected to the Internet. By the end of 1997, more than 100 million were connected.

• Traffic on the Internet doubles every 100 days.

• Business and industry are aggressively investing to build out the Internet. Within the next five years, the vast majority of Americans should be able to interact with the Internet from their television sets

An editor at a Missouri newspaper lays out a page on his desktop computer. A number of the state's dailies and weeklies are among the pacesetters in Internet publishing as well as desktop. © Telegraph Colour Library/FPG International LLC

or watch television on their personal computers—and make telephone calls from both devices.

"Technology is reshaping this economy and transforming businesses and consumers," U.S. Secretary of Commerce William M. Daley said in a speech in early 1998. "In the last five years, information technologies have been responsible for more than one-quarter of real United States growth. . . . There are 7.4 million people working in this field alone. They earn close to $46,000 each annually—64 percent more than the private sector average. And even with the big paychecks, there are more jobs than people with the skills to fill them."

Weaned on Nintendo and Sega in the 1980s, kids are moving up to personal computers and the Internet in staggering numbers. The positive experience of these kids with computers heralds deep changes in society and presents tremendous challenges for the commercial, public, and academic sectors in every state.

Missouri is ready to meet that challenge.

AHEAD OF THE GAME

The offices of the governor, secretary of state, department of economic development, and others have joined in triggering statewide initiatives. And they are not latecomers to the challenge. In the mid-1990s, for example, the governor appointed a commission on information technology to plot Missouri's route into the new millennium.

In the private sector, Missouri always has been a media leader. My own company, the Pulitzer Publishing Company, has been an innovator in both print and broadcast journalism. Its *St. Louis Post-Dispatch,* the first newspaper in America to engage in investigative journalism, was also among the first to offer color graphics; the first major metropolitan paper to use offset printing; and one of the first

KIDS' EXPERIENCE WITH COMPUTERS HERALDS DEEP CHANGES IN SOCIETY AND CHALLENGES FOR THE COMMERCIAL, PUBLIC, AND ACADEMIC SECTORS

to paginate the entire paper. In broadcast journalism, Pulitzer was one of the first companies west of the Mississippi River to offer commercial radio and to build a post–World War II television station.

The *Kansas City Star* has marked similar high points in its long and legendary existence. Kansas City and St. Louis have been joined in the electronic journalism revolution by papers from Springfield to St. Joseph to Columbia to Cape Girardeau. A large percentage of the daily and weekly newspapers affiliated with the Missouri Press Association (MPA) is among the pacesetters in moving effectively into the cyber age and Internet "publishing."

In academia, the University of Missouri–Columbia School of Journalism, the world's top-rated school of journalism, occupies an equally lofty position in the media's digital revolution. The *Digital Missourian* is one of this country's foremost on-line electronic newspapers—in the private sector as well as the academic world.

That new millennium of tomorrow actually began yesterday. Missouri was there then. It is taking big steps toward being there in the years to come. Anything else would be unacceptable if the state is to be a major player in the economic, cultural, and social world of the twenty-first century.

A sound mixer in the control room of a recording studio does his best to ensure that perfectly balanced tones reach the audience. From broadcast journalism to opinion pieces and music, radio is part of the information revolution that has reshaped society. © Lonnie Duka/Tony Stone Images

COORDINATED HEALTH CARE 2000

JOHN A. O'ROURKE
*Chairman, President, and Chief Executive Officer,
RightCHOICE Managed Care, Inc.*

John O'Rourke came to RightCHOICE in 1997 with a multifaceted background in health care, including provider, government, and managed care positions. Before coming to St. Louis in 1985 to head HealthLink, Inc., he was director of the Department of Economic Research for the American Medical Association and deputy director of the Office of Health Maintenance Organizations of the U.S. Department of Health and Human Services. He serves on the board of directors of the Blue Cross and Blue Shield Association and is president of the St. Louis Managed Care Group and past president of the Missouri Managed Care Association.

Health insurance got its start in 1929 when the first predecessor of the Blue Cross and Blue Shield system began offering prepaid hospital benefits. People paid fifty cents a month and could receive up to twenty-one days of inpatient care at Baylor University Hospital in Dallas. Coverage was soon expanded to include medical-surgical benefits, and for the next fifty years the health insurance industry settled down to the business of processing claims and paying bills.

Then came the cost explosion of the 1980s. Health care costs, and consequently health insurance costs, soared, making the market cry for relief. Insurers responded with preferred provider organizations (PPOs), health maintenance organizations (HMOs), point of service (POS) programs, disease and demand management—all the options designed to bring cost-sensitive accountability to health care delivery decisions.

That's health insurance today.

THE HUMANISTIC ASPECT OF HELPING PEOPLE AVOID THE PAIN AND SUFFERING OF LUNG CANCER IS IMMEASURABLE

TRACKING TREATMENT OUTCOMES

The challenge for the industry tomorrow is to organize a cooperative effort that helps members, providers, and payers make rational health care choices, grounded in fact and centered on bringing about the best possible outcome for the patient. These choices have to be predicated on the knowledge that treatment A works better than treatment B, that drug C works better for a certain medical condition than surgery D.

Health statistics tell us, for example, that a woman with breast cancer is more likely to have a mastectomy if she lives in the South than if she lives in some other part of the country. They don't yet tell us whether women in the South who undergo mastectomy live longer and have a better quality of life than women who undergo less radical treatment in the Midwest or the Northeast.

Solid, broad-based data can provide these kinds of answers. We must know, as best we can,

Trained to perceive subtle differences in patients and make appropriate treatment decisions, a physician confers by phone from the X-ray room. © Eric Myer/FPG International LLC

the relationships between medical interventions and health outcomes. Such knowledge can only come from a systematic, thorough tracking and measurement of the effects of care. It requires evaluating the impact of specific treatments and then sharing that information with health care providers, patients, and payers.

This kind of database is the logical next step for managed care, and it is crucial to the health care industry's move into the next century. It isn't meant to bring about a "cookbook" type of medicine that would require physicians to deliver care based on a standard set of guidelines. Because medicine is both a science and an art, the database would become a resource providers could use to improve their patients' results.

NO HEALTH CARE SYSTEM HAS VALUE UNLESS IT OFFERS ACCESS TO EFFECTIVE CARE, AND NO SYSTEM HAS VALUE IF IT BECOMES UNAFFORDABLE

Physicians are best attuned to the subtle differences among patients that need be taken into account in making treatment decisions. However, health care decision making must be a shared process. The patient, provider, and payer need to be involved, and it is requisite that each have the tools necessary to know what health care option works best. Together they can make a decision, with the welfare of the patient always the final determinant of care.

BENEFITS OF PREVENTIVE CARE

It is also essential that health insurers take a leadership role as advocates of preventive care and early intervention. In today's health care system, it is far less costly to support antismoking programs than to pay for the treatment of lung cancer. But the gains go far beyond the financial aspects of care. There is no way to measure the humanistic aspect of helping people avoid the pain and suffering of lung cancer. Similarly, supporting members through "healthy heart" education programs is of far greater value than covering even the newest heart surgery advances.

Health insurers need to convey these messages to their members and encourage the physicians who treat them to reinforce them as well.

The last century has taught us that there are seemingly no limits to the possibilities of medical technology. Once-dreaded diseases such as polio and smallpox have all but disappeared. Magnetic resonance imaging (MRI), laser surgery, and organ transplants—once the stuff of science fiction—are now commonplace. But the last *decade* has taught us a lesson as well: no health care system has value unless it offers access to effective care. Similarly, no system has value if it becomes so expensive that people cannot afford it. Unless we control the costs of our burgeoning health care system, we may be denied the miracles of this marvelous medical technology.

There is only one constant in today's health care industry: change. But no matter how persistent the change or what new tools and mechanisms the industry adopts, our dominant concern must remain the same as it was in 1929: helping people have coordinated access to effective health care programs.

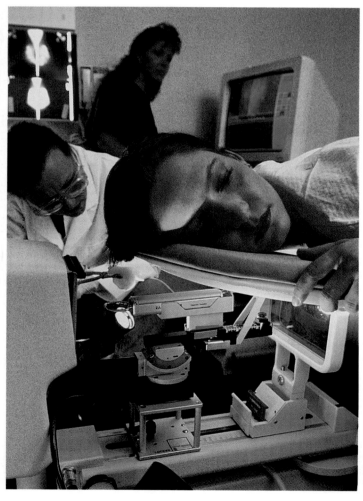

In this stereotactic biopsy, a series of images has located the lump in the patient's breast. A radiologist enters the data into a computer, which positions the needle. © Charles Thatcher/Tony Stone Images

DELIVERING WORKFORCE READINESS

DR. KALA M. STROUP
Missouri Commissioner of Higher Education

Dr. Kala Stroup was appointed commissioner of higher education in September 1995; the next year she implemented a new strategic plan for Missouri higher education. Prior to her appointment, she had been president of Southeast Missouri State University and, earlier, Murray State University in Kentucky. Dr. Stroup has authored books, articles, and numerous published addresses; she has been recognized in *Who's Who in America* and selected for both the University of Kansas Women's Hall of Fame and the Ohio Valley Conference Hall of Fame. Dr. Stroup served as chair of the National Small Business Development Centers Advisory Board of the National Postsecondary Education Cooperative Group on Workforce Development Policies.

Missouri's economy and the world of work are significantly different than they were just ten years ago. The rate of change has exploded. Owing to technology, information doubles every twelve to eighteen months, affecting work security, productivity, technical skills, and global competition. If that trajectory continues, by the year 2020 information will double every seventy-three days.

We have learned in Missouri that tomorrow's economy and quality of life are inextricably linked to the educational level of our citizens.

> **TOMORROW'S ECONOMY AND QUALITY OF LIFE ARE INEXTRICABLY LINKED TO OUR CITIZENS' EDUCATIONAL LEVEL**

The information explosion means that individuals in the workforce need to adapt even more rapidly than in the past, making continuous education essential. Unless our citizens are highly capable, we will be unable to attract new industry to Missouri, much less keep what we have. In plain words, our future depends on the number of qualified people Missouri's educational system can provide business and industry and the means by which this workforce can keep learning while employed.

LAUNCHING A PLAN

In the early 1990s, numerous studies in Missouri examined issues relating to the state's economy and the role higher education plays in strengthening the state's economic competitiveness. The studies were undertaken by a number of different groups comprising representatives of business and industry, state legislators and government officials, and school, college, and university officials and governing board members.

The overarching theme of these reports was the need to evaluate the barriers and constraints, both geographic and programmatic, that prevented students from acquiring the skills necessary to achieve career development, employability, and advanced technical skill sets for the twenty-first century.

A department head receives customized computer training as part of Missouri's plan to provide workers with the skills needed for the new millennium. © Telegraph Colour Library/FPG International LLC

In 1991 the Missouri Business and Education Partnership Commission recommended that the state's system of postsecondary vocational technical education be strengthened. The Coordinating Board for Higher Education responded by establishing a citizen-based task force to develop a cost-effective, high-quality, accessible system of higher education for Missouri. Part of that vision was the development of a more comprehensive technical education system that would provide the workforce with the highly developed skills needed to fuel Missouri's economic engine on an ongoing basis.

Missouri's general assembly joined with the coordinating board in identifying the need to strengthen the state's delivery system of postsecondary vocational technical education through its passage of Senate Bill 101 in 1995. In that legislation, the coordinating board was directed to complete, in cooperation with the state board of education, a comprehensive assessment of postsecondary vocational technical education in the state and prepare a plan for the delivery of that education to all Missourians at the postsecondary level.

In 1996 the coordinating board launched the postsecondary technical education plan, designed to deliver associate of applied science (AAS) degree programs through the state's fifty-seven area vocational technical schools and target selected baccalaureate and master's degree–granting institutions to provide access to applied technology degree programs beyond the AAS degree.

This extensive delivery system provides a full range of one-, two-, and four-year programs, as well as services and activities, for Missourians. The publicly supported schools and institutions include 424 comprehensive high school districts (53 of which are within the area vocational technical school network), 12 community college districts with 17 campuses (4 within area vocational schools), 1 state technical college, and 7 four-year public institutions. Nearly 95 percent of the population now resides within twenty-five minutes of an area vocational technical school in partnership with a community college.

MISSOURI HAS SUCCESSFULLY PREPARED AN INFRASTRUCTURE FOR THE ONGOING TRAINING AND EDUCATION OF ITS WORKFORCE

SOLID FOUNDATION

By the end of this millennium, Missouri will have invested an additional $70 million toward improving the geographic access, program capacity, and opportunities for student success in the workplace. Nearly 300,000 high school students and adults will have taken part in vocational/technical programs, including approximately 120,000 secondary and 48,000 postsecondary students, 100,000 adults, and 40,000 employees, through customized and contract training.

Clearly, the economic and social climate in Missouri is one of readiness to build the capacity for economic competitiveness. Missouri has successfully prepared an infrastructure for the ongoing training and education of its workforce, and the people, the legislators, and industry itself are increasingly optimistic about the future. In addition, Missourians are talking about a systematic rethinking of the actual nature of technical education. In partnership with business and government, educators are designing, building, and delivering workforce readiness for the twenty-first century.

Formulas for supply and demand keep an economics class fascinated. Courtesy, Missouri Dept. of Education

TELECOMMUNICATIONS

BEYOND THE IMAGINATION

TOM RACKERS
Public Affairs Manager, Sprint

In 1964 Tom Rackers joined the engineering staff of Sprint, then known as Capital City Telephone Company. After cross-functional assignments in the district engineering operation and in the commercial sector, he entered customer relations management in 1981. He has been public affairs manager since 1989. Rackers's extensive background in public service includes terms as chairman of the Missouri Development Finance Board, the Jefferson City Board of Education, the Jefferson City Area Chamber of Commerce, the Jefferson City Area United Way, and the Capital Region Medical Center Board of Trustees. He currently is a member of the Missouri Mansion Preservations Board of Directors.

It all began in 1876, over a network of wires, with the simple phrase "Mr. Watson, come here, I need you." Today that simple invention, the telephone, is used to make more than a billion calls a day, has spawned a multibillion-dollar industry affecting trillions of dollars in business around the globe, and has provided the foundation for newer innovations such as the Internet, wireless phones, and even the 911 emergency number.

In the 1870s the idea of a telephone was not just foreign, it was feared—but as fascination with the new invention grew, so did the number of uses for it. At the turn of the century, the popularity of the telephone had carried it beyond its

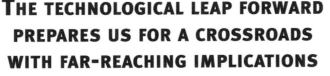

THE TECHNOLOGICAL LEAP FORWARD PREPARES US FOR A CROSSROADS WITH FAR-REACHING IMPLICATIONS

original use as a tool for businesses and the upper classes to serving as truly a "people's phone," with 855,900 subscribers. In 1929 President Herbert Hoover became the 15 millionth phone customer; in 1952 President Dwight Eisenhower had the country's 50 millionth telephone installed on his desk.

It can easily be said that the 1960s were a decade of change, not only in the country's social fabric but in telecommunications as well. The decade's first major telecommunications change was the beginning of the seven-digit telephone number. And by the end of the 1960s the first cordless phones were being tested. The proliferation of telephones also led to the creation of an emergency number that was easy to remember: 911.

RACING AHEAD
By 1979 the number of U.S. telephone subscribers had grown to 175 million. The fast-paced technological innovation of the 1980s that spawned the introduction of the Macintosh

Sophisticated switching equipment such as this helps process the more than a billion calls a day made throughout the world. © Tom Tracy/FPG International LLC

computer also led to several new developments in the telecommunications industry. Among them were the first mobile wireless telephones, a service that began in 1983; by 1987 there were more than 1 million cellular subscribers. And the court-ordered breakup of AT&T in 1984, of course, was the starting gun for the telecommunications race we've seen during the latter years of this century.

The last eight years of the 1990s represent a period of fast growth and rapid change for the telecommunications industry and technology in general. Technology, in effect, forced deregulation. The U.S. Congress's passing of the Telecommunications Act of 1996 opened the door for new companies to offer value-added services to consumers and businesses. The 1990s have witnessed the emergence of the Internet along with the proliferation of electronic mail, paging, and wireless phones based on personal communications services (PCS) technology. Today every company with more than 100 employees has access to the Internet, according to a study by International Data Corporation (IDC).

And in an industry where technology is moving at an astonishing speed, it appears the pace of change is only beginning to gather momentum. It's been more than two decades since Moore's Law correctly predicted a doubling of processing power every eighteen months. Now we are witnessing a powerful new force in the form of rapidly increasing capacity on the telecommunications network. For example, in 1999 Sprint's network will be able to carry, by itself, all the long-distance traffic in the United States today—and from a capacity standpoint, we would be able to carry it on a single pair of fibers.

AN INCREASINGLY DIGITAL SOCIETY

The technological leap forward prepares us for a crossroads with far-reaching

implications. Today telecommunications networks carry about 80 percent voice calls and 20 percent data. According to some projections, those proportions will be reversed in as little as six years, with much of this explosion in data due to the Internet. The dramatic shift from today's voice-dominated traffic patterns to the rapidly growing demand for high-bandwidth data applications is just one indicator of the accelerating rate of change throughout the information industry.

> **TODAY TELECOMMUNICATIONS NETWORKS CARRY ABOUT 80% VOICE CALLS AND 20% DATA; THIS COULD BE REVERSED IN AS LITTLE AS SIX YEARS**

The pace of change may outstrip our ability to imagine all its consequences. While nothing can ever replace the sound and importance of human voices over the telephone, the last decade of the 1900s clearly demonstrates the significance of data communications to both businesses and consumers. And while there's every reason to believe that the current growth cycle in telecommunications will not only continue but accelerate, we already have incredibly powerful tools at our disposal. Whether the user is a small U.S. company doing business with a major European corporation or a father traveling on business who sends an E-mail to his child, highly sophisticated forms of current technologies will keep us in touch—and will do it in an integrated, effective way. As we become an increasingly digital society, the future of telecommunications innovation has no limits.

An out-of-town executive uses his cell phone to touch base with his office. The first mobile wireless telephones were introduced in 1983—just seventeen years ago. Today more than 1 million people subscribe. © Adamsmith/FPG International LLC

FROM TWAIN TO THE 21ST CENTURY

PETER F. HERSCHEND
Vice Chairman, Silver Dollar City, Inc.

Peter Herschend and his brother Jack put out the welcome mat for 11 million visitors a year at twelve major tourist attractions in Pigeon Forge, Tennessee; Myrtle Beach, South Carolina; Atlanta, Georgia; and Branson, Missouri. In addition to his role as vice chairman of Silver Dollar City, Herschend has chaired various organizations, including the Missouri State Board of Education, the Missouri Tourism Commission, the Missouri Travel Federation, and the Ozark Marketing Council, and has served on the board of directors of the Missouri Chamber of Commerce, the International Association of Amusement Parks and Attractions, the Travel Industry Association of America, and the U.S. Senate Travel and Tourism Industry Advisory Council.

All the grand stories that brought fame to author Mark Twain were set in his beloved Missouri. Those stories cast a favorable light on this great state, creating what marketing experts today call a "unique position." As awareness grew of Twain's writings, so grew an awareness of Missouri's character and personality.

Another well-known writer, Harold Bell Wright, inspired millions with his tale of triumph of good over evil, *The Shepherd of the Hills*. It was an enticing love story, a tragedy, and a chronicle of heroism based on real people in the rugged Missouri Ozark Mountains. When the Missouri Pacific Railroad came to the Ozarks in 1913, visitors came from all around to meet the people and see the sights described in Wright's book.

> **BRANSON MADE HISTORY IN THE REALM OF RURAL TOURISM DEVELOPMENT BETWEEN THE '60S AND '90S**

Missouri's "Show Me" moniker has been around for nearly a century, ever since Missouri Congressman Willard Duncan Vandiver exclaimed, during a speech in Philadelphia in 1899, "I'm from Missouri! You'll have to show me!" For better or for worse, Missouri became known as the Show Me State, further defining our character and differentiating us from any other place.

The men mentioned above didn't set out to develop tourism. The extensive railroad passenger system was not built for that purpose. Nonetheless, all played a role in developing tourism in the first half of the twentieth century. Famous words created images in the minds of people, and the railroad gave people a way to go see the images with their own eyes.

AN INDUSTRY EVOLVES

In the second half of the century, the interstate highway system gave people even more freedom to travel, because their cars could go places the railroad couldn't. Missouri, under Governor Warren Hearnes, glimpsed the economic promise of tourism and formed the Missouri Tourism Commission, for the first time allocating funds for marketing. It took years to see results, but in time, tourism grew to become one of Missouri's top three industries.

Part of a working crafts colony in Branson's Silver Dollar City theme park, a costumed blacksmith demonstrates the way things were done in Mark Twain's day a century ago. Courtesy, Silver Dollar City

History was made in the realm of rural tourism development in Branson. While my family helped lay the foundation, the Branson boom outstripped anything we imagined. In retrospect, the ingredients of success are evident: mountains, lakes, a marketing force significant enough to start building a visitor base—in other words, synergy, timing, and a magical combination of attractions.

From 1960 into the 1980s, Silver Dollar City targeted marketing efforts at attracting daytime visitors to our theme park. The early Branson music shows filled a void in evening entertainment, setting the stage for Branson's music industry to take off—it entered the national spotlight in the early 1990s.

LEADERS OF TOURISM IN THE 21ST CENTURY NEED TO 'THINK OUTSIDE OF THE BOX' AS PLANNERS AND BE TRUSTWORTHY AS LEADERS

Scores of famous entertainers discovered Branson as a performance venue, and their celebrity presence added to the city's tourism appeal.

Air travel made it possible for people to come from farther away to see a Branson music show or the state's unique landmarks—St. Louis's Gateway Arch, Springfield's Bass Pro Shops Outdoor World, and Kansas City's Country Club Plaza.

APPROACH FOR THE NEXT CENTURY

Expanded air service to Missouri airports has led to plans for international tourism, an effort that is worthwhile as long as we carefully focus marketing efforts and don't neglect our strength, those visitors who travel here by car (80 percent). My nomination for the international marketing focus is Canada, specifically Toronto. This is based on the marketing maxim "behavior follows belief," meaning that people must be aware of what Missouri offers before they will visit. Because of proximity,

Canadians are much more likely to know about Missouri than are Europeans or Asians.

Focus on the right geographic markets and target audiences is key for the twenty-first century. Missouri must become more sophisticated and less shotgun in its approach to marketing. Technological advances make it possible, yet more complicated, to focus marketing efforts. Cable television has divided the market into many smaller pieces. As the Internet and other means of reaching people further divide the market, Missouri is challenged to get in front of the changes. That means understanding things like the fiber-optic network and the impact of the AT&T/TCI merger. It also means diligent study of basic questions: Who are the next customers? What are their interests? What message will appeal to them? What do they believe about Missouri now?

In addition to having marketing and technological skills, leaders of tourism in the twenty-first century need to "think outside of the box" as planners and be trustworthy as leaders. Their ability to get results through other people will be the ultimate measure of how successful they will be. Those who are not trusted and who do not have people's confidence will not last. Character counts; it always has and it always will.

Symbol of the westward pioneers' courage, Gateway Arch rises from its riverside park to frame downtown St. Louis . . . and beckon visitors. © James Blank

TRANSPORTATION

EMBRACING CHANGE

W. L. (BARRY) ORSCHELN
President, Orscheln Industries

W. L. (Barry) Orscheln joined Orscheln Industries in August 1977 and, after serving in various capacities, was appointed president in October 1990. The privately owned group of companies is engaged in manufacturing parts for the OEM automotive industry, retail agricultural and hardware sales, real estate development, and a host of other diversified interests. Orscheln currently serves as director on the boards of UMB Financial Corporation and UMB Bank, N.A., Kansas City; the Missouri Hawthorn Foundation; William Woods University; and the Midwest U.S.–Japan Association; he was elected to a two-year term as chairman of the Missouri Chamber of Commerce in 1997. Orscheln is also serving a six-year term as commissioner on the Missouri Highway and Transportation Commission.

One of the most important changes affecting Missouri business during the twentieth century has been the development of the state's transportation infrastructure. From the early 1900s, when horses and wagons carried goods from small towns to large cities over dirt roads, to the superhighways that will carry "horseless carriages" into the twenty-first century, transportation has been key to both the social and economic fabric of the state.

Legislators, business leaders, and everyday citizens recognized the necessity of a good highway system as automobiles became common. Early efforts to "get Missouri out of the mud" resulted in passage of the Centennial Road Law of 1921 and formation of the present-day Department of Transportation. Over the years, businesses relied on a strong highway network to get goods they produced to both domestic and, ultimately, foreign markets. A sound transportation network has helped businesses expand and diversify to provide needed goods and services.

> **MISSOURI WAS THE FIRST STATE IN THE NATION TO BEGIN CONSTRUCTION ON AN INTERSTATE HIGHWAY PROJECT**

I'm fortunate to view transportation from two perspectives—as a businessman and a member of the Missouri Highway and Transportation Commission, the body that guides development and construction of the state's transportation improvements. The commission recognizes the importance of an interconnected transportation system that moves people and goods efficiently. A major factor influencing a company's decision to locate in a particular area is access to transportation. Location next to a river, airport, railhead, or four-lane highway lowers transportation costs, increases commerce, and provides potential for continued growth. These factors appeal to business now and will be even more important in the future.

HIGHWAY TO THE WORLD

The single most significant transportation

A road along Lake of the Ozarks near Bagnell Dam is part of the sound Missouri transportation network that has helped businesses expand and diversify. © James Blank

achievement of the twentieth century was the creation of the interstate highway system, the world's largest public works project. Missouri played a key role in that system by being the first state in the nation to begin construction on an interstate highway project in 1956. Eventual completion of that highway system has helped position Missouri as a transportation and economic leader. Modern highways carry goods to railheads, ports, and airports for shipment around the country and around the world.

A company based in any Missouri town no longer competes in a local market, thanks to both an improved transportation network and vast changes in the way we communicate. The computer age has made communication with Paris, France, as easy as communication with Paris, Missouri. Goods and packages are tracked with ease; order placement and confirmation occur instantaneously and business is conducted around the clock, around the world. Advances in cellular phones and computers have put information within reach of more people. The advent of the Internet has expanded the marketplace to the entire world. For many Missouri firms, the Internet will be the key to opening new markets.

INTELLIGENT TRANSPORTATION SYSTEMS WILL EASE TRAFFIC FLOW, REDUCE CONGESTION, AND PROVIDE MOTORISTS 'REAL TIME' INFORMATION

CAPITALIZING ON CHANGE

What does the twenty-first century hold for Missouri businesses? Success in the next century will depend on many of the qualities needed today—planning, dedication, hard work, creativity, excellent customer service, financial acumen, and a finger on the pulse of the world marketplace. Innovations in shipping and manufacturing processes will result in more just-in-time deliveries and more precise control of inventories. And transportation system improvements will be vital to delivering those goods in record time. Intelligent transportation systems are being developed to increase traffic flow, reduce congestion, and provide "real time" information to motorists.

Success will also depend on how well the business world embraces change and capitalizes on it. Operating from a "we've always done it that way" perspective will doom a company to extinction. Business will have to adapt to changes in the workforce and embrace change instead of tradition. A challenge facing transportation providers will be recruiting and training a workforce to take the place of those who brought the interstate highway system to fruition. Successful Missouri businesses of the twenty-first century will focus globally and develop partnerships beyond state and national borders. Companies will also need to know their customers and provide personalized services to retain them.

The new century offers challenge and opportunity for Missouri. Finding transportation solutions will continue to be important as demands for infrastructure improvement increase. Creating innovative mechanisms to fund those improvements will also be a formidable challenge. Transportation is one of the keys to Missouri's economic and social well-being. Working in connection with citizens, businesses, and communities, the state's transportation leaders will build and maintain the infrastructure that will propel Missouri into the twenty-first century.

Success in the next century will depend on intelligent transportation systems such as light rail, shown here, that help reduce congestion.
© Nick Gunderson/Tony Stone Images

BIBLIOGRAPHY

Alampi, Gary, ed. *Gale State Rankings Reporter.* Gale Research, Inc., 1994.

Albee, Robin, and J. Sanford Rikoon (with Michael Seipel and Daryl Hobbs). *The State of Rural Missouri.* Columbia, Mo.: Missouri Agricultural Experiment Station Special Report 487, September 1995.

AlliedSignal. "AlliedSignal, Corporate Information, A Brief History." <http://www.alliedsignal.com/corpinfo/index.html> (1998).

Ameren. "AmerenUE History (About Ameren, Power Plants, and Union Electric)." <http://www.ameren.com> (1998).

American Automobile Association. *Arkansas/Kansas/Missouri/Oklahoma TourBook.* Heathrow, Fla.: AAA Publishing, 1997.

———. *Arkansas/Kansas/Missouri/Oklahoma TourBook.* Heathrow, Fla.: AAA Publishing, 1998.

American Home Products Corporation. <http://www.ahp.com> (1998).

Amtrak. <http://www.amtrak.com/amtrak/news/critical.html> (5 June 1998).

ASARCO Lead Co. <http://www.asarco.com> (20 June 1998).

Balaban, Dan. "Bringing the Best Science to KC." *Kansas City Business Journal,* 2 March 1998. <http://www.amcity.com/kansascity/stories/030298/story4.html>.

———. "Cashing In on Casinos." *Kansas City Business Journal,* 6 January 1997. <http://www.amcity.com/kansascity/stories/010697/story2.html>.

Barry, Tom, director of continuing education, University of Missouri–Kansas City, and former director of technology for the Missouri Department of Economic Development. Interview by author. 18 May 1998.

"Baseball in America: Jackie Robinson on Branch Rickey." *Reader's Digest,* 11 April 1997. <http://www.readersdigest.com/rdmagazine/specfeat/archives/jackierob.htm.>.

Behan, Gary W. *1992 Missouri New and Expanding Industry.* Jefferson City, Mo.: Research and Planning Program, Missouri Department of Economic Development, June 1993.

Black, Melissa. "Into the Future: Research—A Tool of Our Past, Present and Future." *Pathways: A Quarterly Magazine of the Missouri Department of Transportation* (fall 1996): 10–15.

The Boeing Company. "The New Boeing Begins Operations as a Single Company." <http://www.boeing.com/news/releases/1997/news_release_970804.html> (4 August 1997).

Borgmeyer, Bill, Office of Productivity, Business Development Group, Missouri Department of Economic Development. Interview by author. 7 May 1998.

Brockhoff, Anne. "Casinos Draw Conventions with Mix of Entertainment." *Kansas City Business Journal,* 7 April 1997. <http://www.amcity.com/kansascity/stories/040797/focus2.html>.

"Brownfields '97: Partnering for a Greener Tomorrow." <http://www.kcmo.org/environ/brownfld.htm>.

Brown Group, Inc. <http://www.browngroup.com/corporate/index.html> (27 July 1998).

Bullock, J. Bruce, Department of Agricultural Economics, University of Missouri–Columbia. Interview by author. 5 May 1998.

Burlington Northern Railway. <http://www.bnsf.com/about_bnsf/html/history.html> (8 June 1998).

"Business Development Blueprint for Rural Communities Using Advanced Telecommunications." <http://www.ctr.cstp.umkc.edu/nevada/progress.9602.html> (1998).

Carlsen, Frances L., ed. *1997 Missouri Directory of Manufacturers.* Twinsburg, Ohio: Harris InfoSource International, 1997.

Center for Telecomputing Research, University of Missouri–Kansas City. <http://ctr.cstp.umkc.edu/welcome.html> (5 May 1998).

Central Methodist College. <http://cmc2.cmc.edu> (31 July 1998).

Central Missouri State University. <http://cmsuvmb.cmsu.edu> (30 July 1998).

Clements, John. *Missouri Facts: Flying the Colors.* Dallas, Tex.: Clements Research II, Inc., 1991.

Coleman, Jim, and Melissa Kent. "75 Years: A Brief History of How We've Gotten from Here to There, from Then to Now." *Pathways: A Quarterly Magazine of the Missouri Department of Transportation* (summer 1996): 15–19.

College of the Ozarks. <http://www.cofo.edu> (30 July 1998).

Conard, Howard L., ed. *Encyclopedia of the History of Missouri.* 6 vols. New York: Southern History Company, 1901.

Conrad, Lee. "Consulting Overtakes Audit Work at Ernst, Deloitte." *St. Louis Business Journal,* 3 February 1997. <http://www.amcity.com/stlouis/stories/020397/focus3.html>.

———. "Ozarks Visitor Bureau Draws Leads from Satellite Office Here." *St. Louis Business Journal,* 17 March 1997. <http://www.amcity.com/stlouis/stories/031797/focus5.html>.

Convention and Visitors Bureau of Greater Kansas City. *Experience Kansas City.* Kansas City, Mo.: Convention and Visitors Bureau of Greater Kansas City, 1997.

Darling, Peter. "Polymetallics in the Heartland of the Union." *International Mining,* October 1989.

Davis, Jim. "Local Market Yet to Cool Off." *Kansas City Business Journal,* 9 June 1997. <http://www.amcity.com/kansascity/stories/060997/newscolumn4.html>.

———. "Postal Service to Sign, Seal Deal for Sears Warehouse." *Kansas City Business Journal,* 11 November 1996. <http://www.amcity.com/kansascity/stories/111196/story6.html>.

———. "Sprint Rehearsing Big Move." *Kansas City Business Journal,* 26 January 1998. <http://www.amcity.com/kansascity/stories/112497/newscolumn2.html>.

Deloitte & Touche. <http://www.us.deloitte.com> (1998).

Desloge, Rick. "Techno Town: Computer Companies Dominate Fastest-Growing Private Firms List." *St. Louis Business Journal,* 9 June 1997. <http://www.amcity.com/stlouis/stories/060997/story4.html>.

———. "Who's Who in Health Care: Professional Services." *St. Louis Business Journal,* 10 February 1997. <http://www.amcity.com/stlouis/stories/021097/focus8.html>.

Desloge, Rick, and Stephen Roth. "Architectural Consultants Merging with St. Louis Firm." *Kansas City Business Journal,* 19 January 1998. <http://www.amcity.com/kansascity/stories/011998/story8.html>.

Division of Labor Standards, Department of Labor and Industrial Relations, State of Missouri. *1989 Statistical Report: Mining.*

Dodd, Donald B., and Wynelle S. Dodd. *Historical Statistics of the United States, 1790–1970.* Vol. 2: *The Midwest.* University, Ala.: University of Alabama Press, 1976.

The Doe Run Company. <http://www.doerun.com/index.htm> (22 June 1998).

Downs, Peter. "Chemical Warfare Comes to the Ozarks." *In These Times,* 8 October 1998, 5–6.

Driskill, Joseph L. *Economically Speaking. News Releases 1997–1998.* Jefferson City, Mo.: Missouri Department of Economic Development. <http://www.ecodev.state.mo.us/ded/column.html>.

Dufur, Brett. *Exploring Missouri Wine Country.* Columbia, Mo.: Pebble Publishing, 1997.

"Earnings by Industry." *Demographics Journal* (American City Business Journals), 10 March 1998. <http://www.amcity.com/journals/demographics>.

Emerson Electric Co. <http://emersonelectric.com> (27 July 1998).

Encyclopedia Americana–International Edition, 1996, s.v. "Missouri."

"Environmental Management." <http://www.kcmo.org/environ>.

Ernst & Young, Inc. <http://www.eyi.com> (29 June 1998).

Famighetti, Robert, ed. *The World Almanac and Book of Facts 1997.* Mahwah, N.J.: World Almanac Books, 1997.

Faultless Starch/Bon Ami Company. <http://faultless.com> (27 July 1998).

Faust, Fred. "Gambling Pumps $759 Million into State." *St. Louis Post-Dispatch,* 26 April 1998. <http://archives.stlnet.com/archives/pdarc98.net>.

Flannery, William. "Trade Marked St. Louis Ranked No. 2 Place to Start Companies." *St. Louis Post-Dispatch,* 16 September 1997. <http://archives.stlnet.com/archives/news/pdtoday97.net>.

Food and Agricultural Policy Research Institute. *10-Year Agricultural Outlook.* Columbia, Mo.: Missouri Agricultural Experiment Station Special Report 492, September 1995.

"Forbes, Fortune Rank Top Missouri Companies." *The Missouri Enterprise* 9 (August 1989): 11.

Fradin, Dennis Brindell, and Judith Bloom Fradin. *From Sea to Shining Sea: Missouri.* Chicago: Childrens Press, 1994.

Gist, Noel P., Thomas C. Morlock, Clarence M. Tucker, and W. Francis English, eds. *Missouri: Its Resources, People, and Institutions.* Columbia, Mo.: Curators of the University of Missouri, 1950.

Gordon, Daniel R., and J. Bruce Bullock (with Michael Seipel, J. Sanford Rikoon, and Daryl Hobbs). *The Status and Potential of Missouri Agriculture.* Columbia, Mo.: Missouri Agricultural Experiment Station Special Report 488, September 1995.

———. *The Status of Selected Natural Resources in Missouri.* Columbia, Mo.: Missouri Agricultural Experiment Station Special Report 490, September 1995.

Gray, Lisa Waterman. "Technology and Turnover Boost Demand for Management Consultants." *Kansas City Business Journal,* 28 October 1996. <http://www.amcity.com/kansascity/stories/102896/focus3.html>.

Greater Kansas City Chamber of Commerce. *Greater Kansas City: The Good Life.* 1996.

———. *1997 Economic Forecast.* 1997.

Grebing, Jim, ed. *Official Manual, State of Missouri 1997–98.* Jefferson City, Mo.: Office of the Secretary of State, 1998.

Gwinn, Mary Ann. "Ribbon of Rust." *Missouri Life,* January–February 1982, 24–30.

Hall, John. "Railroad Revival: Amtrak, the Ann Rutledge, and the Missouri Mule." *Missouri Life,* November–December 1980, 38–41.

Harley-Davidson Company. <http://www.harley-davidson.com> (26 January 1998).

Hast, Adele, ed. *International Directory of Company Histories.* 5 vols. Chicago: St. James Press, 1991.

Hayes, David. "Opportunity for Sound Beginning: Technology Companies Find Kansas City Area a Good Place to Launch their Businesses." *Kansas City Star,* 20 April 1997. <http://www.kcstar.com>.

Hayhow, Joyce, pub. *Book of Lists, Top 25 Addendum.* Special Supplement to the *Kansas City Business Journal* (29 May 1998).

Heffernen, William D., Department of Rural Sociology, University of Missouri–Columbia. Interview by author. 7 May 1998.

Heritage of Missouri. State Publishing Company, 1963.

Hoechst Marion Roussel USA. <http://www.hmri.com/company/usbgd.html> (23 June 1998).

Holt, Douglas L. *Missouri's Food Processing Industry.* Columbia, Mo.: Missouri Agricultural Experiment Station Special Report 491, September 1995.

Hopkins, Sondra, project coord. *Book of Lists, 1996–97.* Columbia, Mo.: Mid-Missouri Business Journal, 1996.

H&R Block, Inc. <http://www.hrblock.com> (29 June 1998).

Institute of Management Consultants. <http://www.imcusa.org/imcinfo.html> (28 June 1998).

Jacks, Howard, project mgr. *Nevada Telecommunity Project Status,* February 1996. <http://www.ctr.cstp.umkc.edu/nevada/progress.9602.html>.

Janecke, Ron. "Center Asks Manufacturers What Keeps Them up at Night." *St. Louis Business Journal,* 9 September 1996. <http://www.amcity.com/stlouis/stories/090996/smallb2.html>.

———. "Engineering a Comeback." *St. Louis Business Journal,* 12 January 1998. <http://www.amcity.com/stlouis/stories/011298/smallb1.html>.

———. "Savala Engineers $12.8 Million at ASTEC." *St. Louis Business Journal,* 1 September 1997. <http://www.amcity.com/stlouis/stories/090197/smallb1.html>.

Jean-Pierre Rampal Plays Scott Joplin. Liner notes. CBS compact disc digital audio MK 37818.

John, Lisa Stevens. "American Meat Co. Growth Soars over Past Dozen Years." *Kansas City Business Journal,* 22 June 1998. <http://www.amcity.com/kansascity/stories/062298/focus5.html>.

Kane, Joseph Nathan. *Famous First Facts.* 3rd ed. New York: H. W. Wilson Co., 1964.

Kansas City Area Development Council. *Profile: Greater Kansas City, What's New? Business & Industry.* 1998. <http://www.smartcities.com/sections/profiledocs/busind.html>.

Kansas City International Airport. <http://www.kcairports.org/kci/history.htm> (21 June 1998).

Kansas City Metropolitan Community Colleges. <http://www.kcmetro.cc.mo.us> (30 July 1998).

"Kansas City, Missouri: Business and Industry." <http://www.edcks.com/html/2d_indust.html> (11 July 1998).

Kansas City Power & Light. <http://www.kcpl.com/kcplinfo/aboutus.htm> (1 June 1998).

Kemper Military School and College. <http://www.kemper.org> (31 July 1998).

King, Suzanne, *Kansas City Business Journal.* Interview by author. 26 May 1998.

King, Suzanne. "Buyer for Lee's Summit AT&T Plant." *Kansas City Business Journal,* 22 September 1997. <http://www.amcity.com/kansascity/stories/092297/story8.html>.

———. "FabTech Proving Value of High Tech in KC." *Kansas City Business Journal,* 29 September 1997. <http://www.amcity.com/kansascity/stories/092997/story.html>.

———. "High-Tech Allies Pool Resources." *Kansas City Business Journal,* 5 January 1998. <http://www.amcity.com/kansascity/stories/010598/story3.html>.

Kirkendall, Richard S. *A History of Missouri, 1919–1953.* Vol. 5. Columbia, Mo.: University of Missouri Press, 1986.

Kirksville College of Osteopathic Medicine. <http://www.kcom.edu/welcom/history.ssi> (23 June 1998).

Laclede Gas Company. <http://www.lacledegas.com/frconten.htm> (21 June 1998).

Lakes Area Chamber of Commerce and Convention and Visitor Bureau. *Slip Away to Branson: 1997 Vacation Guide.* 1997.

Levey, Judith S., and Agnes Greenhall, eds. *The Concise Columbia Encyclopedia,* s.v. "Reinhold Niebuhr." New York: Avon Books, 1983.

Linafelt, Tom. "Management Consulting: Clean-up Call." *Kansas City Business Journal,* 28 October 1996. <http://www.amcity.com/kansascity/stories/102896/focus1.html>.

Lincoln University. <http://www.lincolnu.edu> (30 July 1998).

Lipton, Inc. "About Wishbone: History." 1998. <http://www.wish-bone.com/company/history.html>.

Little, Wayne, SmartCities, Kansas City Area Development Council. Interview by author. 26 May 1998.

Mallinckrodt. <http://www.mkg.com> (26 June 1998).

"Mallinckrodt Head Resigns; AT&T, SBC Talk Merger." *St. Louis Business Journal,* 2 June 1997. <http://www.amcity.com/stlouis/stories/060297/weekinbiz.html>.

Mallory, Charles. "The Orschelns." *Missouri Life,* May–June 1983, 11–14.

MAMTC (Mid-America Manufacturing Technology Center). <http://www.mamtc.com/light> (26 July 1998).

Mannies, Jo. "River Gambling: It's a Horserace." *St. Louis Post-Dispatch,* 3 April 1991. http://archives.stlnet.com/archives/pdarc.net>.

Manning, Margie. "Lost Souls, Lost Dollars." *St. Louis Business Journal,* 20 July 1998. <http://www.amcity.com/stlouis/stories/072098/story2.html>.

"Manufacturing Growth." *Demographics Journal* (American City Business Journals), 2 March 1998. <http://www.amcity.com/journals/demographics>.

March, David D. *The History of Missouri.* 4 vols. New York: Lewis Historical Publishing Co., 1967.

Margolies, Dan. "Costs, Clients Drive Big Law Firms to Merge." *Kansas City Business Journal,* 20 April 1998. <http://search.amcity.com/kansascity/stories/042098/story1.html>.

Mayer, Bob. "Kansas City's Riverfront Running out of Patience." *Kansas City Business Journal,* 10 November 1997. <http://www.amcity.com/kansascity/stories/111097/editorial4.html>.

McKinnell, Henry, executive vice president of Pfizer, Inc. "From Machine Age to Information Age: Health Care in the Twenty-First Century." Speech presented to World Economic Forum, Davos, Switzerland, 2 February 1998. <http://www.pfizer.com/pfizerinc/policy/21century.html>.

McLaughlin, Tim. "Developing St. Louis." *St. Louis Business Journal,* 14 April 1997. <http://www.amcity.com/stlouis/stories/041497/story7.html>.

———. "Technology Applications Building $5 Million Office." *St. Louis Business Journal,* 4 November 1996. <http://www.amcity.com/stlouis/stories/110496/story6.html>.

McReynold, Edwin C. *Missouri: A History of the Crossroads State.* Norman, Okla.: University of Oklahoma Press, 1962.

MEMC Electronic Materials, Inc. <http://www.memc.com> (27 July 1998).

Merriam Webster's Encyclopedia of Literature, s.v. "Langston Hughes," 1995.

Ibid., s.v. "Laura Ingalls Wilder."

Microsoft Encarta, s.v. "Angelou, Maya." Microsoft Corporation, 1994. Funk & Wagnalls Corporation, 1994.

Ibid., s.v. "Baker, Josephine."

Ibid., s.v. "Carver, George Washington."

Ibid., s.v. "Cronkite, Walter (Leland, Jr.)."

Ibid., s.v. "Eames, Charles."

Ibid., s.v. "Niebuhr, Reinhold."

Midwest Research Institute. <http://www.mriresearch.org> (23 June 1998).

Midwest Research Institute. "Missouri Research Labs: A Brief History of MRI." <http://www.moimpact.com/research/mri/mrioverview.html>.

Midwest Research Institute and Capper Press, comp. *The Missouri Quick-Fact Book.* Topeka, Kans.: Capper Press, 1991.

Miklasz, Bernie. "There's Only One McGwire." *St. Louis Post-Dispatch,* 14 October 1998. <http://www.fastball.com/cardinals/archives/stories/1998/70mikl.html>.

Miller, Tom. "Tracking the Future of Highways." *Pathways: A Quarterly Magazine of the Missouri Department of Transportation* (summer 1996): 12–14.

Mineral Area College. <http://www.mac.cc.mo.us> (31 July 1998). *Missouri Agricultural and Food Industry in the Next Decade: Issues and Challenges, Perspectives on Agriculture, Food and Natural Resources,* Part II. Columbia, Mo.: Missouri Agricultural Experiment Station Special Report, n.d.

"Missouri, Area Development Online (Site and Facility Planning)." <http://www.area-development.com/MISSOU97.HTM> (10 July 1998).

Missouri Arthritis Rehabilitation Research and Training Center. <http://www.hsc.missouri.edu/arthritis/text/marrtc.html> (23 June 1998).

"Missouri Business Climate Rated Best in the Midwest by Study." *The Missouri Enterprise* 9 (August 1989).

Missouri Coordinating Board of Higher Education. *Overview of Higher Education: Trends and Issues in Missouri.* Charles J. McClain, Commissioner of Higher Education, State of Missouri, July 1990.

Missouri Corporation for Science and Technology. *1990 Annual Report.* Jefferson City, Mo.: Missouri Corporation for Science and Technology, 1990.

Missouri Department of Agriculture. *Missouri Farm Facts 97.* 1997.

Missouri Department of Economic Development. *Office of Productivity.* 1998.

———. *Missouri's Economic Development Status, 1993.* 9 December 1993.

———. *Missouri's Economic Forecast: 1995.* 30 December 1994.

———. *Welcome to Missouri: The State of the World Today.* 1998.

Missouri Department of Economic Development, Business Development Group. *Missouri's Opportunity to Lead in Microelectronics.* 18 August 1997.

Missouri Department of Health, State Center for Health Statistics. *Missouri Health Manpower: 1993,* Publication No. 230. 1993.

Missouri Department of Insurance. *1997 Annual Report.* August 1997.

Missouri Department of Natural Resources. "Hazardous Waste Program." <http://www.dnr.state.mo.us/deq/hwp/fac_list.htm> (20 June 1998).

———. *Missouri Coal.* n.d.

Missouri Division of Tourism. *Destination Missouri: 1996/1997 Multi-Cultural Travel & Tour Guide.* 1997.

———. *Missouri Calendar of Events January–December 1998.* 1998

———. *Missouri 1997 Calendar of Events.* 1997.

———. *Missouri 1997 Travel Guide.* 1997.

———. *The 1998 Official Missouri Travel Guide.* 1998.

———. *Official Missouri Travel Guide, 1998.* St. Louis, Missouri: Missouri Division of Tourism in cooperation with Publishing Concepts, a division of Commerce Publishing Company, 1998.

———. *Wake Up to Missouri: Facts & Figures.* July 1995.

The Missouri Gaming Commission. *1994 Annual Report to the General Assembly.* Robert L. Wolfson, chairman.

Missouri Highway and Transportation Commission. *Show Me Transportation: Strategies for Action into the Twenty-First Century (Linking Missouri Through Quality).* 1995.

Missouri Institute for Information Technology, University of Missouri–Kansas City. <http://www.miit.org>.

Missouri Military Academy. <http://www.iolaks.com/mma/html> (31 July 1998).

The Missouri Quick-Fact Book. Topeka, Kans.: Capper Press, 1991.

Missouri Public Service Commission 1995 Annual Report. 3 December 1996. <http://www.ecodev.state.mo.us/psc/summ.htm>.

Missouri Secretary of State. *Official Manual of Missouri.* 1997.

Missouri Western State College. <http://www.mwsc.edu> (30 July 1998).

Moberly Junior College. <http://www.macc.cc.mo.us> (31 July 1998).

Morgan Quitno Press. *State Rankings 1997: A Statistical View of the Fifty United States.* Lawrence, Kans.: Morgan Quitno Press, 1997.

Morgan Quitno Press. *State Rankings 1998: A Statistical View of the Fifty United States.* Lawrence, Kans.: Morgan Quitno Press, 1998.

Nagel, Paul C. *Missouri: A Bicentennial History.* New York: W. W. Norton & Co., 1977.

Nellcor Puritan Bennett. <http://www.nellcorpb.com> (26 June 1998).

Northwest Missouri State University. <http://www.nwmissouri.edu> (30 July 1998).

Office of Social and Economic Data Analysis, University Extension, University of Missouri–Columbia. *The State of the State Revisited 1994.* 1994. <http://www.oseda.missouri.edu/sos94/>.

Parrish, Wm. E., Charles T. Jones Jr., and Lawrence O. Christensen. *Missouri: The Heart of the Nation.* 2nd ed. Arlington Heights, Ill.: Harlan Davidson, Inc., 1992.

Priddy, Bob. "The Tale of Missouri's Trains from Mule Power to MOPAC."

Missouri Life, November–December 1980, 45–50.

"Pulling the Lead out for Missouri." *St. Louis Commerce,* August 1989.

Quick Facts about Lambert Field, St. Louis. <http://www.st-louis.mo.us/st-louis/airport/cell1a/quickfaq.html> (21 June 1998).

Rafferty, Milton D. *Historical Atlas of Missouri.* Norman, Okla.: University of Oklahoma Press, 1982.

Robertson, Tommy. "League, Other Officials Urge Push for High Tech Corridor." *St. Charles Post,* 19 June 1998. <http://archives.stlnet.com/archives>.

Rosenberg, Martin. "Regional Technology Saluted." *Kansas City Star,* 28 October 1994. <http://www.kcstar.com>.

Roth, Melinda. "Their Cross to Bear." *The Riverfront Times,* 29 April–5 May 1998, 17–18.

Roth, Stephen. "AlliedSignal Plant Brings Cedar Creek to Life." *Kansas City Business Journal,* 26 May 1997. <http://www.amcity.com/kansascity/stories/052697/story6.html>.

———. "Cramer Inc. Not Resting on Its Laurels." *Kansas City Business Journal,* 29 June 1998. <http://www.amcity.com/kansascity/stories/062998/newscolumn5.html>.

———. "The Friendly Skies Above KCI." *Kansas City Business Journal,* 6 April 1998. <http://www.amcity.com/kansascity/stories/040698/newscolumn6.html>.

St. Louis Community College. <http://www.stlcc.cc.mo.us> (30 July 1998).

St. Louis Regional Commerce and Growth Association's Economic Development. *Greater St. Louis: America's Center for Technology.* 1997. <http://www.econdev.stlrcga.org>.

———. *RCGA: Technology Gateway Alliance.* 1997. <http://www.econdev.stlrcga.org>.

———. *St. Louis: America's Center for Business.* 1997. <http://www.econdev.stlrcga.org>.

———. *What's New?* 1997. <http://www.econdev.stlrcga.org>.

Sallee, Tommy, Vicki Pauley, and Sally Oxenhandler. *1996 Missouri Farm Facts.* Compiled by Missouri Agricultural Statistics Service and issued cooperatively by the Missouri Department of Agriculture and the U.S. Department of Agriculture, September 1996.

Savage, W. Sherman. *History of Lincoln University.* Jefferson City, Mo.: Lincoln University, 1939.

Savageau, David, and Geoffrey Loftus. *Places Rated Almanac.* Macmillan USA. Macmillan Travel, 1996.

Seipel, Michael. *Selected Characteristics of the Missouri Horticultural Industry.* Columbia, Mo.: Missouri Agricultural Experiment Station Special Report 489, September 1995.

Seipel, Michael, et. al. *The Social and Economic Organization of Missouri Agriculture, 1964–1992.* Columbia, Mo.: Missouri Agricultural Experiment Station Special Report 486, September 1995.

Sherberg, Ellen, pub. *Book of Lists,* 1998 Edition. *St. Louis Business Journal,* 1 January 1998.

The Silicon Prairie Technology Association. <http://www.silicon-prairie.org>.

SmartCities, Kansas City Area Development Council. <http://www.smartcities.com> (8 May 1998).

Southeast Missouri State University. <http://www2.semo.edu> (30 July 1998).

Southwest Missouri State University. <http://www.smsu.edu> (30 July 1998).

Spain, Patrick J., and James R. Talbot, eds. *Hoover's Handbook of American Business:* 1996. Austin, Tex.: The Reference Press, Inc., 1995.

Springfield Chamber of Commerce. *Springfield, Missouri U.S.A. Demographic Profile.* <http://www.spfld-mo-chamber.com/demo.htm> (21 June 1998).

State of Missouri. *The Missouri Report: Achieving the National Education Goals, 1993.* 28 September 1993.

Statistical Abstract for Missouri. Columbia, Mo.: College of Business and Public Administration, University of Missouri, July 1996.

Stetson Hats. <http://www.stetsonhat.com/history.htm> (26 July 1998).

Steyer, Robert. "Monsanto Seeks $80 Million to Build Plant Research Center" *St. Louis Post-Dispatch,* 11 June 1998. <http://archives.stlnet.com/archives>.

———. "Plant Research Center in Planning Stages Here, Four Institutions to be Centerpieces." *St. Louis Post-Dispatch,* 5 May 1998.

Stout, Larry, and David Hoffman. *An Introduction to Missouri's Geologic Environment.* Educational Series, No. 3. Rolla, Mo.: Missouri Geological Survey and Water Resources, 1973.

Strauser, Claude N. *Restoration of the Middle Mississippi River by the Army Engineers.* April 1978. <http://1ms61.mvs.usace.army.mil/restore.html>.

Sverdrup Corporation. <http://www.sverdrup.com> (19 June 1998).

Trans World Airlines. <http://www.twa.com> (21 June 1998).

Truman State University. <http://www.truman.edu> (31 July 1998).

Union Pacific Railway. <http://www.unionpacific.com/overview/history.htm> (5 June 1998).

U.S. Army Corps of Engineers, Missouri River Division. *Missouri River Master Water Control Manual.* Vol. 6A; Economic Studies: Navigation Economics. August 1994.

U.S. Bureau of the Census. *U.S. Census of Population: 1990.* Washington, D.C.: Bureau of the Census, 1993.

U.S. Department of Commerce. *State and Metropolitan Area Data Book, 1997–98: A Statistical Abstract Supplement.* 5th ed. 1998.

University of Missouri–Kansas City. <http://www.umkc.edu> (30 July 1998).

University of Missouri–Kansas City, Missouri Institute for Information Technology. "Computer Science Telecommunications Program: Center for Telecomputing Research." <http://www.ctr.cstp.umkc.edu>.

University of Missouri–Rolla. <http://www.umr.edu> (30 July 1998).

University of Missouri–St. Louis. <http://www.umsl.edu> (30 July 1998).

University of Missouri System. <http://www.system.missouri.edu/urel/main> (30 July 1998).

Vespereny, Cynthia. "State Venture Capital up 129 Percent." *St. Louis Business Journal,* 23 February 1998. <http://www.amcity.com/stlouis/stories/022398/story1.html>.

Washington University. <http://wupa.wustl.edu> (30 July 1998).

Wasson, Tyler, ed. *Nobel Prize Winners.* New York: The H.W. Wilson Company, 1987.

"What Is MOREnet?" <http://www.more.net/infoserv/tour_morenet/history.html>.

"Who's Who in Technology." *St. Louis Business Journal,* 12 May 1997. <http://www.amcity.com/stlouis/stories/051297/focus1.html>.

William Jewell College. <http://www.jewell.edu> (31 July 1998).

Williams, Walter. *The State of Missouri: An Autobiography.* Columbia, Mo.: Press of E. W. Stephens, 1904.

"Wine Country of Missouri." <http://www.wine-mo.com>.

Zarkowsky, Daniel. "Warehouses 96 Percent Occupied." *St. Louis Business Journal,* 18 August 1997.

The Web sites of the following companies, places, organizations, and electronic publications were also consulted for this book: Anheuser-Busch Companies, Inc.; Bass Pro Shops; Blue Cross and Blue Shield; the *Concise Columbia Electronic Encyclopedia,* 3rd ed., 1994; Hallmark Cards, Inc.; Kansas City, Missouri; the *Kansas City Star;* Lake of the Ozarks; Midwest Research Institute; the Missouri Coalition for the Environment; Ralston Purina Company; Safety-Kleen Corporation; Saint Louis University School of Medicine; Science City at Union Station; Sister Cities International; SmithKline Beecham; Trinity Lutheran Hospital; Western Auto; and Washington University Medical School.

The following Web sites were also consulted: www.cityview.com; www.conservation.state.mo.us/conmag/1996/jul/1.html; www.littleblue.com/kcradio/hist/kc/wdaf.html; www.nationalparks.org/; www.sfo.com/~itc/baseball/national/buschs.htm; www.sprint.com; www.stlouiswalkoffame.org/inductees/branch-rickey.html; www.wish-bone.com/company/history.html.

INDEX